Write a Children's Book
And Get it Published

Write a Children's Book And Get it Published

Allan Frewin Jones and
Lesley Pollinger

For UK order enquiries: please contact Bookpoint Ltd,
130 Milton Park, Abingdon, Oxon OX14 4SB.
Telephone: +44 (0) 1235 827720. *Fax:* +44 (0) 1235 400454.
Lines are open 09.00–17.00, Monday to Saturday, with a 24-hour
message answering service. Details about our titles and how to
order are available at www.teachyourself.com

For USA order enquiries: please contact McGraw-Hill
Customer Services, PO Box 545, Blacklick, OH 43004-0545,
USA. *Telephone:* 1-800-722-4726. *Fax:* 1-614-755-5645.

For Canada order enquiries: please contact McGraw-Hill
Ryerson Ltd, 300 Water St, Whitby, Ontario L1N 9B6, Canada.
Telephone: 905 430 5000. *Fax:* 905 430 5020.

Long renowned as the authoritative source for self-guided
learning – with more than 50 million copies sold worldwide –
the **Teach Yourself** series includes over 500 titles in the fields of
languages, crafts, hobbies, business, computing and education.

British Library Cataloguing in Publication Data: a catalogue
record for this title is available from the British Library.

Library of Congress Catalog Card Number: on file.

First published in UK 2006 by Hodder Education, part of
Hachette UK, 338 Euston Road, London NW1 3BH.

First published in US 2006 by The McGraw-Hill Companies, Inc.

This edition published 2010.

Previously published as *Teach Yourself Writing for Children*.

The **Teach Yourself** name is a registered trade mark of
Hodder Headline.

Typeset by MPS Limited, a Macmillan Company.

Printed in Great Britain for Hodder Education, an Hachette UK
Company, 338 Euston Road, London NW1 3BH, by CPI Cox &
Wyman, Reading, Berkshire RG1 8EX.

The publisher has used its best endeavours to ensure that the URLs
for external websites referred to in this book are correct and active
at the time of going to press. However, the publisher and the author
have no responsibility for the websites and can make no guarantee
that a site will remain live or that the content will remain relevant,
decent or appropriate.

Hachette UK's policy is to use papers that are natural, renewable
and recyclable products and made from wood grown in sustainable
forests. The logging and manufacturing processes are expected to
conform to the environmental regulations of the country of origin.

Impression number   10 9 8 7 6 5 4 3 2 1

Year   2014 2013 2012 2011 2010

Acknowledgements

In the preparation of this book, we received help, support and advice from many people, including those who kindly responded to our research questionnaires. If we have forgotten to list anyone, please forgive us. With thanks to Stephen Aucutt, Giles N Clark, Amber Caraveo, Michael Coleman, Suzanne Collier, Peter Clover, Vince Cross, Andrew Dalton, John Goodwin, Joanna Devereux, Catherine Fisher, Jennifer Flannery, Alison Allen-Gray, Lisa Grey, Philip Gross, Bethany and Crystal Hadcroft, Frances Hendry, Barry Kernon, Penny Morris, Sue Mongredien, Christopher Norris, Kate Paice, Gary Paulsen, Kate Pool, Brandon Robshaw, Victoria Roddam, Gillie Russell, Fay Sampson, Andrew Sharpe, Kevin Stewart, Sue Welford, David Neville Williams, Adrian Whittaker, Hayley Yeeles and all the staff at Pollinger Limited.

Contents

Meet the authors

Welcome to *Write a Children's Book And Get it Published*!

Allan Frewin Jones

When I first decided I would like to see some of my writing in print, way back in the mists of time, I found a book on how to write. I have now only one clear memory of that book – in the introduction the author made the following comment: 'There are no dumb Miltons out there.'

Hmmmm. Interesting. I took the gist of this observation to be that 'talent will out' or, to put it another way: if you're any good, you will be published. He should have added the caveat: ... eventually, and if you really work at it.

I found this really rather inspiring, which is why I now pass it on to you, amended to chime with the times, and more than three decades and close to 100 published children's books down the line: There are no dumb J. K. Rowlings out there.

I was told early on that a writer's life is one of 'famine and feast' – and that is certainly true for those of us who don't immediately strike commercial gold. I carried on working full time for five years after my first book was published, although in that time another seven books of mine hit the shops.

Luck also comes into the equation. I was made redundant at the same time as a 'book packager' was on the lookout for people to write a mystery series. My redundancy pay allowed me to buy a word processor, and I got busy. Within ten months I was a full-time writer.

Over the years I have adapted to writing in different genres –
romance, adventure, detective, supernatural and fantasy – and
for different markets ranging from younger readers to teens.

What I love about the writing business is the fact that, once
published, you step onto the first rung of a ladder which can
take you anywhere.

Lesley Pollinger

I've read a great many children's books, written a handful, and
grew up and now work in the publishing and media industry.
I have an idea of how it all works, what works, who does what,
what's happening next trend-wise, and I also get the tingles
when I discover a new writer or a piece of work which I just
know I can get published in some format.

I spent much of my childhood reading. At home, when I wasn't
dancing, singing, climbing trees or building dens I was reading,
reading, reading. I read all the Katy books, the affordable
Ladybird series, Greek myths, Grimm's tales, Arthurian tales,
historical fiction, classics, every war story, escape adventure and
Paul Brickhill book I could find. I devoured science fiction, Pan
books of horror stories, non-fiction, comics, and joined the
I SPY club, buying the whole series.

I joined my father's authors' agency in 1985, cutting my teeth
on women's short story fiction. Being a late starter to publishing
(I moved to the agency from a job in the police force) I went
on Book House Training Centre courses (later becoming an
occasional lecturer), made firm friends through the Society of
Young Publishers, Federation of Children's Book Groups,
Women in Publishing and the Children's Book Circle, and
opened and ran a children's bookshop. I took on the role of
creating a bespoke children's author list at the agency, and there
came across a client called Allan Frewin Jones. After reading one
of his scripts, *The Mole and Beverley Miller*, I thought 'Wow!',

and that was the really the beginning of my professional career in the world of children's writing. What happened next would take up a whole book, so for another instalment, you'll need to check out the website which accompanies this book and I'll tell you some more stories!

Only got a minute?

From your imagination to the printed page, the process that turns a talented amateur writer of children's books into a published author is a complicated one.

At a basic level, you need to think about where ideas come from, how they clash and combine to produce fresh concepts. How do you make sure a good idea is not lost in the hurly-burly of everyday life? One important thing to do from the start is set up a writing zone for yourself. Then you need to equip yourself with whatever tools you need. For the modern writer, computers and the internet have become indispensable.

There are specific problems and challenges facing the writer of children's books, and an understanding of them will increase your chances of success. You need to consider your market and target audience carefully. Think about the full diversity of the markets that are aimed at children – from first-readers for toddlers, through to stand-alone novels for young adults, from non-fiction to full-colour picture books, from series fiction to 'issue' books, covering every subject from genetics to school bullying.

Acquiring the knowledge of how to approach publishers and literary agents in a professional and arresting way is invaluable. There are professional skills and techniques to learn that will engage commissioning editors and draw their attention, setting you apart from the amateur pack.

When your book attracts the interest of the publishing world, it will be just the beginning of a process that takes your original book or concept to the next level – and then on to the point where it becomes a publishable product.

5 Only got five minutes?

Writing for children is not an easy option. It is part of a highly diverse marketplace that calls for many specific skills and abilities.

Some of these may be quite basic. From the very beginning, it is essential that you organize your working day, whether your writing time-frame is early morning, snatched lunch-hours or late evenings. You also need to create a work space for yourself, and think about what basic equipment you need.

To succeed in writing for children, you need to be able to adapt your work for every possible age-range and interest level. It's a big wide world out there, and the more you know the better equipped you will be to thrive in it. Research and familiarity with your audience is of huge importance. Think about how to suit your language to your audience, and how to get yourself inside the head of the child you hope to entertain with your writing.

Getting your work noticed by commissioning editors and literary agents is notoriously difficult, but the publishing world is always on the lookout for new ideas by new writers, or for writers who can take an old idea and dress it up in some new clothes. Take a look at some bestselling children's fiction – most of them have at their heart a fairly old idea, dressed up for a modern readership. *Harry Potter*? There have always been books about magic and magicians. *Twilight*? The first sexually charged blockbusting vampire novel was written by Bram Stoker in 1897.

If you are thinking of adding illustrations to your book, think about what form these would take: a few line drawings, or page after page of full-colour illustrations? If you are writing a non-fiction work, research will be of primary importance but you also need to think about how to present your work – and who to present it to. Not all publishers publish non-fiction, not all non-fiction publishers publish non-fiction for children and not all non-fiction children's publishers accept unsolicited work.

There's a good chance that your first attempt at being published will fail. This is quite normal, and rejection is something every author has to get used to. Are you being told your book is just plain bad, or are you being told how to improve it? Should you do more work on your book, or should you put it to sleep and try again with something completely different? You can build on this experience, but working on other projects while you're waiting for a response from a publisher or literary agent is a good idea.

If you decide that you need to see your work in print at whatever cost, there are plenty of internet publishing houses out there that will publish anything so long as the author pays for it – think carefully about whether this is the best way forward for you.

When your book is accepted by a publisher, the chances are you have quite a few more hoops to jump through before it appears on the shelves. The publisher may want you to rewrite half of your book. How important to you is it that your work is not changed by publishers? Usually the needs and wishes of publishers and writers can be balanced.

Once your book has been accepted, an understanding of the publishing process is useful even if it is pretty much out of your hands: cover designs, logos, dump-bins for bookshops, publicity, book signing tours, internet publicity and personal websites will all form part of your book's life. Getting your first work published is only the start of it. Then there is your advance payment and how the tax system works to think about, and, of course, what happens next in your writing career!

10 Only got ten minutes?

Once upon a time, a happy little elf wrote a children's book. A fairy carriage took it away to the publisher who lived in the jewelled castle on the hill. The kindly old publisher loved the book and decreed that the Court Magician should make millions of copies that would be carried throughout the land by good-hearted imps and goblins. Every child in the kingdom loved the book and a statue of white marble was erected to the writer, upon whom gold and silver cascaded in a constant rain.

Now we've got the fairy tales out of the way, it's time to wake up and smell the napalm. The only part of that tale that's true – or at least analogous to real life, is the fact that as far as you are concerned, the publisher lives in a fortified castle – and your job if you want to be a published writer for children is to find some way of breaking into that castle and getting noticed.

Writers are not somehow 'special' or 'different' from ordinary folk. Anyone who can harness their imagination to the plough of commitment and hard work has the potential for success. On the other hand, not everyone can do it! It isn't as easy as it might look. Amusing your own kids or grandkids with a made-up bedtime story is a million miles away from getting those stories published. It will take a lot of hard work, patience, determination and a hefty serving of good luck.

Take a quick look at the competition out there. Some estimates suggest that over 250,000 books are published worldwide each year, aimed at the children's and young adults' market. Can you really hope to compete against such a riptide of writing? Of course you can. The one constant in all the endless flux of fashions and trends within the big wide world of children's publishing is that new writers are in constant demand. There is no reason at all why you can't be the publishing world's Next Great Thing.

We assume at this point that you are not a published writer; but that you wish to become one. Here's a quick list of the things you will need to get started:

- ▶ imagination
- ▶ dedication
- ▶ persistence
- ▶ flexibility
- ▶ adaptability
- ▶ patience
- ▶ self-discipline
- ▶ drive
- ▶ ambition
- ▶ hunger
- ▶ need
- ▶ desire
- ▶ a very thick skin.

As far as 'natural talent' goes, the ability to write well is as much a slow-learned process as a 'gift'. You certainly need to have good ideas, and you do need to be able to string words together, but most of the rest of getting from bedroom-scribbler to published author is a process of learning and adapting and persistent hard work.

Let's assume you have some idea of what you want to write. Before you start, you'll need to engage in some way with the market that is already out there. Read as many books as you can manage, preferably within the genre or age-range for which you are hoping to write. If you have a great idea for a school-based book or series of books, then go out and buy up all the school-based books you can find. Learn what works and what doesn't. Learn why things that used to work no longer work. Find out what kind of characters are popular at the moment. (Look for character descriptions of female main characters – nine times out of ten you will discover the word 'feisty' in there somewhere. Few girls these days are allowed out without being 'feisty'.)

Teach yourself the different word-lengths expected from the various types of book. How many words does a picture book aimed at six- to eight-year-olds have? What's the average length of a young adult novel? If you're writing a sci-fi book aimed at young adult girls, what are your chances of getting a publisher interested? How many such books are already out there? Lots? Any at all? If none, why none? Is it a gap in the market, or is it a black hole?

Learn the basic rules of writing. You don't have to be an expert in linguistics to put an appealing sentence together, but you do need to be able to spot the difference between something that is entertaining and something that is not. Be your own harshest critic. Examine every sentence you write. Rewrite and rewrite and rewrite until you are certain it's the very best you can do. Come to terms with the fact that an editor, should you encounter one, will most likely blow your favourite writing out of the water. Can you cope with that? Can you come back smiling and rewrite stuff that you think is perfect, just because an editor prefers it be done another way? Welcome to the world of professional writing.

Do you want to write for toddlers? Have you got a house full of picture books and a head full of ideas for even better picture books? Then you need to study the books you already have, in order to learn the very specific and demanding skills needed in order to present a publisher with your new idea. And you might want to know that getting a 70,000-word young adult book published is far easier than getting an 800-word picture book into the stores.

Do you have ideas for a pre-teen age-range? Do you know how books are banded by publishers, age-wise? Find out *before* you start writing. Few books appeal across the ages – a book aimed at six-year-olds is rarely appreciated by 15-year-olds. Books filled with girls characters are rarely going to be read by an audience of boys.

And what about those young adult books? What exactly is a young adult anyway? And how do you appeal to them?

The children's book market is tough and getting tougher all the time, but the good news is that it is also a very hungry market and needs a lot of feeding. Writing for children is not an easy option, but the skills can be learned by anyone of any age, so long as they are prepared to bend their muse to the needs of the marketplace.

A question that professional writers are often asked is: where do you get your ideas from? Almost as though some people imagine there is a specific method of picking up ideas, like tuning in to a radio channel. Ideas come from everywhere around you. They can be sparked by an item on the news channel on television, by a single sentence in a magazine article or by a phrase in a book or poem, or an overheard conversation. More often than not, the idea will be sparked by the collision of two things in your head. My little brother was always a pest. I like movies about vampires. My little brother is a vampire! Of course he is. It all makes perfect sense now.

This only scratches the surface, but hopefully you now have a clearer idea of the daunting task ahead of you. Still want to write for children? Then off you go. And remember what I said earlier: someone has to be the next generation's Next Big Thing – why not you?

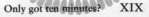

Foreword

Many years ago when I was first starting to write, one of those ridiculous writing magazines that tell you how easy it all is had an interview with Gore Vidal. When asked if he had any advice to give young (or new) writers, he said (paraphrasing – it has, after all, been some 30 years), 'Don't do it. The competition is too hard and you'll never make it. Stay out of it.'

Anger at the statement kept me going for months, but in the event he was only being honest. The competition is hard, almost impossible – you have about as much chance of selling your first book as winning the lottery. And the second one is harder. Publishers will say one thing and do the opposite, or – more likely – nothing. Agents will fudge the truth, or at least exaggerate horrendously, and movie people ... well, let's just say if you get far enough along the food chain to deal with movie people, prepare yourself for what amounts to life on another planet.

Don't do it. Stay out of it. It's too hard and will break you.

Pause.

If you're still here – as I expect you will be and as I was – and are thinking of sticking with it though you paper your house with rejections, though you spend all your extra time, money, life, on Making It Work; if you are still here then there are three primary things to take into consideration if you're going to write for young people.

Do not write down. (They are smarter than you and will smell it coming and stop reading, which is the very worst thing you can have happen as a writer.)

Do not preach. (See above.)

Do not overwrite. (See above.)

As for all the rest – dealing with publishers and editors and agents and printers and distributors and truck drivers and first readers and second readers and movie people and paper people and proof readers and editorial assistants and your cousin Fanny who read your manuscript and thinks it's '... just precious' – as for all that, read this book.

Gary Paulsen

1

Writing for children: an easy option?

In this chapter you will learn:
- *that writing for children is not an easy option*
- *that getting your material published is going to be hard work*
- *some basic guidelines to help increase your chances of getting published.*

Once upon a time, someone had a great idea for a story ...

Are you that person? Do you have a great idea in your head right now? Then you need to get it out of your head and onto paper or into your computer. If you don't have a computer or any paper to hand, use your mobile phone, blackberry or whatever other electronic device you currently carry around with you. If you don't have *any* of these things, borrow a pen from a stranger and scribble your idea down in the back of this book. Just get it written down – ideas can easily get lost in all the chaos of modern life, and you are going to kick yourself if your great idea goes down the drain because your boss suddenly gave you an insane deadline, or your children need help with their homework or you're distracted by a bee, or whatever.

Trust us – ideas can come and go really quickly if you don't pay them enough attention. And the other thing is that once you start recording ideas, they can snowball unexpectedly until suddenly you have a complete plot or storyline figured out. Don't let anyone get in the way of your great idea. There was a famous poet called Samuel Taylor Coleridge. He woke up after an amazing dream and started writing the dream down – and it turned into the poem *Kubla Khan*. It was going to be an epic, but 54 lines in, someone turned up at his house and broke his concentration – and the poem was never completed because all the rest of Samuel's ideas got knocked out of his head by his unexpected guest.

Don't let that happen to you. Don't pay any attention to the doorbell or the telephone or a text message until you have the whole of your idea written down.

How to use this book

So, what is it with books anyway? People have been prophesying the death of the printed word for years. *'In the future there will be no books. Everything will be electronic.'* Well, possibly – but we don't think so, and it certainly isn't going to happen any time soon. Handheld readers are additional ways of accessing books and information, not necessarily replacements for the sight, touch and smell of paper. Of course the internet has changed the way people read and research, especially when it comes to factual stuff – but when they're reading a good story, the majority of people still like the feel of a book in their hands – perhaps especially so for children. And even if books do eventually become 'ear-pods' or 'story-screens' – someone still needs to write them – and that's where you come in – and that's where this book comes in to help you out.

People collect expensive first editions of favourite books and keep them sealed behind glass. Good for them – why not? But books aren't ornaments – they exist to be handled and stuffed into pockets and bags and to be dropped in the bathwater and mauled around a bit... and to be *read*. Okay, so maybe we were brought up to treat books with care and reverence and not to scribble on them or fold down the corners or anything like that. Well, you can forget all of that with this book.

Exercise 1

We want you to go and buy a coloured highlighter pen, and we want you to highlight passages or lines in this book that interest you. We want you to turn the corners down and scribble in the margins. We want you to cover it in Post-it® notes. This book is a tool – like a textbook in an 'open page' exam. Its only purpose is to help you – treat it mean. *Use it!*

This book isn't like one of those writers' courses you see advertised everywhere – we don't guarantee that by the final chapter you'll have recouped your outlay from work you've had published. There are no promises like that on offer – but we do believe that by the time you've read the book, you'll have taken on board a whole lot of useful practical advice and know-how that will help you to get published – if you have the talent and the determination to really go for it.

By the way – this book isn't intended for writers who have already got published work out there; it's aimed at people who have been quietly and diligently creating stories for their own pleasure, or to amuse their own children, but who don't know how to turn their work into something that will appeal to a wider audience. Or maybe you're thinking – 'Hey, I'd like to try writing a children's book. I just bet I can do it. But how do I go about it?' Well, read on – we're here to help. Or it could be that you've been sending your work off to publishers for a while, and you're getting tired of getting rejection letters back. These days publishers don't have a lot of time to explain what you're doing wrong – but *we* do. Let us show you how you can turn rejections into signed contracts and to books on shelves.

STARTING WITH THE BASICS

We have a bit of a problem at this point. We have no idea how much you already know about writing children's books and trying to get them published. You may be on the brink of having your first piece of work accepted, or you may never before have even thought of contacting a publisher. We have to work on the basis that you know absolutely nothing, and build up from there, so we hope those of you with a higher level of knowledge will bear with us while we go through the basics.

First off, there is no right or wrong way to write for children, but getting a handle on some of the basic guidelines will increase your chances of being published. Use this book as a study aid and you'll get to where you need to be far more quickly than by going it alone. At least, that's the plan, and the fact that we're working on a fourth reprint right now suggests the plan is working fine. When we originally put this book together, we sent out a whole bunch of questionnaires to authors and publishers and literary agents (we'll fill you in on what they are later) involved in the world of children's books. These people were glad and eager to help – even the slowest, longest reply only took ten days to arrive, and a lot of people emailed or wrote back the same day. This made one thing really obvious to us – people in the book business want to help new writers and are happy to share their expertise, as well at to point out the mistakes they made along the way and what worked and didn't work for them.

When we repeated the process for this new edition, we found things had changed a little. Far fewer people responded. What should we make of this? Maybe agents and editors and authors are busier now, and don't have the time to fill out questionnaires. Maybe the world has grown harsher and more callous over the past decade? Whatever is going on, it's as well for you to be aware that, in the words of one publisher we spoke with: *'The children's market is brutal right now ...'* But brutal or not, we hope you stay with us – the world needs writers and storytellers.

The responses we got to our questionnaires covered the whole range of human emotions and experience – from laugh-out-loud hilarious (but eye-poppingly unprintable) to grim and grisly and horribly sobering. You'll spot these handy first-hand insights scattered throughout the book. We hope you'll find them as useful as we did. Here's one to be getting on with:

Insight

> Write something every day. Anything. Even if it's utter garbage. Just write.

Myth-busting

First the harsh news: if you thought writing for children was an easy option, forget it. It's probably more difficult to write the text of a 400-word picture book for the very young and get it published than it is to sell a 100,000-word novel for adults. These days it's hard for any new author to get their foot in the door, and the children's market is certainly no exception. Why so? Well here are a few of the reasons. Large book store chains will usually have a central buying policy which means they tend to buy books that will show a quick profit in all of their stores – meaning books already earmarked as bestsellers by known authors. Books by established authors or known celebrity 'names' will be given large marketing budgets, get all the publicity and go straight to the top of the buying list. As chains of book stores merge and are bought up, this just gets worse. Supermarkets and similar outlets are also in the book-selling game – 'stacking 'em high and selling 'em cheap' and not always at a profit – which is good if you are a recognized bestselling author, but it does unknown writers no favours at all. It's called 'catch-22': if no one knows who you are, how do you get publishers to pay you any attention? If your book is not advertised and broadcast to the book trade – how will buyers find out about it? 'Come back when you're better known and we'll do business together' is all very well – but how do you *get* better known? No experience could mean no publishing deal – but without getting anything published, how do you learn the trade, and how do you get your foot in the door? Read on, and we'll show you the best way of maximizing your chances.

MYTH 1: WRITING FOR CHILDREN IS EASIER THAN WRITING FOR ADULTS

At lot of people – even those who should know better – think that writing for children is going to be easier than writing for adults.

They've got that wrong.

Even famous authors of books for the over-16s have found that they can't make a go of writing for a younger readership. An author needs special and specific skills if they're going to crack the children's market.

When you write for adults, there are no real limits on the language you can use. You can also be as oblique and complex as you like in your plotting and presentation. You can write in whatever style takes your fancy, and write about pretty much anything you can think of, and you can still find publishers who will give your work a chance.

Not so in the children's market. You're going to have to come to terms with a whole heap of important new issues and concerns. Consider this for a start: what age children are you aiming your story at? Toddlers who are just starting to learn the alphabet? Five-year-olds who want an adult to read to them while they look at lots of brightly coloured pictures? Eight-year-old boys with the attention span of a fruit fly? Twelve-year-old girls who hang out in gangs in the Mall and are desperate to be 16? Soul-searching Goth teens who want to fall in love with a cute-but-dangerous vampire? Each of these target audiences will have different language skills and each will expect different things from storytellers. When you decide whom you want to write for, you then have to find yourself a publisher who works in that zone.

And there will be fewer of these than in the world of grown-up literature.

By the way, if UK readers are wondering why we don't just say 'the adult market' when we're talking about books for the over-16s – it's because in some countries the 'adult market' means erotica and porn.

If you want to crack the children's market, you're going to need a few elements working for you right from the start. You're going to need inspiration and luck. You're going to need persistence and adaptability. Then you're going to need to grow a thick skin to deal with all the harsh criticism you're going to encounter. You also have to want to write, and yet to have fun at the same time.

Think about this: in the children's market a great idea, badly written, has more chance of being picked up by a publisher than a weak idea written wonderfully well. This is because a publisher may latch onto an outstanding concept, as they know that the bad writing can be put right when it gets edited. The same publisher may be impressed by the technical expertise of wonderful writing, but if the story being told does not grab them, the book will not be taken on. In other words, there is no place in children's writing for the abstract, abstruse or overly complicated; the job of a children's writer is to tell a story – simply and entertainingly.

But is this an *easy* option? Of course it isn't, although plenty of people both outside and inside the business still don't get how hard and demanding it is.

Here's part of an actual letter from an editor who usually works on adult-interest books, in response to the submission of a children's short story by a well known author:

> *It would do you some good to make heavier demands of your art and yourself. Although you have a gift of writing both poems and fiction for children, and there is no reason*

why you shouldn't continue to cultivate it, I do worry that you may be clinging to those habits as a form of security.

In other words, stop dabbling in 'easy option' kids' books and get out in the real world. Tell that to the people who have created all the unforgettable heroes and heroines of children's literature down the years. Tell that to the creators of Alice in Wonderland, Toad of Toad Hall, the Wizard of Oz, Winnie the Pooh, Bilbo Baggins, Harry Potter and Lyra Belacqua. Tell them that all they did was to cling to children's storytelling as a form of security. It may comfort you to know that the author concerned is now a Professor of Creative Writing at a university encouraging budding writers.

No one should look upon writing for children as a soft option. Okay, it is in some ways simpler than writing for adults – the books might be shorter, the ideas less complex – but you need a particular type of ability to do it well. An ability to become a child, to get right inside the minds of your child characters, to see through their eyes and with their experience – while at the same time, remaining your adult self, sifting and selecting as you write.

MYTH 2: THE GOOD OLD DAYS OF PUBLISHING

The story goes that in the 'good old days', a publisher who liked your book would just go right ahead and make you a tasty offer on it. No problems. No delays. A handshake over lunch and it was a done deal. We're not sure it was ever quite that simple, but these days it's *certainly* a whole lot more complicated.

In the modern world, it's extremely rare that a single person has the power to make those kinds of deals. A publisher, or a commissioning editor who works for a large publisher, might think your book is great – they might love it to bits, but before they can make you an offer, they're almost always going to have to run it past an 'acquisitions meeting' where the suits and the accountants are in control. (If this reminds you of Hollywood, it should.

Money people have taken over the book world in the same way that they took over the movie world.) Companies have merged, staffs have been rationalized and pressure has been applied to cut costs and increase profits. The good old days have been replaced by tough new days.

Today, an editor has to present your book to a meeting of sales people, marketing people and hard-nosed accountants whose sole interest is in profit margins – and all of these suits have to be convinced that your book is going to reach its projected sales target before it will be taken on. These people have little interest in whether your book has literary merit or deals with an important or significant topic – of course it needs to be well-written and have *some* value, or it wouldn't have got this far – but the suits are still looking for mass-appeal and high turnover, and unfortunately at these meetings profits are always the bottom line, and a 'minority interest' classic would have a real fight on its hands, no matter how well-crafted it might be.

What these people like is to be told that a new book will be a cross between *His Dark Materials* and *Twilight*, or *Warriors* meets *Harry Potter*. This they will understand – this they will 'green light'. Tell them it's a totally original concept, and they'll shrink away from it like snails curling up in sunlight. But don't panic – brand new ideas can still force their way into the light. It's just not quite so simple to sell them to a cautious publishing world.

In such a climate it makes sense to play safe and to publish the tried and tested author, rather than to gamble on an unknown. There will always be the 'hot property' exceptions, but on the whole you need to bear in mind that in most cases you are going to be The Unknown.

It is said that everyone has a story to tell. The question that occupies the minds of publishers is whether that story will be of any interest to anyone outside the author's immediate circle of friends and relations.

MYTH 3: ONLY CHILDREN BUY THE BOOKS

Another thing you need to bear in mind is that, as with children's clothes and children's toys, the majority of children's books are *not* bought by children. They are bought by booksellers and librarians, by teachers and bulk-buying distributors. They are bought by parents and relatives, or by adult collectors and dedicated followers of a particular author's work.

In other words, your children's book or *proposed* children's book has mainly to attract and gain the interest of an adult audience. It is absolutely true that the manuscript of Tolkien's *The Hobbit* was handed by the publisher Sir Stanley Unwin to his ten-year-old son Rayner for an appraisal. The boy liked it – and the book got published. These days – no chance. Forget it.

Something else to think about is that there are fewer children in a population than there are adults, so the children's market is obviously going to be smaller than the adult market. Getting the picture? Children's publishing is a very tough and competitive market.

What if your great idea is for a picture book? Picture books are an even smaller slice of the market, and you also have to allow for a whole number of writing and marketing guidelines that are out of your control, and possibly subject to a shifting social perspective way beyond your knowledge. Therefore, your 400-word picture book idea will have to conform to a specific set of rules, and only then will it be able to take a leap into the competitive world of potentially publishable material.

Time for some good news. Just when you were about to give the whole thing up as a waste of time, there's one positive thing we can tell you: the writing for children's market is actually healthy and expanding. And not only for books, but for websites and educational resources. Governments are aware of literacy needs – if you can't read, you will find it difficult to use a keyboard. The phenomenon of Harry Potter has also allowed it to be okay for adults and young adults, who would have never previously been seen reading a 'children's book' in public, to be out in broad daylight with one. It is also heartening to know that in a recent UK survey, three out of the top five 'Favourite Books of the Twentieth Century' were actually children's books.

A vital resource

No matter what sparked your interest in writing for children, it is worth pausing a moment to consider how important books are for children. If people do not learn to enjoy reading as children, their chances of picking up the habit at a later age are pretty limited.

We mentioned earlier the predictions about the death of the printed word, and that e-devices are going to take over the world. Take a look on a bus or train or airplane and you'll see that it's just not true, there are still plenty of people with their noses in real books. People still respond to the portability and ease-of-access of a book, magazine or newspaper. You don't need to turn them on, you don't need to plug them in or insert batteries. You can read a book wherever you like: in the bath; up a tree; on a beach. It's also still far quicker to look up an unknown word in the dictionary than it is to switch on a computer and access the right web page – especially if you are in the bath or up a tree at the time.

How are children intended to gain access to knowledge and information if they never learn to read and write? A reasonable level of literacy is absolutely vital in life. Try playing a new computer game without being able to read the instructions. Almost every device or product you buy comes with a list of dire warnings or a great fat instruction manual. Try overthrowing the old order without being able to read *Computers for Dummies*. It's not going to happen.

On a wider scale – how do you apply for a job without being able to complete an application form? How do you find your way around if you can't read street signs, or use technology to search for the address? How do you communicate if you don't even have the basic skills to text? The truth is that the ability to write and type goes hand-in-hand with the practice of reading. While modern society is crying out for increased levels of literacy, these standards are not only failing to be maintained, but in many places are falling, as statistics frequently published in newspaper articles will show. Basic literacy skills are a vital resource for anyone wishing to communicate on any level above the purely verbal.

Many people complain that emails and texting are wrecking the English language. So long as children are taught the rules of spelling and grammar and syntax, and understand why it is important to have a written system that everyone can understand, what's the problem if they then go off and use slang and text-speak among their friends? LOL*!

FYI – a healthy language is in a constant state of flux, with words dropping out of use and new words entering the vocabulary all the time. The important thing for a writer to achieve is a modern voice, although at the same time you have to avoid falling into the trap of using the kind of ephemeral street slang that can outdate a book within a period of months. Words, like clothes fashion, can change with every season.

*Just in case: 'LOL' – laugh out loud; 'FYI' – for your information. See, you're getting it already.

Exercise 2

Add your own words to this list of popular expressions, which over the years have meant 'good'. Use your own experience, or think of lines heard in films from different eras:

1960s – Groovy! Fab!
1970s – Far out! Right on!
1980s – Baad! Wicked!
1990s – High five! Cool!
2000s – Safe! Awesome! Sick!

Not everyone's contribution to society can be as clear-cut as that of a doctor, a lifeboat crew member or a charity aid worker. A children's author may never know how much joy, understanding, problem solving and information their work has given to children all over the world, and in every situation. If your writing cheers one single child, if it provides escapism for a short time from some harsh reality, or if it teaches one new word or comprehension of a problem, then you've done a good thing and should feel proud of yourself.

Books are essential for children and have an important and significant role to play. There is no better medium for firing the imagination. Nowadays, humans need the skills of literacy and communication more than ever before. A large part of that learning process and literacy will involve books.

Take heart

Remember the questionnaires we mentioned earlier? Among those people we canvassed were prizewinners and full-time professional authors; and one of the questions we posed concerned the most useful piece of advice given to them when they were starting out on their writing career. Check out some of their answers:

Your readers will only read this <u>once</u>. You've got to get them <u>first</u> time.

Keep trying, don't give up in the face of innumerable rejection slips. If you really believe in yourself you will eventually succeed.

Critics are often, though not necessarily, wrong – especially if you live with them.

Learn to cope with rejection. Be yourself. Write what you want to write, and strive to find your own voice, not a pale imitation of somebody else's. Write the sort of material you

*enjoy reading, and ask yourself if you would read with
pleasure the book you have just written!*

*Talking to other writers is really helpful, as well as
interesting. I also used to be part of a creative writing group
where we discussed each other's work every week. It was
terrifying at first, having complete strangers telling me what
they thought of my writing, but getting such feedback and
insight was incredibly useful, and gave me the confidence to
show my work to professional editors.*

Don't give up your day job.

The real world

In our experience, it takes any regularly published author about
eight years to go from publication of a first work to the point
where a living wage can be earned. (This is based on at least one
book coming out every year – some writers manage a lot more
than that, but for most, it's going to be a lot less). The exception
would be for someone producing an instant worldwide bestseller.
Of course, if you don't need to go out and earn a living, then you
might be able to carve a few years off the end of this timescale, but
that's all. It's still a long process.

The average author has to love writing; it's pointless going into
the writing business expecting to get rich and famous. It simply
doesn't work like that. You'll need a lot of patience and plenty
of perseverance, and you may never make a fortune or be a
recognizable celebrity. Full-time writers will also tell you that it can
be a very lonely existence – just you and your computer and four
walls for hours and days and sometimes weeks on end. Can you
deal with that?

At the start you shouldn't try! If you have a job, keep it: you're
going to need the money. If you're totally dedicated to writing

for a living, explore the possibilities of job-sharing or part-time work, so that you can be sure of a regular and reliable income. Writing, like many freelance occupations, can be a case of swings and roundabouts, feast or famine. Gradually an author will start to receive income from royalties, advances and so on, which will help through the lean times, but there is no substitute for the security of a separate safe salary. Think of that salary before handing in your resignation.

Besides needing some other source of income, you'll also need to get out into the real world to keep the creative juices flowing, and to keep a balanced view of life. Working, travelling, and socializing with other people, meeting new faces, experiencing novel or unusual situations and listening to the experiences of others will give you plenty of fuel for to your imagination. Being alone, with only the radio or social networking websites for company could seriously limit your individual creativity.

Your own experiences, and those of people around you, are a good source of ideas. I find that early writings have more resonance if they are based on something you already know. Always keep your eyes and ears open. Observe how people behave, and listen to what they say. If you want your books to be peopled with real characters, you need to become something of an expert on human behavior.

Exercise 3

Hopefully, you already have plenty of ideas for stories, so all you want from us is to learn how to polish them up so they'll appeal to a publisher. But before you go any further, you're going to need to check that your idea is as original as you think. There's always the chance that someone else has beaten you to it – and if they have, you don't want to be wasting your time working on something that is already on the bestseller list with its own brand of soft toys, T-shirts,

(Contd)

and a movie that's about to hit the market. So, if you have
an idea already, do a little research to find out how just
original it may be.

You may be stuck with only half an idea, or no ideas at all. You
might have just spent two hours staring at a blank computer screen
without a single creative thought in your head. Your muse may
have switched off the light and gone out clubbing – muses can
do that to you. It's fine – it happens to the best of writers – you'll
get over it.

But there are cunning ways of dealing with this kind of 'dead air'.
If you have writers' genes, the chances are that part of your brain
is always on the lookout for new ideas. Latch onto these things
and keep a tight hold on them. Anything potentially interesting
should be noted as a reminder for later. It's also worth knowing
that a single idea is often not enough. Real creativity starts to flow
when two opposing ideas collide. When you mash three or four
ideas together – you're probably well on the way to plotting out
an entire book.

Insight
Get yourself a notebook or some e-device you can use to leave
yourself reminders or suggestions – something you can keep
in a pocket or bag and carry around with you all the time.

You can record or make notes on your mobile, you could use
someone else's phone to call and leave yourself a message on your
home answerphone. You could scribble an idea on the back of a
receipt. The point is that you should always be on the look out
for potential ideas – and you should always have some method of
recording these ideas. Don't rely on your memory unless you know
for sure that it's totally infallible.

Become an 'ideas scanner'. Look, listen and learn from everything
that is going on around you. Make the most of any contact you

have with children and check out everything that forms part of a child's world. Watch children's television programmes, buy children's magazines and check out internet websites aimed at children. Be sensible about how you use the internet – browsing websites aimed at children is fine, but never involve yourself in young people's chat-rooms or anything of that nature, even if your interest is for research purposes and entirely innocent.

Insight

Visit toyshops, mooch around shopping centres and malls at the weekend or during school holidays. Go to a park or other place where you know kids hang out. Maybe even take your life in your hands and get on board a bus when the schools are emptying out in the afternoon. You'll learn some new stuff, we can promise you that – although how much of it will be printable, is another matter!

Conversations overheard between kids in queues, fast-food restaurants or on street corners or railway platforms will probably astound and astonish you. When they think there are no adults around to hear them, even the most sweet and doe-eyed teens can out-swear a whole unit of battle-hardened paratroopers. If you find yourself within earshot of startling and shocking language or behaviour, bear in mind that although publishers are always on the look out for 'reality' there are limits to what can be put into print. Similarly, behaviour between children can be alarmingly cruel and violent and full of casual abuse – not to mention breathtakingly and publicly sexual. This level of 'reality' *can* form part of your book – but sex, violence and bad language will only get through the net of fashion and political correctness if there is a very good reason for it. Even then, books with such content may well be banned from schools and libraries and so on. In other words – be real, be true – but remember that there are going to be limits.

Train yourself to spot the differences in behaviour between children. Do boys behave differently from girls? If so, in what ways? And why? Do girls behave differently in front of boys than they do with other girls, and vice versa? Do they all behave differently with adults? Jot down ideas in your notebook or on your e-device. And if you suddenly remember something from your own childhood – note it before you forget it again.

I get my ideas from books, places, TV, from myths and legends and from using archetypal storylines. I have a notebook, nothing else.

I put my useful ideas down longhand in a little blue book. The little black book is for something else …

Alongside using your favourite way of saving notes, you should also be starting a scrapbook of some kind – a cuttings file that will become your 'Ideas File'. A large envelope would do the job, an empty drawer, a concertina file – or you could go crazy and set up an alphabetical or cross-referenced subject filing system. Or keep it all on computer – hard-copy information could also be scanned and saved easily enough. Whatever system you use, fill it with newspaper or magazine clippings – eye-catching headlines or entire articles, pictures of people, buildings, scenery, cartoons, work by an inspirational artist, copy and paste downloads from interesting websites – anything, in fact, which you think might inspire you one day. You never know what might come in handy further down the line. Suck it all up and put it somewhere that's easy to find again. Do whatever works for you.

For character ideas, I cut out photos from magazines/papers/ catalogues. I make a pinboard for each book, with notes beside pictures for age, character, links with others, etc.

Insight

Later in this book we will start suggesting uses for your 'Ideas File', so it is best to start gathering material now. The larger your collection, the more useful it will become.

Think about it: a video stream of a child being rescued from a burning building may be the kernel from which a whole book could grow; a newspaper article about curriculum changes in education may be the seed for a non-fiction work; a face in a magazine may awaken in you the entire personality of a central character for a book.

For many years I have kept an 'Ideas Folder'. Whenever an idea comes to me, even if only a snippet, or a funny or intriguing remark I have heard someone say in the street, I immediately put it in my folder. Ideas can linger therein for years before finally being put to good use.

The electronic age

Things have changed a lot since we started on the first edition of this book way back in 1995. In those days it was quite unusual for us ordinary people to have computers, but now they're available to almost everyone and many children have their own computers in their bedrooms.

Writing my book on a computer has proved invaluable. All my notes/ideas/drafts/research are there in one file, only a finger-click away.

In 1995, that seemed like a really interesting thing for a writer to tell us – now, it's as though they were explaining how a thing called a 'pen' and a sheet of a substance called 'paper' were amazingly helpful.

Then there was that remarkable new invention called 'the World Wide Web'. We spent a lot of time a few years back explaining how that worked. No need to bother now – there's a good chance that you bought this book from an online store. By the time this book is a year old, we know technology will have leapt even further forward. Ease of access to computers and broadband technology has speeded up the connection to an astonishing

universe of information and research material. In the words of
one publisher:

> *These days, for writers, the computer is no longer an*
> *optional extra – it is a vital tool.*

Yes, it is. But we do need to pause for just a moment. If you're
not plugged into the internet revolution, you will find you have
an additional hurdle to overcome in the race to being published.
These days the vast majority of communication between an editor
and a writer will be via emails. The work you are writing may not
actually ever appear on paper – in 'hard-copy' form – until the
finished and published book lands on your doorstep. The whole
process will very likely take place on a computer – with copies
flying back and forth via emails while it's being edited. Publishing
agreements increasingly include a clause that insists that the writer
must submit the work on disk or electronically. In other words,
unless you have a computer, you may not even get a contract.
Think about *that* for a while if you're still using pen and paper.

But the computer and internet revolution has had enormous
benefits for a writer capable of taking advantage of it.

> *I would never have written novels, I suspect, before word-*
> *processors. Editing – for myself, back and forth with editors –*
> *is really well served by email.*

(For our younger readers: 'word processors' were early computers.)

> *You can work on more than one project at a time. A finger-*
> *click and everything's filed away, neat and tidy. Also, editing*
> *has become a dream where it used to be a nightmare of*
> *messy crossing out, tipped and spilled coffee!!*

Once again, the above comments speak with awe and glee of
something that has now become quite ordinary. Let's check out
quickly how the internet can help you with your writing. Imagine
you're writing an adventure story set in a remote part of China

and you live in Europe or America. The characters canoe down a river – one of them falls in and becomes ill – and it might be cholera. You want to make this as realistic as possible. You don't have the resources to visit China, you don't know a canoe from a banana and you have no idea of the symptoms of cholera. Easy-peasy these days!

Get on the internet, open your favoured search engine and type 'cholera symptoms'. A few seconds later and there you go – all the information you could possibly want, delivered to your computer instantly and in huge amounts. We just tried this ourselves – and came up with 1,380,000 references. One online encyclopaedia, Wikipedia, is also a huge source of information, although it has been suggested that double-checking entries on any such 'public access' site may be a good idea, as misinformation and errors can creep in when the general public is allowed to write and edit entries. MySpace, Facebook, Bebo, Twitter and other social networking sites can also open your search to a whole world of people who may already know what you need to find out. Use whatever resources the internet offers – dive right in! But if the information you want is of a factual kind (like with cholera symptoms), then cross-reference the answers you discover – make sure you're not quoting someone with a website and an over-active imagination but with no actual grasp of the facts. Don't get caught out by some random blogger's world of wishful thinking. Research selectively and only use reference answers you're sure are correct.

If you prefer your information in hard-copy form, you can log onto an internet bookshop and buy yourself a 'Lonely Planet' guide to China. Then add to your information pool by clicking onto something like Google Earth for the location or tourist sites where travellers have posted their own photos of China – that way you can actually see what the area you're writing about looks like.

Let's run a little further with the China thing. Your characters are in China, and you live in the United Kingdom. You know about Chinese food, but you suddenly realize that you don't have the faintest idea what Chinese families eat for breakfast. Into the search engine: 'Chinese breakfast'. Ten seconds later you'll have in front of you menus for a whole range of Chinese breakfasts. For those of us who have grown up doing this kind of research the hard way, the internet revolution is miraculous!

The difference between internet information and that accessed from books, is that most non-fiction and reference books will have been written by an expert, checked again and again by editors and other experts, and as correct as humanly possible at the time of going to the printers.

We've all heard people say: *I read it in the newspaper therefore it must be true.* Any of you who have ever been involved in some way with something you have then read about in the newspaper will know how many inaccuracies can get reported. Be cynical, use your common sense, and double check your facts before repeating what could become a 'Chinese whisper'.

Exercise 4

Become an Instant Expert:

Spend no more than ten minutes searching the internet on a subject you know absolutely nothing about. It could be the sewer system under a city, the effects on sea life of an oil spill from a tanker, or the sleeping habits of a sloth. Try to focus on the most useful sites – not just those that appear on the first page. Look for sites that appear to have credentials – do they come from a recognized organization? Jot down some notes, and then either write, dictate, or tell a friend what you have learned.

Did you search worldwide, or just home country sites? Did you want to get distracted and go searching for the effects of sleep deprivation instead of sloths? Have you found out enough about your subject in the time allowed? Is it accurate? Would you feel confident enough to use the information in a work you were writing without further research? Have you found a new topic of conversation you could bluff another person about? Does what you have found given you any ideas that could link into a plot idea you have?

There is more about research in Chapter 2, but a reminder here that despite ease of access to a whole world of wonder, you don't want to become an 'internet potato'. You still have to get out there into the real world sometimes and see what real people are getting up to – don't let yourself overdose on the internet and forget what is happening beyond your front door.

Computers save writers an amazing amount of time. Only a few years ago, any changes to a script would have to be laboriously cut and pasted into the pages of a hard-copy manuscript. If there were too many changes, or if they were scattered all over the script, then the entire manuscript would need to be retyped – a time-consuming ordeal if you were doing it yourself, and an expensive one if you hired a ten-fingered typist.

These days, say an editor likes your book but wants the main character's name changed from Prudence to Jade. A nightmare of work a few years back – but now you just press FIND, type in 'Prudence' – press REPLACE – type in 'Jade' – and it's done – in a moment 'Prudence' is replaced by 'Jade' right through the manuscript. But watch out – if you're hero is called Tom and needs to be called Frank, and you do 'find and replace' on 'Tom' – you might find that words like 'tomato' and 'bottom' have suddenly become 'Frankato' and botFrank' – and once you've made that mistake you've opened yourself to a world of pain.

Even in a pre-edit phase of writing your book, you can make big changes very easily. Scenes can be highlighted and moved about in the manuscript. Paragraphs, incidents, conversations, revelations, explanations, can be taken out, rewritten, expanded, tweaked, twisted and rearranged – and all with an ease that would have had Tolkien dancing in the streets.

In other words, if you can possibly afford to buy a computer – or if you can beg or borrow one or find access to one for your writing-stints – then you must! This is a revolution in writing that you really cannot ignore; as one writer expressed it:

> *I can hardly believe it now, but I used to write everything in longhand and then type it up on a clanky old typewriter! I still can't type 'properly', but nowadays everything goes straight onto the computer; for anyone wanting to be taken seriously as a professional author, a computer is not just useful, it is an absolute necessity – and so far as research is concerned, the internet has now become my very best friend.*

10 THINGS TO REMEMBER

1 *Immediately begin making a record of ideas the moment you have them.*

2 *Don't be afraid to annotate this book so you can easily find information of particular interest to you.*

3 *Realize that publishing is a business and you need to be business-minded and professional.*

4 *The children's market is naturally going to be smaller than the adult market.*

5 *Your writing will form part of a child's education.*

6 *You are unlikely to get rich quick through writing for children.*

7 *Keep your day job – for security and for inspiration.*

8 *Start an 'Ideas File'.*

9 *Get access to a computer and become computer and keyboard literate.*

10 *Learn how to search the internet effectively.*

2

A professional approach

In this chapter you will learn:
- *how to approach the craft of writing in a professional way*
- *the importance of researching the children's market*
- *how to maintain contact with the children's world and the world of children's publishing.*

People want to write for children for all kinds of reasons.

> *I used to work in children's publishing, and when I left work to bring up my children, writing for that market seemed a very family-friendly thing to do.*

> *At first, I wrote books so that I could read them – it was only later on that I considered the possibility of any audience other than my own children.*

At one and of the spectrum, you may have a job in the publishing industry and think you know enough about how it works to join in on the creative side; alternatively, you might be someone who is full of stories that you write for your own entertainment, but which you now think other people might enjoy. Either way, the path to publication is a long and twisty one – the gulf between writing for your own pleasure (or the pleasure of friends and family) and writing professionally for a larger audience is wide and deep.

If all you're interested in is entertaining your friends and family, than you don't need to teach yourself how to get published – all you probably want is a book that shows you how to improve your storytelling skills, and even then you can choose to ignore the advice if it doesn't appeal to you. There are a lot of non-professional ways of getting your work out there: fanzine fiction has become increasingly popular with the rise of the internet: stories inspired by fans of *Star Trek* or *Doctor Who* or *Twilight*, etc., written and read by a small band of enthusiasts. Or you can just print your work out and hand it around to receptive friends – there's nothing wrong with doing that. But in this book, we assume you want to learn how to become a professional – how to get your work published and get paid for it – and that is an entirely different thing.

Insight

As with any profession, you will need to learn your trade. If you are a true beginner, you will have to accept that you probably have a challenging learning curve to negotiate before you should consider presenting your work to a potential publisher.

So, let's get going with the absolute basics of this apprenticeship. First of all, you will want to know as much as possible about your intended market. This means research.

Research

If you have only just begun to write and to think about seeking a publisher for your work, the chances are you will know practically nothing about the battle you are about to undertake. The world of publishing is a fortified citadel with towering walls and a wide moat – you need all the tactics, wiles, weapons and skills you can accumulate if you are going to attack and conquer it. Keep in mind that you are not the only person trying to get in – you're going to have some stiff opposition from your fellow writers.

Remember the old gag about the two men running from the lion. One says, 'We'll never outrun the lion!' The other one replies, 'I don't have to; I just need to outrun *you*.'

If this sounds a bit cut-throat and callous, then welcome to the world of publishing! Get used to it. A publisher told us this:

> *My advice is to read a lot of children's books, and visit many children's bookshops. Too many would-be writers have no idea what's in the marketplace or what may appeal to their readers.*

THE IMPORTANCE OF RESEARCHING YOUR MARKET

If you're starting to wonder when we're going to get to the actual *writing* part of teaching yourself how to write for children, then you're in for a disappointment. Not yet. There's some really important stuff we have to get through first.

You're going to have to take a long, hard look at the market for your work.

You are planning on presenting a publisher with a product that will make everyone plenty of money. By the way, money may not be at the top of your list of priorities while you are writing, but it will be way up there for the publisher. They are in the business of selling books, making a profit, and buying more books to sell to make more money. Publishers are looking for books with very strong marketing angles.

Imagine for a moment that you are an inventor – working away in the shed at the bottom of your garden, perfecting some marvellous new device intended to make everyone's life easier. How are you going to feel if you present your invention to a manufacturer, only to find it already exists?

You are going to feel like an idiot. By doing some simple research you could have saved yourself weeks and months of pointless labour. Worse – had you known that a similar device was already out there, you might have been in a position to come up with a 'new improved' version.

Similarly with publishers, they're not going to publish a book that is exactly the same as something already in the bestsellers' lists. But – and this is a useful *but* to remember – they might well be interested in a book that looks at a bestselling concept in a new way, or which compellingly combines two well-loved themes.

While we are writing this, the books and the movie *Twilight* are making big bucks. *Twilight* just takes the thoroughly road-tested 'bad boy' concept and runs an extra mile with it – the bad boyfriend is a *vampire*. There's nothing new about vampire stories, and there's nothing new about stories of teen girls falling in love with bad boys. But slam the two ideas together and you're on a roll.

But let's get back to that inventor as he returns to his shed, a sadder and wiser person. With any luck our inventor will have learned to research the market before starting on anything new. The bottom line is, research will save you a lot of wasted time.

Look at it from a different point of view. Imagine you're going to a job interview. The wise applicant would dress correctly, behave appropriately, and find out as much about the company they want to work for as possible. Think about it. The interview is almost over, you think you've done reasonably well – then comes the dreaded question – '… and do you have anything you would like to ask us?' How great would it be to say: 'Actually, yes – I noticed your market share in the mid-west is down by 17 per cent for the first quarter of this year, and I was wondering if your advertising policy might be to blame. I have here a few ideas I'd like to run past you…'

Of course, if the Chief Executive who is interviewing you came up with the ad campaign, you might be in trouble, but on the whole the interview panel will be impressed that you have done … what's that word …? … homework … background … there it is: research!

The authors responding to our questionnaire said:

> *The most useful piece of advice anyone gave me was, 'Go to
> the library and see what sort of books other people write.'
> This will give you an idea of what publishers want.*
>
> *Research, read and target your market.*
>
> *If you want to get published, then you have to write
> something publishers are looking for. Find out what is
> selling (or even better – what is going to sell next year) and
> then write something which will fit the bill.*
>
> *It's important to think about your market, age-ranges,
> current tastes and issues before you start writing.*

As well as researching the market, find out about the publishers.
Not all publishers publish children's books. Not all children's book
publishers publish non-fiction books. Teenage magazine publishers
do not necessarily publish magazines for the pre-school age group.
It is a waste of everyone's time to submit a project to the wrong
publisher. Research will tell you where your work is most likely
to be accepted, and even if you're not successful straight away,
at least you'll be heading in the right direction.

WHERE TO START RESEARCHING

Access to the internet gives you a quick and user-friendly way of
finding things out. Most publishers will have a website that you
can access – and plenty of Literary Agents and authors also have
their own official sites, as well as a presence on social networking

sites. The websites run by publishers will give you plenty of information about what kind of books they publish and usually have a section on how to approach them with an unsolicited manuscript. You will also find many websites relating to authors, from the Society of Authors, to the Federation of Children's Book Groups, to children's book review sites. We've included some useful address at the end of this book.

I use the internet all the time – I have it open constantly as I write, both on the thesaurus page and on Google so I can type in a word or phrase and see the information I need right away.

TIPS FOR SEARCHING THE INTERNET EFFECTIVELY

▶ *Get access to the internet and type in 'how to search the internet effectively' and read thoroughly a couple of the very useful articles you will find. Print out the pages or make notes to remind yourself later.*

▶ *Use different search engines regularly, don't just stick to your favourite. Type in 'search engine' and look at the range available from the listings.*

▶ *Pick a topic you want to look at, and experiment with different search engines to see how the results to your query vary. Search 'the web', and search 'pages from the UK' or your country. Note the different results. We find searching for home-based sites can speed the process, rather than being led at tangents in all different directions.*

▶ *Be selective. Do not feel you have to look through all the search results returned. Often you will find an appropriate site within the first couple of pages of results.*

▶ *Type in 'writing for children' and look at the results. Also look at the 'searches related' topics that may help focus and link to the areas you are most interested in.*

▶ *Set yourself a time limit. You can get too easily distracted by internet research. It's good fun, but bear in mind that while the internet is an excellent tool, it can also turn into a time-consuming toy – don't let yourself be led astray.*

Exercise 5

Go online and type 'online bookshops' into your favourite
search box. Scroll down several pages and look at the
range out there. Some are purely online stores, and have no
retail shops at all. Do the same or similar word search in
'Shopping'. Search the bestsellers lists for children's books
and then search for that book title under a 'News' search,
then an 'Image' search, and lastly a general worldwide search.
Look for information about the author, the publisher and for
any reviews or press coverage. What have you discovered?

Next pick a bestselling adult interest bestselling title and
repeat the search. You'll find out which books are the
highest sellers and what types of books are getting a big
promotional push – useful things to know for the budding
professional. You may also be able to read both an inhouse
review of the book and comments by readers. Although
the latter will always be subjective, a book that received
unanimous five-star reviews has got to be worth investigating
further. You will almost certainly find that the press
coverage or information on an adult title will be far greater
than that for a children's title. What does that tell you?

Insight

Checking out the websites of published authors is always
helpful, and many authors spawn official and unofficial
fansites where you will be able to learn first-hand from their
readers what it is that they love about the writer and the
work being discussed.

There are now so many useful websites out there, from schools,
to organizations local to you. The internet can also put you in
touch with writing groups and creative writing websites, where

you can have online discussions with other trainee writers. Beware of signing up to any group that asks for fees up-front, which may lead to a hard sell of a writing or editing service you don't yet need. The more you research, the more you'll find as links lead you in random but possibly inspirational directions.

Insight

Do be very wary of online publishers who guarantee to publish your work. The whole idea is that publishers should be paying you – not the other way around. Our advice at this stage is *never* pay to be published. More about this in Chapter 12.

Get out and visit your local bookshops, and join your local library – you will probably find they all have websites of their own which you can investigate first. Your library, civic hall, community centre, museum and local council area may well have regular talks along with inspirational exhibitions. Look for adverts in the 'What's On' sections for your area and in local newspapers. There is probably a lot more going on than you realized. After that, visit every bookshop and library you come across. Widen your area of research as far as you can. If you are away from home, check out any 'book places' you may happen across. There are a few specialist children's bookshops, but it is a good idea to root around in regular bookshops, too, and look at all other retail outlets where children's books are being sold.

Children's books are sold in all manner of places, from newsagents to service stations, from supermarkets to market stalls, from garden centres to mail-order clubs and leaflets, from television shopping channels to online booksellers, from toy shops to school book fairs and clubs.

Bargain and remainder bookshops are worth investigating, too. They will give you an idea of books which have not done well, and which are being sold cheaply. There are publishers who produce glossy-but-cheap books specifically aimed at this market, and some titles may have been bought in as 'damaged stock' – these could well be bestsellers. Take the time to browse and observe. If you need to increase your stock of ideas or reference books for use at home, don't forget to check out charity shops and other places where you might pick up second-hand books at a reasonable cost.

> **Insight**
> Treat all your research visits as a learning process. Unless you have already chosen a specific area of writing, look at everything. It will help you understand the market.

As far as libraries are concerned, check out the opening times before you head off, particularly if you want to look at a specialist children's section, as library opening times do vary. They stock large-print books, audio books, CDs and DVDs. They often have resource centres where you can access the internet and reference material. Some small towns and suburbs without libraries have travelling libraries which visit once a week and can offer a much more personal service. Libraries stock far fewer hardback titles and more paperbacks these days. Many children's publishers no longer produce original fiction in hardback at all. Some hardbacks have been replaced with what are called 'trade paperbacks'; these books are aimed mainly at the schools and library markets because of their durability. Trade paperbacks are generally the same size as a hardback, but because of the 'soft' cover are less expensive both to produce and to buy.

During your research, if you are lucky enough to encounter a specialist children's librarian, you should talk to them. These people are very widely read and knowledgeable in their field. Pick an appropriate time to approach them, or arrange to go back and speak with them at a more convenient time. You never know, a good library and its staff could prove a gold mine of reference and research material if approached in the right way. Look out for information leaflets, recommended reading lists, competitions and children's events run by your library or visiting library.

One author said this:

> *A children's writer's best friend is her librarian – cultivate the local children's library or department, useful for research/publicity/contacts/sales.*

Try to visit bookstores at times when they are not crowded out. This might give you the opportunity to approach staff and speak with them. You never know, you might encounter someone with both the time and the knowledge to be a help to you. For example, they may be able to tell you what the bestselling titles are in their shop. Many bookshops that are part of a group or chain have central buyers who make the purchasing decisions for the whole group; however, if you come across a person who actually buys the books for the store, you could ask them about their favourites. Ask them what titles or subjects publishers' reps or the book trade magazine *The Bookseller* are pushing hardest at the moment, and also what kind of things customers most frequently request. That way you can discover both what the publishing world is trying to sell, and what customers are looking for.

You may discover that customers want books on coping with examination stress at school. Are there such books? If so, what do they look like? What age-range are they intended for? Where are they located in the shop? If there are no such books, you may have just discovered every author's potential crock of gold: a gap in the market.

FINDING YOUR WRITING ZONE

If you know the genre or book and the age-group for which you want to write, make a point of investigating other books in that field. Make notes of what you find out. How many pages long are the books? How large is the typeface, and what style is it? Does the font size and type make it easy to read? Roughly calculate the average text length of the books and note the differing needs of different age groups. Do the books have illustrations? If so, are they in colour or black and white? Are they full page, half page or positioned amongst the text? Are there a lot of titles by the same author? Do the books form part of a series?

You will come across a lot of 'series' books identifiable by their series titles or visual style. Some series may be about one set of characters and written by a single author – or at least, bearing a single author's name. (A series may very well be written by several authors, but be published under a single 'brand name' for ease-of-identification and bookshelf placement.) Other series may have a specific theme: horror stories, for instance, or romance, or maybe a non-fiction series by different authors, but sharing the same jacket logo, name and style. Series aimed at younger readers – storybooks for instance – may have colour-coded or numbered recommended reading age guidelines.

CALCULATING THE LENGTH OF A BOOK

Count the number of words in ten average-length lines of print. Divide the total by ten to give an average number of words per line. Look at several pages of text and note the average number of lines per page. Multiply the average number of words per line by the average number of lines per page. This will give you a rough idea as to the number of words per page. Multiply this figure by the number of pages in the book. You now have a good working idea of how many words there are in the entire book.

Example: 10 words per line × 25 lines per page × 100 pages in a book = a 25,000 word text.

Make some allowance in your total figure for illustrations, chapter openings and where chapters end part-way down the page and so on.

RESEARCH ON YOUR DOORSTEP

There could be many reasons why you may not be able to visit libraries and bookshops as often as you might wish. First, take a look around your home, and those you visit. What books, or audio books or downloads do you own? What reference books or material do you have? Any storybooks from your childhood? If so, why did you keep them? Why did you like them? If your friends or family have children, ask them about the books, magazines, comics, audios, downloads, games and films they have, who bought them and where and when, and why they like or dislike them.

A fair amount of information can be delivered to your door. Investigate one of the mail-order book clubs that include many children's books and often advertise in newspaper magazines. Many books are especially printed for book clubs (known as 'book club editions') and can be cheaper than those from other retail outlets.

Some book clubs ask you to buy a certain number of books, DVDs etc. annually, along with postage and packing costs, so you might want to think that over before you sign up.

On the other hand, the brochures will show you the most popular titles, and buying books, DVDs or audio books from book clubs will be useful to your research as they will give you a good idea of what kind of material is in fashion.

Insight

Don't forget to keep your receipts or invoices for purchases made in connection with your writing business, as these expenses may be offset against tax (see the section 'Tax and accounts' in Chapter 12).

Many societies and organizations produce their own magazines which can be sent to your home, and don't forget to search through any junk mail which lands on your doorstep before throwing it in the recycling bin. Looking at the latest branded merchandising for children will show you what's in fashion, and you can spot for those products based on books or film/TV to see where the inspiration has come from.

There are also various magazines aimed at teachers, parents and buyers of children's books. These might be worthwhile subscribing to as they contain author interviews, reviews, news of awards and event details. The reviews, for example, cover a whole list of subject matter and, among other things, may save you from wasting your time on a project which someone else has just had published.

Other trends to keep an eye on include those in toys, clothing, merchandising, film and the media. This is known as 'riding the Zeitgeist' or – more plainly – giving the audience what it wants. But beware: you must avoid writing a book on a subject that is all the rage now but which will be out of date by the time it hits the shelves. Contemporary writing needs to be able to survive short-lived fashions and to avoid becoming rapidly dated. In other words, follow the latest trends, but don't get dazzled by them. It can take a couple of years for a book to reach publication. Retro spinning tops and licensed film character crazes may reach epidemic proportions every Christmas, but in two years' time a book devoted to this year's obsession is likely to be old news as new fads are promoted. Keep attuned to what is happening in the marketplace and, if possible, think of what might be coming next.

Educational periodicals (whether hard copy or online) are good sources of information if you are thinking of writing non-fiction or entering the educational market. These publications discuss issues and trends in education, as well as containing reviews and details of educational websites. Some newspapers review children's books and materials, and have occasional or seasonal children's book supplements.

Radio, television, and the magazine market can keep you fairly well informed. Listen to and watch children's and teen-based programmes, as well as broadcasts for schools (often shown during the day). You should be interested particularly in book reviews, readings from books, and dramatized shows on terrestrial, digital, cable and satellite television, especially those based on books. Search your interactive TV menu if you have access, for programmes that may not be otherwise widely broadcast, but are book shop sponsored children's book review programmes. Set your TV recorder to catch programmes that are broadcast at inconvenient times, to watch when it suits you. This will also allow you to hit the pause button if you are making notes. Many radio and television programmes can also be accessed via your computer if you've missed their immediate broadcast. Record relevant radio shows for future play-back – radio is more word-heavy than TV, and you may miss something important or useful in a single hearing.

Watch as wide a variety of TV programmes as you can, and work out why particular series are popular and successful. Remember that someone created the idea, and someone had to write the script.

Insight
To compete with what's already been or about to be published, your idea will have to be original and imaginative.

I have a lot of contact with children through family, friends and regular visits to schools. I find it enormously important to keep a feel for the way children talk and behave and think ... and also to know a little about current trends and interests. Watching television is particularly useful.

Buy a variety of children's comics and teen magazines on a fairly regular basis. Take a look at the features and letters pages. If you are an adult and you're not familiar with today's teen magazines, you will probably be surprised or even shocked by the topics covered, but you need to know what your audience is up to if you want to communicate effectively with them. Remember – these kids are possibly a lot more worldly-wise than you were at their age. Talk down to them and you'll be dead meat.

Exercise 6

Take a newspaper, or turn to a 24-hour TV or radio news channel, or open a news page on the internet, or search for the latest video clips. Take two totally random headlines or stories. For instance: 'Mum let son believe he was ill' and 'Kid stuck in skate park bowl'; 'Ducks quack in different languages' and 'Angry baby says monkey hit me'; 'More help needed for young runaways' and 'Sat Nav for disappearing puffins'. We found these in seconds from a newspaper and the web.

Ask yourself a relevant question, such as: do these young runaways have anything to do with the disappearing puffins? Or: are the puffins themselves the young runaways – and if so, where are they running to, and why?

Now write a paragraph-length synopsis of a story linking the news items that have caught your eye. Or you could try a very short story, or even a poem or limerick incorporating your news items.

Seems a bit arbitrary? It certainly is – and the less relevant the two items are to one another, the more fun you can have coming up with ways to link them together.

This technique of randomly selecting unrelated ideas can also oil the pistons of a seized-up imagination.

Those more interested in writing non-fiction can use an encyclopaedia, or reference/technical website. Randomly select a heading and write down all you know on that subject, even if very little, before comparing your piece with the entry. If you select two headings, stimulate the brain cells by seeing if you can form a connection, however tenuous the link.

Meeting your audience

Some authors claim to have very little contact with children, yet are still able to produce marvellous work time and time again. They are able to remember their own feelings and experiences and access their 'inner child' to create works that are avidly read and which receive ecstatic reviews. These authors clearly recollect what it is like to be a child, and how children think and comprehend the world around them.

I think contact with children can be overrated. The important thing is to remember what it was like to be a child. Their environment may be very different from yours, but their emotions aren't. Children still laugh at the same things you did and cry for the same reasons.

I have little direct contact with children other than visiting schools to do book talks. I don't actually know any children and have thus come to conclude that it is not important. More important is to be flexible in your thoughts, keep abreast of modern trends and perhaps above all to go back and become as a child.

I teach in a primary school and see children a lot. It is important, especially if you're used to reading aloud to them, so that you know how they respond to books. Having said that, I don't think about the reader much at all when I write, being so caught up with the story and satisfying myself! But the knowledge of probable responses must be there deep down.

What about the publishers of children's books and their staff? You'd be surprised at how little contact many of them have had with children since leaving school. Many young people work in editorial, production and marketing positions, and they don't always have families of their own, so their recent experience of children can be very limited. It's often the case that these young editors will come from a middle-class university graduate background and know nothing about life 'in the hood'. Publishers will point to the years of experience that senior editors have in the world of children's publishing – and to their great knowledge of what works and what doesn't – but the reality is that you may find yourself facing a very inexperienced editor who, for workload reasons, has to make critical decisions with limited knowledge and very scanty senior advice. Some enlightened publishers do send staff into schools on a regular basis and use this to get feedback on potential projects. Others use focus groups of children for feedback on projects. However, an editor's possible lack of child contact and experience, and the people who buy children's books, should be borne in mind when working with a publisher, or coping with rejection letters.

You may be one of those people who seem to have a sixth sense for what will appeal to both children and publishers but, on the whole, successful children's authors whom we contacted felt that it is very important to keep in regular contact with children and their world.

I need to stay in touch with children. Language, tastes and outlook change all the time.

Have as much contact as you can stand!

How do you know what children like to read if you don't have contact?

You may have children of your own, in which case you can use them as a starting point. But don't kid yourself into thinking that a bedtime story which proves a roaring success at home will necessarily interest an outside audience. Most children love to be read to, and simply enjoy the attention and experience. A young child might well be perfectly happy to have an attentive parent's lulling voice reading names from a telephone directory prior to lights out.

My elder two children always said, 'I loved that book, Mum. You're really good.' The youngest is more critical. I like the first reaction best!

CHILDREN'S SCHOOLS AND INTERESTS

The friends, hobbies, schooling and interests of your own children can be very useful. Authors with children (and grandchildren) will already know what clothes, books and toys are appealing, as well as what films and television programmes are popular. They will also know what is 'hot' and what is definitely 'not'.

Your own upbringing will always narrow your field of experience. Unless you have lived with and worked with a broad cross-section of society, you are almost bound to have a limited understanding of other lifestyles. Therefore, it makes sense to write about situations you understand rather than experimenting with those you have never encountered. The former will always ring truer to the reader. For example, if you have daily contact with pre-school children but hardly ever meet young adults, it may be a mistake to try to write realistically on teenage subjects. The language and attitudes of young adults change rapidly. Finding out what they read and watch will broaden your experience.

Sadly I don't have much contact with children, very important from the view of listening to speech patterns and current colloquialisms.

Your own children may have grown up and there are no grandchildren to hand. In this situation, it may be hard to remember the language and abilities of, say, a two-year-old toddler. A good parenting book or website will provide the answers. For example, say your story idea concerns the activities of a naughty 12-month-old baby: such a parenting source will remind you that some babies are talking at this age while others are not, and some are walking when others are still zipping about on all fours.

If your children are of school age, then it is relatively easy for you to join in and meet other families and children from a wide range of backgrounds. Most schools and playgroups welcome parental assistance. An hour or two when you get the chance will provide you with a great deal of information. You could choose to listen to children reading, and will discover the enormous range of reading and language abilities. You will find out about favourite books and topics, humour and concerns, as well as getting an insight into your local education system. You will learn the way children are taught to read, and the reading schemes and methods used. If the non-fiction area interests you, then it may be possible to help or work as a classroom assistant on project work. This will help you to understand the educational curriculum requirements, the texts children presently work from and their ability to tackle practical work. You will also find that teachers are a valuable source of information and opinion.

I think contact with children is vitally important. I have my own, plus the children I meet at the school book club I run.

One of the exercises I do on school visits is to ask a class to create characters and a storyline which we then jot down. The crazier the ideas, the more we laugh and also keep their interest. If I am stuck with a storyline, there is nothing better than turning it into an imaginative game, telling my nieces and nephews the outline and asking what they would do to make it better, or what it would need to make them want to read such a story.

Some schools may welcome help from you even if you are not a parent, but these days it is essential for them to obtain references and other official checks to reassure themselves that you are an appropriate person to work with children – for obvious reasons. A clearance for working with one age group, may not allow you to work with another age group.

If you have no children and are unable to get to a school during working hours, then there are plenty of other organizations that would welcome your involvement subject to Criminal Records Board or similar clearances. These range from your local church youth group, or charity run club organizations, to after schools clubs, youth clubs, outdoor activity movements or first-aid organizations. Ask at your library, your council, or search the internet – there are hundreds of activities where volunteers would be welcome or where you can get involved, and the choice from sporting activities to wildlife walks and talks is huge. A few hours on a regular or even occasional basis may give you all the feedback and inspiration you need for your writing.

If you're interested in the young adult market, then an educational course could provide the answer. Attending a school or college-run course in a subject which teenagers are taking or retaking will give you very interesting company. You could be learning keyboarding skills in order to type faster and without getting repetitive strain injury, or how to use graphics software while finding out about modern study methods and the social behaviour of young people.

In the previous chapter, we mentioned the importance of becoming an ideas detective. Watch, listen and learn when you are out and about and ideas will come to you, as the following author discovered:

> *I was stuck on a story about goats! Two months later I was walking past a bus stop where a gang of aggressive-looking bikers in full leathers was standing. I was a bit nervous, and could see plenty of things dangling from the belt of the ugliest one who had a brass studded leather cap. As I tiptoed past, I heard Studded-Cap say: 'Yeah, I was scared to cut my budgie's toenails in case I hurt his feet, so I took him to the vet. It doesn't cost much ...' I realized that the things*

dangling from his belt were a pair of nail clippers and a bottle opener, not knuckle dusters. A biker with a heart of budgie feathers brought my story to a riotous conclusion.

Listen to young people, get used to the things they talk about and the way they talk about them. Kids, especially those unaware that they are being overheard, will scare the life out of you with their 'bad' language and their choice of topics. We heard about a mother of a sweet-faced 11-year-old, who happened to see a signing-off email to a friend – 'Gotta go – gotta do f***ing homework!' The girl, so far as her (perhaps naïve) mother was aware, didn't even know such words, never mind use them so casually. We guess that mostly adults will be buying this book, adults who know how to spell. But the offending word will not be printed in full here. It will have been 'edited out'. It will almost certainly be edited out of any young adult book you may write even if used in context.

If you present a publisher with a book full of undiluted swearing and street-talk, you'll find out that their desire for realism has its limits. Okay, strong language and extreme behaviour among kids go on all the time, but grown-ups buying books probably won't want to see it in print and every society has its legal and social methods of censoring the things that are seen as stepping outside accepted conventions – either by not publishing them in the first place or by them being banned at point-of-sale subsequent to publication.

It is true that a bit of outrage by 'concerned citizens' can boost sales – all children will be drawn to something that they are told is 'bad' for them – but this is not an area to approach lightly and could prove disastrous for your publishing future. Courting controversy is not necessarily a good career move for the hopeful first-time author. This includes anything you may have done in your life whether deliberate or by accident which could prove detrimental to your book sales when discovered.

'Political correctness' is an ongoing and ever-changing quagmire for writers. As we write this, one media organization has changed the last line of the nursery rhyme 'Humpty Dumpty', to explain that he is not a real person getting hurt. We probably all know of books published in the past that have been edited or modified in their new editions so as not to be offensive to a modern buyer or reader. You will need to strike a sensitive balance between reality and acceptability. Use your common sense. Be subtle, but try not to be bland either.

Insight

Read recent books and articles to see how others write about subjects and characters from different backgrounds and different situations, and to learn how they deal with any issues.

If in doubt, leave it out. You can't provoke an editor into publishing your work, any more than you can judge a book by its cover.

The publishing world

There are plenty of societies and organized events that you'll find useful. Details can be found in the weekly book trade magazine, writers' reference books, libraries and so on. You'll be able to subscribe to most of these societies (although some will require that you have had at least one book published). Your membership will usually bring you regular mailings of information about the world of publishing as well as the latest developments, conferences, lectures and services. Details of some of the well-known ones are given at the back of this book.

Many lectures and talks will be free to members, and not too expensive for non-members, and some conferences can be very good value. You'll learn a lot and you'll get the opportunity to meet other people with the same interests, as well as those who work in the publishing industry. Some conferences organized by professional bodies can prove very expensive; these might include, for instance, conferences on technology developments, copyright, and intellectual property rights in the electronic publishing world. This is all fairly highbrow stuff for the beginner, and you should think carefully before committing a lot of money to such an event.

Book fairs or educational/game/computer/licensing/merchandising fairs can prove invaluable research venues. You will see the latest trends and developments in the publishing and related industries. You will discover who are the biggest companies and the breadth of their product ranges – and you will get a look at the sometimes daunting competition. You might find that your latest brainwave is already on the production schedules of half a dozen other companies. Or you may spot a gap in the market. Whatever you find, there is no need to be intimidated by the sheer range and quantity. All you need to know is that the majority of material is of a very high standard, and has been thoroughly researched as a saleable commodity before it was put into production. These fairs will teach you that publishing is big business.

You do need to understand exactly what is going on at a trade fair or exhibition. Basically, the exhibitors are selling their products to each other, not to the general public. They could be selling books, e-books or online content to distributors and retailers, or 'rights' (paid permission for translating a book, or any other selling area different from the original printed work) to the home or overseas markets. In any event, your presence, while encouraged as a potential individual customer, is not always entirely welcomed by busy sales people working under great pressure and within strict time limits. Try to take everything in while keeping a reasonably low profile.

The Bologna Children's Book Fair is the largest of all specialist children's book fairs and has been held in northern Italy in spring for nearly 50 years. More than 1,300 exhibitors and 5,000 publishing and media related professionals attend from over 70 countries. These people are buying and selling rights, and products related to the world of children's books to each other's companies, and viewing the competition. If it sounds very business-like: it is.

Every hotel and flight is booked solid by the publishing trade from one year to the next and there is a tendency for prices to treble during the week of the fair. In other words, this fair may not be the best place for a budding author to visit.

A similar story can be told of the Frankfurt Book Fair, which takes place in Germany every October. Here, the entire range of book and related product manufacturers meet for the same purpose. The fair in Frankfurt is frantic and frenetic. It may well be worth attending a national event such as the London Book Fair, which is also held annually in spring, especially if it is within travelling distance and your budget.

Some dos and don'ts when attending fairs and exhibitions

- ▶ *Book fairs and other children's product-related fairs will be advertised on the web and in trade magazines. Pre-registration can often mean free entry tickets. Large fairs may also organize discounted travel and accommodation packages if you live too far away for a day visit. You will need to book early.*
- ▶ *Wear comfortable shoes and smart clothes (smile, look professional and interested, and someone may have a moment to talk to you).*
- ▶ *Take a bag or rucksack to carry home the free catalogues and information exhibitors give away, but be selective about what you take. At the end of the last day, some exhibitors sell off display material at bargain prices.*
- ▶ *Look, listen and learn. Note potential publishers for your work. If possible, go with an interested friend, so you can chat about what you see.*

(Contd)

> ▶ *Never interrupt exhibitors who are obviously in the middle of a business meeting.*
> ▶ *Don't try to show or sell your work to anyone at a fair. The chances are that you will be speaking to the wrong people anyway and, in any event, 'cold-calling' at an exhibition is considered unprofessional and could make you very unpopular. Take a card or catalogue and make a note to research the company and follow up later.*
> ▶ *Don't be intimidated by the seemingly crowded nature of the market. Publishers are always on the lookout for new talent with innovative ideas.*

How to annoy publishers

We asked publishers what they hated most about the unsolicited submissions they receive. The replies were very similar. Read these extracts and remember.

> *Anthropomorphic animals, absolutely! Anything with a heavy-handed message. Several ideas on a page, requesting an opinion on which of them are worth working up.*

> *People who have no idea how high the standard of writing is nowadays, and who assume because their text is for children, poor quality writing doesn't matter. People who, in their submission letter, say how much their own children, or their neighbours' children/class at school/etc. love the story (of course they do!).*

> *The most ridiculous stories we receive usually involve the animation of inanimate objects (characters generally have*

*alliterative names): Elmer the Elevator whose day has its ups
and downs; Bertha the Bathtub who is worried about her
bathtub ring; or the chocolate bar who runs down the street
and melts on the sidewalk.*

*A story starting with breakfast in the summer holidays.
Elves, pixies and fairies. Things like Cuthbert the Cucumber,
Larry Lighthouse, Freddy Foghorn, Oscar Ozone – all actual
examples, I'm afraid.*

*Our website says, 'We don't accept unsolicited manuscripts.'
There is no footnote saying, 'Unless it's you.' No, it's
not a test. No, we won't be impressed by your daring and
perseverance if you send your MS anyway. No, we
won't read it. (I would actually love it if we had the time
and resources to look at unsolicited MSS and respond
personally and helpfully to aspiring authors, but we
just don't.)*

*If the website/Artists and Writers entry/lady on the phone
says, 'We do not publish picture books', that's because we
do not publish picture books. We're not lying. And we're not
going to start publishing picture books just for you. If you
didn't send an SSAE you're not getting it back. I'm not made
of stamps. I didn't turn your MS down because you're not
part of my exclusive publishing clique where it's all about
who you know. I turned it down because it wasn't very
good. Sorry.*

There you go – you've been warned! Although as we go to print,
Elmer the Elevator and Larry Lighthouse are still on the hate
list, other things change. For instance, fantasy is still very sellable
(it is right now, anyway), and you might find a publisher eager
to take up your series about talking animals engaged in exciting
adventures. Or you might not. But if that's your thing, check out
the market as it is when you read this, and then make an informed
decision.

Exercise 7

For the next chapter you'll need a sample of your writing.
Yes, you read that correctly – we're moving on to actual
writing now. We're not concerned with style or content just
yet, so if you don't have something obvious to hand, then a
letter to a friend or a diary entry will do, or your comments
on a book you have read recently, or even your opinion on a
news item. It doesn't matter what the subject is: just aim to
write or type about two pages of stuff.

10 THINGS TO REMEMBER

1 *Think about why you want to write.*

2 *Research is very important if you want to reach a marketable audience.*

3 *Target and understand your market through contact with children and reading books for children.*

4 *Use the internet as a research tool and get familiar with the children's resource websites.*

5 *Get out there, visit bookshops, libraries, schools. Make notes about what you find, and speak to people with children's book knowledge.*

6 *Discover your own 'writing zone' and create your own space.*

7 *Establish how useful you personally find contact with children.*

8 *Think about how easy you personally find it to interact and empathize with the world of the modern child/young adult.*

9 *Think about how best to navigate the tricky waters of political correctness to avoid upsetting people.*

10 *Get to know publishers' pet hates and use that knowledge.*

3

Getting started: the tools
of the trade

In this chapter you will learn:
- *how to prepare yourself and your environment for writing*
- *how to gather, file and create storyline ideas.*

Write it down

You have a great idea. It could be for a picture book, a storybook,
or a full-length book. It could even be for a series. It could be
fiction, non-fiction or educational.

So, what to do next?

Telling your family and friends about it is easy. With an email you
can send it to people all around the globe. You could post it online,
you can blog, podcast, tweet and social network the idea about.
Some famous writers have written internet-only books – selling them
to fans one chapter at a time. But you are not a famous writer and
there aren't many people who are going to pay you for a download –
even if they manage to find your work in the first place among all the
millions of websites. The bottom line is you still need a publisher to
help you get your work across to your potential audience. In order
to present it to a publisher, you have to write it down in one form or
another; and to do that you will need some basic equipment.

A pen and a notebook will do for a start, but regular access to a computer to get the text down is close to essential, especially once your book has been accepted. Virtually all correspondence between writers and publishers these days is by email. However, there are ways around this:

> *I've reluctantly moved from a typewriter to a word processor – but I've refused to have a computer. My sister looks after my website, and my agent rings me or posts things.*

> *I can't use a computer. Basic email is my limit. I write my books down longhand in a large notebook. Then when I'm happy, I give this to a friend who types it all out, and brainstorms any corrections.*

These two authors are well known, and can just about get away with how they are working – for now. You can get your email via mobile phones, and televisions, but for writing books, nothing will beat having your own computer, e-notebook or whatever has been developed since this book was printed.

Before you start work you need to have a good grasp of the language in which you will be writing. Let's assume you're writing in the same language as the publisher. (Occasionally a book is first released by a foreign publisher in another language, but we don't need to worry about that right now.) Later on we'll look at the way in which different writing areas require differing tones, styles and contents, but right now you need to address the level of your own language skills.

Words, words, words

Many people these days speak more than one language, but the majority are most fluent in the language they were brought up with. Are you writing in a language that you learned as an adult? For instance, you might be an American who went to live in

France, and who now wishes to write a book in French for the French market. If so, there may be areas in which you'll need help, perhaps with the language subtlety of an indigenous speaker. There may be other reasons why your use of language is not as skilled as you'd like it to be. You need to work on this – your writing will need to be understood by a whole variety of people.

Language works on many levels. It ranges from eloquence to street-slang, from 'Good morning, and how do you do this bright and sunny day?' to 'Yo, bro! Wassup?' From ancient to modern. From 'Hail and well met, good fellow!' to 'Hiya!' As we mentioned before, language is in a constant state of flux, with old words falling out of favour, the meaning of words changing and new words entering common usage every year. Just take a look at some old movies to see how significantly language has altered over the past few decades. In the 1930s, a female movie actor could ask her male co-star, 'Are you making love to me?' In the 1970s she might ask, 'Are you chatting me up?' – and these days it's unlikely she'd bother saying anything at all, as she'd just as likely be the one making the running.

Nothing is more fun than knowing the latest catch phrases and buzzwords. Some of these come from the street – some from industry or science or the internet (24/7, AI, FYI and so on). A few of these words and phrases slip into general use, but many are only ever understood by a small number of people, and could be misconstrued by others in different industries. AI can mean anything from Advance Information for a book about to be published, to Artificial Intelligence, to the interpretation a farmer or vet might put on AI. Do you know what 'horizontal communication" means? Or how about 'four-quadrant' or 'viral marketing'? Probably not – and the last two are currently big in the media industry.

Using this jargon is fun, and it can make sense to use it, so long as the person you're corresponding with knows the same set of buzzwords and shortenings. But if you want to communicate with people outside your own group, you're going to need to dump the slang unless you're absolutely certain a much wider audience will get it, and it won't date disastrously.

Language is there to help people communicate – and usually the purpose of writing things down is so that you can communicate with the widest possible audience. This means some common ground needs to be found – common ground that will allow your work to survive. To do this, you're going to need to know to use correct language, with accurate grammar and spelling.

Another thing to keep in mind is that, especially if writing for younger children, your work will form part of that child's education. An enthusiastic person with poor language skills may do just fine, but probably not as well as they might if their language skills were better. These skills give confidence both to the user and to the person on the receiving end.

At the publishing house the person who receives your work is likely to be someone educated up to, and possibly beyond, university level. Their language knowledge should be good, and their expectations high. A submission full of spelling mistakes and bad grammar will not go down well. If you want to be taken seriously, then you have to approach them in a professional way.

Almost every publisher we contacted commented on the spelling and the grammatical content of the scripts and the covering letters they receive. Here are some of their comments:

Call me pedantic, but it's immediately off-putting to receive a badly presented, misspelt, grammatically incorrect manuscript. Ask someone to check your spelling!

Badly written letters, or proposals containing poor spelling and punctuation usually get rejected. If a writer is incapable of checking an introductory letter then there's precious little chance that he/she is going to take care over a manuscript.

Spelling mistakes. It makes my blood boil when I see really common mistakes like there/their and apostrophes in the wrong places.

IMPROVING YOUR LANGUAGE SKILLS

In Exercise 7 in the previous chapter, we asked you to come up with a piece of writing. What you need to do with it now, if you can, is to show it to someone with good language skills. Maybe you know a friendly teacher, or someone with a degree in language, or similar skills. Give them a couple of pages of your work and ask them to go through it, highlighting with absolute honesty anything that is wrong. Explain to them that you're not asking for their opinion on the story or whatever it is, but on the grammatical accuracy.

If you have no school or college qualifications, are dyslexic or already aware that your writing lacks polish, then there are various ways in which you can get help.

Further education

First, there is further education. There are adult education language courses to suit everyone's ability and budget. These may be run via local schools and colleges, or job/careers centres. In such classes you will find people of your own level of ability who are willing and enthusiastic to learn. You will also meet teachers who really want to teach you. If you have grim memories of your own schooldays, just remember that every student is there because they want to be. Not only will you be learning, but you'll meet new people and have some interesting experiences for your Ideas File.

If, for any reason, you are unable to attend classes outside your own home, then there are correspondence and online courses available. These are advertised in newspapers, magazines and on websites, and range from private companies to recognized correspondence universities with radio, television and summer-school lectures. Private editorial help is also available through writers' magazines, directories of freelance editors and children's writing organizations. Be selective and cynical about publishing companies or creative writing courses that ask for very large amounts of money. Can you afford it at this stage? Be sure of what you will get: you don't want to be handing out money – you want to be making it. Get online – find an independent site where people write about their experiences with these companies or organizations – then make your decision.

Writing is usually a solitary pastime, but you'll have noticed by now that the world of writing is full of possible contacts and with people who can help you. For instance, there are creative writing organizations and societies that run workshops, lectures and creative writing weeks. Writers' groups and adult education creative writing courses may also be taking place near where you live. These can be very rewarding: you may be set tasks, be asked to read out your work in front of the class, discuss your own and others' work, and have your writing corrected if it needs it. In these cases, a little investment could benefit you greatly.

There are also MA and BA courses in creative writing in colleges and universities where you can learn how to write 'properly'. Even if you plan on creating a brand new way of telling stories that throws all the old conventions out of the window, you ought to know the rules before you dump them. Remember, Picasso was a brilliant draughtsman before he got into Cubism and all that other avant-garde stuff.

If you've been writing solo until now, the thought of showing your work to other people might give you the screaming willies. Or, you might be one of those people who can't wait to get up in front of an audience and show them what you've got. Either way, you're going to need to develop a thick skin. Your writings are your babies, the fruits of your heart and soul, the result of days, weeks and months of effort. No matter how you view your writing, it's certainly going to be very personal to you and revealing it to other people will be a major – and for some, traumatic – experience.

HOW GOOD ARE YOU AT DEALING WITH CRITICISM?

Insight

A writer has to get used to being rejected and criticized. Even bestselling authors attract bad reviews and unpleasant put-downs.

Check out an online bookstore that has readers' reviews – click on your favourite author and favourite books and go to the one-star reviews – most will have a few, for sure. You'll be amazed how vicious and dismissive people can be when they are hidden behind the safety of their computers.

You're just starting out – so think carefully before you decide you're ready for the Great Public. If you have doubts about how well you are writing, you don't want them magnified by a whole bunch of other people. One thing we can tell you with total conviction: the more you write, the better you will get. The last thing you need is to be crushed by adverse criticism when you're just getting going.

In a creative writing class, do keep an open mind about criticism and advice. Be selective that the advice or criticism you are receiving is useful to you. What is your gut feeling? If the person advising you has had only one book published, say, 40 years ago on techniques in postmodernist beekeeping, then you'd do well to ask yourself if he or she is really in any position to comment on your brilliant new idea for a young adult novel or pre-school picture book.

Insight

Believe in yourself, but keep in mind that the publishing market has its own needs and demands. If you have a fantastic idea, don't tell everyone – keep it to yourself. You don't want someone else to sneak off and write it first.

People may not deliberately steal your idea, but once it's 'out there' your chances of keeping it under wraps will rapidly disappear. The point of going to creative writing courses, or belonging to online writing groups, is to learn the ropes, not to hand over great ideas to other people.

You may feel confident in your language skills, but that might not be enough. You also need to 'sell' your work – which means presenting it in a way that will impress and interest publishers.

You may know stories about people who have broken all the rules and who still became bestselling authors. Forget them! They're irrelevant right now – by picking up this book you've already proved you're not one of them. You want to do it right. You want to be a professional.

CAN YOU TYPE?

You need to be able to type and use a computer. We're not necessarily talking ten-fingered 140-words-a-minute typing but you will have to get used to a keyboard. You can't submit your work in pen and ink and your first letter to a publisher should not be handwritten. Things have moved on from those times. You will need to come to terms with a computer, preferably one with internet access.

Don't let computers scare you – they're just glorified typewriters with vast libraries attached. Learning to get your writing onto a computer file is about as tricky as figuring out a new TV remote once you've mastered the basics. All the freaky little extras can be picked up as you go along. If your computer skills are not as good as you would like, find out about computer courses or 'computers for the terrified' day skills courses.

The thing is, you want to present your work to a publisher in a professional form. This means either in black type on white A4 paper or as an emailed computer file or disc. We'll cover the finer points of professional presentation in Chapter 9, but meanwhile back to the opening question: can you type? If you can't, then you've got problems.

You could always pay a professional typist to do it for you – but who wants to spend all that money? Even if you're the slowest two-finger typist ever, it beats shelling out for someone else to do it for you. And when your book gets accepted, and the publisher comes back at you with a whole bunch of small changes they'd like you to make – what then? Get the typist back in? That's an expensive way to go.

Or you may have a friend who can type. Three or four manuscripts/revisions down the line, that friend may stop answering the phone when you call.

Insight
Trust us on this – learn to type!

Two-, three- or four-fingered typing may suit you best, but if you want to type to a professional standard, typing and keyboard skills courses are available through adult education classes, schools, correspondence courses, software packages for computers, and from teach-yourself-at-home workbooks. You'll be able to learn at your own pace. (If you are presently a two-fingered typist, you could improve your keyboard skills, speed and accuracy and, moreover, prevent the very real risk of repetitive strain injury.) It may mean going back to basics, of course, and unlearning all those bad habits, but the results could be worth the effort.

Basic equipment

You might start off by scribbling ideas down on scraps or paper or in a notebook, or maybe you have a handheld e-notebook or other electronic device that lets you dictate, scribble or type in information. But once you get down to the actual business of writing, you're going to need to make yourself feel comfortable – meaning you need to be somewhere that works for you – and using tools that suit you.

For many years Michael Morpurgo wrote on his bed until there were complaints about ink on the sheets. Louis de Bernières thinks it important to get away from the house and has a shed in the corner of the garden kitted out as his writing room. J. K. Rowling used a series of cafés when she started out, and J. R. R. Tolkien commented that he could not put a word to paper until he was all but obscured in a fug of pipe smoke.

A creative writing student of mine used to set out 20 minutes early to pick up her daughter from playschool. She used that time to sit in the car and write.

PEN AND PAPER

If you choose to write initially in longhand, then you may have a favourite old pencil, or a fountain pen or ballpoint pen. Use whatever instrument suits you best, but remember that this method of working is only temporary – at some point you'll have to use a keyboard.

If you use lined paper, then leave a gap of at least one line between your writing. This will help when you come to revise your work. You might want to write revisions in a different colour pen, so you can see at a glance where you've changed things. Leave wide margins and write only on one side of the paper: then you can use the other side for more revisions, additions and notes.

COMPUTERS

If you don't already have access to a computer, then you'd be wise to start thinking about getting your hands on one right now. Do you use a computer at work? Might you be able to negotiate with your boss to use it for your personal writing in your lunch break, or out of office hours? Do friends or family have a computer that you could use for an hour or so a day if you came to reasonable terms or trade with them? For example, one hour's use = one hour's babysitting or gardening? Does your local library, job club, internet café or day centre have computers you can use. What are the costs? Check out your local papers and internet sites – e.g. freecycle groups. Someone may be giving away or trading their old system for next to nothing. If you don't have any spare cash, check all these potential sources out before you do anything else. If you do decide to get your own computer, do some research – make sure that your buy will give you what you need. If you are thinking of renting or getting a laptop on a monthly contract, check out the small print. Your computer won't need all the buzzers and bells, so the expense needn't be substantial – and you'll quickly discover that the outlay was worth the benefits. You'd be wise to buy your computer from a reputable company with knowledgeable staff and a good after-sale help service. A second-hand computer may come cheaper, but if it goes wrong or crashes it can be frustrating and time consuming getting it to work again.

Why a computer? Well, for a start, it will check your spelling and grammar for you as you go along. A computer file can be altered really easily. On a computer you can make substantial changes in no time at all. You can move words, sentences, paragraphs or entire chapters around within the document any which way you like. You can change the name of a character in moments with 'find and replace'. You can save an original document then make changes on a copy – so you can always go back to the original again if you need to.

Laptop computers and e-notebooks also have their advantages – they are portable for a start, meaning you can work perfectly well when you are away from your normal writing-space, and they will give you the same access to emails and the internet as a desktop computer.

Have you got internet access for your computer? Will you need and can you afford broadband to speed up your access to the internet for your research? There are many Internet Service Providers (ISPs) out there, and each of them will offer a slightly different package, so you should find a provider who will give you what you want at a price you can afford for your locality. This may be via cable or telephone, and may include TV and phone packages. Ask around, ask your neighbours, do some research and read the small print before you decide what will work best for you – your cheap one-off payment will have conditions attached. You may want to start small, and upgrade at a later stage.

The ability to send and receive emails is becoming essential. Although it is still normal for unsolicited manuscripts to be presented to publishers in 'hard-copy' (paper) form, you'll find that an interested editor will want to communicate with you via emails and attachments – especially when you get to the editing and revision phase.

Publishers and agents mostly prefer new writers to submit their work on paper – round-robin emails sent to every publisher you can think of will not endear you to anyone. The day may well come when you get an urgent email requesting biographical details and a photograph by return so that these can be submitted to a committee discussing your book and deciding whether or not to go ahead with it. For this, nothing but email will do the job. As your career progresses, you may even find it worthwhile to have your own website built to publicize your work worldwide and to keep in contact with fans.

One final word – make sure your computer is protected against viruses and other problems by getting a recognized virus checker, spam filter (to avoid unwanted junk mail), and even a 'pop-up' blocker – many are available for free. The last thing you want is for some nasty virus you have read or heard about to infect your computer and destroy days, weeks or months of work. Finally, a power surge-breaker for your plug sockets will also prevent potential problems caused by a disruption to the electricity supply.

SAVE YOUR WORK

When using a computer, it's really important that you remember to save your work. Most computers have an automatic saving system that will save at regular intervals without you needing to take any action.

Insight

At the end of each writing session, make another copy of your work. Save, save, save!

You could save your work on a separate backup disc that should then be labelled and dated, or you could copy it onto a USB pen – also called a memory stick. You might also want to print your day's work to check it over at leisure – but bear in mind that printing it will not save you from typing the whole thing again if you haven't saved it and the computer goes down. You could email your work to a trusted friend to keep safe. Keep your work disks, memory stick, and your printed typescripts in a safe, element-proof place. That way, even if you suffer a catastrophic hard-drive crash, your only immediate concern is finding an alternative computer on which to continue working.

INSURANCE

You should have loss and accident insurance cover for your computer and e-devices both for use at home, or when working on your writing away. Read the small print of your policy. If you don't have one, get one. Some household contents or bank account policies may cover this, but others don't, so check it out. Also, some buildings insurance policies don't cover your home if it's also your workplace, especially if you occasionally receive business visitors, or your name is published. Again, check this out.

Have you got insurance repair cover if your computer fails, or access to an affordable helpline? The last thing you need is an inoperative machine and the prospect of a large bill to get it repaired, not to mention the delay and inconvenience of finding someone to help you repair it. Remember, it is important to get your computer up and running again as quickly as possible – without it you may not be able to work.

REFERENCE BOOKS

There are plenty of books available which can help you with your writing. Authors' societies may have recommended reading lists. You'll probably want to start off with one or two 'beginner's guides' and then expand your collection as your interests and needs evolve. The advantage of books is that they can often lead you to other words or information while you are turning the pages. Checking words online will probably lead you to that word, but a book page will open up other words and other ideas by chance.

Three books will be of particular value.

A dictionary
A dictionary is essential. If you can afford only one book, then it should be an up-to-date dictionary. Do not borrow your great-uncle's school dictionary: language changes quickly. A simple contemporary dictionary should do the trick, and some browsing through the pages may well open your eyes to what words are now in common use and are considered an acceptable part of the language.

A thesaurus
A thesaurus can be really useful when you are stuck for the exact word you need, or if you want to avoid repeating a word or phrase. A thesaurus will provide you with lists of alternatives to keep your writing sharp and sparkling with interest. Seek the advice of a bookseller or librarian on which thesaurus will best suit your needs.

Of course, both these aids can be found online for free these days if you don't want to buy an actual book. It's a matter of personal taste how you access the information you need. Some people like to have a book at their elbow – others will keep an online thesaurus and dictionary open all the time they are writing, and flip from one to the other as they need them.

A writers' reference book
Any one of the annually updated writers' reference books contain enormous amounts of useful information, from publishers' and literary agents' addresses, to prize awards and guidelines on copyright.

You may find that these particular resources are also available online, but we would still recommend that you buy the books – you will find that it's probably easier for you to place Post-it® notes into the pages of a book to mark relevant words or suggestions or passages than it is to be popping in and out of web pages all the time.

With particular regard to writers' reference books, it is vital that you buy or access the most recent edition. Information about publishers and agents and so on changes rapidly and annually. You do not want to be sending your submission to someone who has not been working at your chosen company for a couple of years.

This is another reason for not trusting what you read on websites:

Spell-checkers

Ode to spell-checkers
I have a spelling checker
I disk covered four my PC.
It plane lee marks four my revue
Miss steaks aye can knot see.
A checker is a blessing.
It freeze yew lodes of thyme.
It helps me right awl stiles two reed,
And aides me when aye rime.

Author unknown

A spell-checker on your computer is a great asset, but don't rely on it to know what you mean all the time, and which word to use in the right place.

Exercise 8

Do you know the difference and when to use: 'there' and 'their', and 'its' and 'it's' 'whether' and 'weather'?

1   *Make a quick list of other words that sound alike, but are not spelt the same, and where confusion in a children's book could cause chaos or make an editor think you are either daft or lazy, e.g. 'bear' and 'bare'.*

> **2**   *We all have words where no matter how hard we try,*
> *we have to think and read back carefully every time*
> *we write them. These could be as simple as: 'form' and*
> *'from', or 'tomorrow' or 'dyslexia'. What are your*
> *words? Writing them down now may remind you*
> *to double check your work, so that when your first*
> *submission letter goes out, you haven't misspelt or*
> *mis-typed a key word in your opening sentence.*

Check whether your computer system is using an American or English spelling list, as many words are spelt differently in Britain and America.

If you're going through a long piece of work which contains made-up words or names, or a non-fiction text full of abbreviations or unusual words, then a spell-checker will go crazy highlighting the whole lot. Add them to the dictionary to make it shut up.

Insight

Never rely on your spell-checker for accuracy. Always read your work through with great care.

Raising funds

One young author without a whole lot of spare money asked her friends and family to help her by buying writing materials for birthday and Christmas presents. This kind of thing is not only of practical value, but as a show of support for a budding writer, it can work wonders.

Start keeping all your receipts for anything you spend money on in direct connection with your writing work. Not just paper, ink, postage and so on, but also internet access, work-related telephone calls, travelling expenses if, say, you visit a museum for research purposes, or for any books you may buy to help you with a writing project. (See the section 'Tax and accounts' in Chapter 12.)

BURSARIES

Bursaries may be available from arts councils, associations or charitable trusts to enable authors to complete a specific project. Conditions vary: money may be made available to a new author, or to an established author who wishes to concentrate on a particular project which would be considered to be of great potential value to the reading public. A fairly detailed explanation of the planned project would be needed, along with some supporting references from people whose opinion would be taken seriously by the judges in the relevant decision-making panel. Such grants and bursaries can be quite large sums of money, enough to enable an author to give up a day job for several months in order to complete a project.

Details are available through libraries, authors' magazines, in writers' reference books and via the web.

DOOR-TO-DOOR

Recently one of us opened the front door to discover a 'would-be' young writer standing on the doorstep, selling her autobiography from door-to-door. The idea was for you to pay for the book up-front and then to receive it through the mail in a couple of months' time. In this way, the author hoped to make enough money in advance to cover the cost of having the book printed. Always being on the look-out to help young hopefuls, money passed from hand to hand and two months later the book duly appeared. The plan had obviously worked!

Another author had his books printed privately, boxed them up and put them in the trunk of his car. He then drove from town to town, selling copies to bookshops all over his local area. Again, this may not be the way you'd want to go – but it worked for him. (And as an aside to this story, the author's books caught the eye of a large publisher, who put him under contract. He discovered that sales of his next book dipped, because to the publisher he was just a small cog in a mighty machine and the personal touch was lost.) We're not suggesting that these are the best ways of getting your book published – they are not – it's hard work and will give you only a very limited audience, depending on how much shoe-leather you're prepared to work through. But it does show that there are alternative ways of financing your work and raising funds.

Writing time

You've set up your Ideas File. You've done plenty of research. You've learned to type, and hopefully, you now have access to a computer. So, what else do you need before you can start work?

Two things:

▶ *space in which to write*
▶ *time in which to write.*

The ideal situation would be to have your own writing space, an area used for nothing else. Some authors have a spare room they can use. Others convert lofts or sheds into an organized (or disorganized) office: computer on desk, comfortable writing table, typist's chair and bookshelf with dictionary, thesaurus and other books at arm's reach.

Whatever space you can squeeze out of the chaos of your life, try to make it as comfortable and convenient for yourself as possible. You can't be creative if you are too hot, too cold, too cramped or crammed into an uncomfortable chair or trying to write on a washing machine in spin mode.

Some authors conduct their business from bed; others work at the kitchen table or a desk in a hallway or under the stairs. Wherever you work, aim to make it somewhere as peaceful as possible so that you are able to concentrate (even if your idea of peace includes Wagner operas or hip-hop as background music).

Quite a few full-time authors and illustrators dislike the solitude of working from home and find that a better working environment is created for them by renting a desk in the corner of a busy office – which proves that peace is a pretty flexible concept. Other authors need absolute silence and solitude if they are going to be able to function at all. The least interruption can close the brain down for hours.

The telephone can certainly drive authors crazy. Imagine: you are in the middle of a complex piece of writing when the telephone rings. You pick it up, have a conversation that lasts only a couple of minutes, and then return to your desk only to find you cannot remember for the life of you what was going to happen next.

Make it clear to friends and relations that working at home does not mean you can be called up every half-hour for a quick chat. A five-minute telephone call can result in the creative part of your brain being scrambled for an hour or more. If you have a real problem with this, then you might be wise to disconnect the telephone for the duration of your writing-stint. Alternatively, put the telephone out of earshot, bury it in the garden or, if you can, buy an answerphone or messaging service and let it take messages until you've finished work.

If you're able to allocate a regular daily or weekly time for writing, then make sure everyone is in no doubt that at those times you are to be left alone, short of winning the lottery or the house catching fire. Ask friends not to drop by for a chat. Tell your partner or your children that you require to be invisible for x amount of time. If all else fails, insert earplugs and lock yourself in your room.

I have to be disciplined about not answering phones and glancing at email pop ups: responding to something here-and-now is so much easier than the long-term rewards of writing. Don't fall for the myth that you can just 'get everything out of the way' before you start: you never will!

Lock the door, take the phone off the hook. Write late at night when everybody's gone to bed, or early in the morning before they've got up. Go for walks, talk the story out to yourself (not aloud, you get funny looks and small boys shout at you) then write it when you get home.

Create a space where you can leave your work and know it won't be messed with. It could be somewhere as simple as a drawer or an out-of-pets-and-children's-reach shelf. Wherever it is, keep it as organized as you can: you don't want to be taking half an hour to get yourself sorted out every time you return to your work. Get into the habit of putting everything away in an orderly and accessible fashion every time you stop.

You don't want to lose the scrap of paper on which you jotted the brilliant but complicated bestselling idea that came to you in the middle of the night. Keep it somewhere safe. Similarly, you don't want your finished manuscript to arrive on a publisher's desk covered in coffee stains, muddy paw-prints or smears of marmalade from a midday snack. An organized approach should prevent all the above problems.

Finding time for writing is very difficult – especially as I have three young children! I would say that frequency of writing is more important than the total number of hours put in. I try to manage an hour a day – after the children have gone to bed, and there are also a couple of mornings where I go to work late and I can write for an hour or so after the kids have gone to school. I always put in a good stint on Sunday mornings while my wife looks after the kids – then I take them out in the afternoon.

The world is full of people who'd love to write a book 'if they could find the time'. My response is quite ruthless. If you are passionate about writing you'll find the time, even if you are bringing up 13 kids and working 12-hour shifts. If you can't squeeze the time out of your daily routine, you should ask yourself just how much you want to be a published writer.

You should treat writing in the same way as you would treat studying for an exam or doing any important job of work. Create a writing routine. If you try to fit it in now and then, you'll get nowhere fast. Pick a time when your mind is at its most alert. You know whether you are a morning or a night person. Write a note in your diary or calendar, set up a reminder alert on your mobile. Make a plan of when to write, and don't be distracted by phone calls inviting you out, or from friends and family wanting to make unexpected visits.

You'll be the best judge of when you can write; the important thing is to fight for your writing time and to make it an absolute habit, breakable by friends and family only on pain of retribution.

Some authors make it a point to produce one finished page per day – about 250 to 280 words. That may not sound like much, but do that for one year and you are looking at a 365-page book. Other full-time authors set themselves specific deadlines, this being the only way they can push themselves to complete a piece of work.

Deadlines can be very helpful because they force you to plan your work systematically, If you are one of those people who have to make time to write then a deadline is invaluable – it makes you put everything on hold while you do the work.

A deadline definitely helps me ... knowing I have to write a certain number of words each day or week or month does get it done.

The ideas mine

Authors get their ideas from absolutely everywhere, but it may help if we divide the harvesting areas into three main categories.

FIRST-HAND

First-hand ideas include things experienced by you personally, or things that happen to people very close to you. They can be events from your own childhood, or from any time in your life, where the experience would relate to something that you could use as the starting-point for a project – for instance, sibling rivalry between you and a sister/brother, or issues between you and close friends. These experiences will range from the traumatic to the hilarious, but the important thing for you to do is to think back though your life and try to revive your feelings of the time.

▶ *You spilt red ink on your mum's favourite cushion while she was out. You put it into the washing machine and then into the tumble drier. Black smoke poured out of the tumble drier and when you opened the door the kitchen was suddenly full of burnt feathers. Not funny at the time – but now it could make the basis of a cute comic short story.*

▶ *Your best friend came to school with unexplained bruises on her arms. What was going on at home? It may be that you never found out – but now it could form the spine of an emotionally engaging story.*

▶ *Your parents separated. How did you cope? What did you feel? Include it in a story.*

Use your own life as an Ideas File. Delve back and into yourself: your experiences may one day help another child to understand his/her own situation, and to realize that other people have had the same problems.

Perhaps you notice that your own child is afraid of thunderstorms. What might help? A picture book, possibly, which explains exactly what thunder and lightning are and why there is no reason to be scared.

If you are a parent, or have regular contact with children, the important thing is to see things from a child's perspective. Adults frequently believe that *their* wishes and opinions should take precedence over those of a child. If you are going to write for children, you must forget all about that. The priorities of children are quite different from those of an adult. Not less important, just *different*.

For example, children perceive time in a very different way from adults. Half an hour can seem like an eternity to a child. The agonizing, anticipatory wait of two whole weeks for a birthday party to take place can reduce a child to a tearful, gibbering wreck on the actual day. You must try to remember what this felt like if you are going to speak believably to children through your work.

Books for young adults often explore the gulf in understanding between parents and children. You can tackle this only if you enter the world of the young person and address the conflict from his/her point of view. Try to remember the battles you had as a teenager with those adults who wielded authority over you, be they parents, teachers, the police or whoever. How did you feel when these people tried to impose their will on you?

Remember your own feelings of enchantment when you were a small child. Think back to the time when quite small things held an entire world of fascination. A walk in a wood where *anything* could be lurking. A secret tunnel known only to you and your friends. The first time you noticed the shadows on the moon. Faces in flames and the shapes to be found in clouds. Desperate alliances and sundered friendships.

The lives of children teem with imperatives. Who is your best friend? Who do you hate most in all the world? Has your dog eaten your homework? Children live on the brink of triumph and disaster minute by minute. You need to live it with them. Never be squeamish: dive in!

Exercise 9

Write a sentence about your earliest memory. Write a paragraph on a smell which brings back a memory and why. Write a page on your most embarrassing moment from childhood.

SECOND-HAND

Second-hand experiences are those that are repeated to you or observed by you, but which do not directly involve you. Such experiences could include, say, an overheard conversation between children on a bus or a train, or happenings related to you by friends or relations.

Obviously you are going to be one step removed from the intensity of such experiences, but your job as an author is to soak up all the elements, be they comic or tragic, and to tuck them into your Ideas File for future reference.

It may be that a single aspect of someone's anecdote sets your story antennae twitching, something quite trivial, said in passing, a throwaway comment, but one that strikes you as having potential. A word of warning here: not everyone relishes the idea that everything they say to you will appear in print. If you hear a story which you just know is a sure-fire winner, then make some careful changes. Adapt it, maybe by changing the sex of the main people, altering the location, or making changes in their social background. Create new characters from aspects of several different people. Edit the story so that the heart of it – the spark that ignited your interest – is still there, but construct around that, a world created in your own imagination. (We will mention libel in Chapter 9.)

Perhaps you notice some piece of social behaviour between children that you find interesting, intriguing or amusing. Jot it down and file it away.

Be particularly aware of the rhythm and dynamics of speech. A good rule of thumb for an author is to keep the mouth shut and the ears open. Listen to the way people speak.

Take an eight-year-old child: how does he/she speak to friends? How does he/she speak to children he/she does not know? How does he/she speak to older children? To younger children? How does he/she speak to adults – parents/guardians/authority figures? It will not take long for you to notice that children use a multitude of differing modes of speech, adapting themselves to their circumstances in a very sophisticated way. A sweet-faced little cherub may be very polite and biddable in front of adults, but may mutate into a bullying, screaming banshee once let loose among his or her peers.

A few words of advice concerning dialogue. The only way you are going to be able to write convincing dialogue is by listening to real people talking to one another. Do not try to learn this from books, television shows, films or radio. In all these media, a filtration and editing process has already taken place. You need conversation in the raw, untouched by any other writer's hand.

Insight

When you have written a piece of speech, read it aloud to check if it feels right in your mouth and whether it sounds natural when it hits the air.

Exercise 10

Think of a daft but true anecdote someone has told you, which made you both laugh. A prank where the prankster became the victim, a misunderstanding, something so coincidental it's hard to believe it's true. Write it down in real time, as if you were hearing it now. Include 'he/she said', 'you said' and all those 'you know' phrases or scattergun words people use in conversation. Did you nod when listening? Did you interrupt to get clarification? At what point did you begin to laugh? How did that change the way the storyteller continued the anecdote? Write those descriptions down too.

Now read the piece back. Is it entertaining? What would you revise or cut to turn it into a dialogue which would make the reader laugh, hold your attention in a book, and perhaps even move the story along in some way? Try some editing, and then read it aloud to see if it still rings true.

THIRD-HAND

The third-hand areas from which you can get ideas are those where you have no personal contact with the story at all. They split into two sub-headings.

Reported

You may notice an item on a television news programme which takes your interest. You may read the report of an incident in a newspaper, from the internet, or hear of a real event via the radio.

A missing eight-year-old boy was rescued today from the basement of a part-demolished building following a two-day search. He was exhausted but unharmed, having fallen through rotting floorboards while exploring with a friend. The delay in discovering the boy was due to the fact that his friend was too scared to tell his parents of the incident as they had been specifically told to keep away from the demolition site.

This story is adapted from a real incident reported in a television news programme. From an author's point of view, it has several areas of interest. There is the incident itself, of course, written as a kind of adventure, but an author will be interested in what was going through the minds of the two boys at the time. One trapped in the dark, the other just as trapped by the fear of recriminations. And then you have that moment when the second boy finally had to tell his parents what had happened. Powerful stuff.

How about taking the lives of the two boys on a few years, and writing a story of them as teenagers? What sort of effect would that incident have on their future relationship? How will the second boy be coping with his feelings of guilt that his delay in telling the truth could easily have been the cause of the other boy's death? What if these two boys are interested in the same girl? Might the boy who was trapped use the story to put the girl off the other boy?

As you can see, the possibilities are endless, and all this from a fleeting snippet of news, jotted down and filed away when everyone else had forgotten all about it by the next day. Similarly, headlines, web pages, odd paragraphs and photographs clipped from newspapers and magazines can have enormous potential. Be constantly on the look-out for these items.

Exercise 11

Where were you when the Berlin Wall came down, on 9/11, when you heard about the death of a famous person who meant a lot to you?

Write a paragraph about your own reactions to a newsworthy event that happened in your childhood. What did it mean to you, and how did you feel? What were you doing before you heard the news – and what impact did it have on you?

Write another paragraph about an event that has occurred in your adulthood. Think about those feelings; think about the different concerns or thoughts you had as a child, and those as an adult. Have you conveyed these reactions in your two pieces? Could you convey those feelings in a work of fiction?

Refried

The previous section on reported events concerned itself with real incidents reported through the media, but the refried third-hand area is where you glean ideas from other authors.

We need to be perfectly clear what we are talking about here. Stealing other people's ideas is not only cheating, it is also illegal. It is called plagiarism and must be avoided. However, this doesn't mean your own imagination can't be sparked by something that happens in a book, play, movie, television or radio programme you happen across.

For example, the author Jean Rhys wrote *Wide Sargasso Sea*, a book that told the story of 'mad' Mrs Rochester from *Jane Eyre*. Mrs Rochester was a shadowy figure kept incarcerated in the attic of the house; her main contribution to the story comes when she escapes and burns the house down. Having read *Jane Eyre*, this author found herself wondering what it must have been like to have been that locked-away woman, and thus her book was born. Similarly, the book *Ophelia* by Lisa Klein tells the story of Shakespeare's play *Hamlet* from the point of view of the character Ophelia, giving her much more depth, and adding a fascinating new twist to the original tale. Other authors have written prequels and sequels to famous classic stories, and some like Charlie Higson, have been commissioned to write authorized stories of a young James Bond.

Consider myths, legends and fairy tales. These tales have survived because they tell a riveting story that has the ability to transcend changes in society, sometimes over many centuries. If you are short of ideas, you could do a lot worse than read a book of Greek, Japanese, Aztec or Russian folk tales and legends.

'Sleeping Beauty' could be brought up to date and written as a story of a girl in a coma and how her boyfriend copes with the situation. 'The Ugly Duckling' is the universally understood story of any child who learns to throw off some burden and be themselves. One editor to whom we spoke commented that Verdi's opera *Rigoletto* had provided at least two storylines for a well-known American teen-fiction book series.

> ## Insight
> By now you will have realized that every single thing that you see or hear can have potential for your work, be it in the world of fiction, non-fiction or education. All you need to do is reach out and grab it, file it and personalize it.

HUNTER/GATHERER

Whatever method you use for recording your thoughts, observations and ideas, you will ultimately want to bring your findings home and make use of them in your Ideas File.

Dr Johnson said that there are two kinds of knowledge: the knowledge that a person carries around in his/her head; and the equally important knowledge of where to find things out. One of the purposes of your Ideas File is to save you the trouble and potential heartache of trying to carry everything around in your head – but it is also important that the material you have accumulated is easily accessible.

Be professional in your approach to your Ideas File. We mentioned earlier the possibilities of a drawer or large envelope. This is fine if you're researching a single project, but if you're on permanent lookout for new ideas (which you should be), then a more user-friendly filing system will be necessary.

The perfect 'hard-copy' solution to this problem is, of course, a proper filing cabinet with a sophisticated index system. This may not be as far out of your reach as you might think, providing you have the space. Ex-office filing cabinets, from small, two-drawer affairs to five- or six-drawer giants, can often be picked up cheap in second-hand office-supply stores. Or again, you could take a look at one of the many 'selling' magazines. An office clearance could land you a real bargain.

Failing this, a drawer in a desk would do the job, or even a drawer in an ordinary cabinet or chest of drawers, provided everyone is told that the drawer is not to be used for anything else. There are also box-filing systems available in stationery stores, in which a fair amount of information can be kept tidily.

Of course, by far the most convenient way to store your ideas is on your computer. Open different folders for different topics. New Work. Current Work. Old Work. Then put carefully titled files into the appropriate folder – preferably with a date on them: 'New Book – working copy – third edit – 12-01-2010 – so you can instantly see which is the latest version of files that have gone through several incarnations. This is particularly important if you're working with a publisher and various copies of your book are flying back and forth with different layers of editing on them. Keep all the versions – just name them accordingly – you never know, an idea edited out at an early stage may need to be re-inserted later on.

If you invest in a scanner or a digital camera, you can scan or photograph items or objects that will be of use to you and have them in a clearly labelled folder for ease of access: 'New Book – newspaper clippings', 'New Book – research photographs'.

The important thing is to set up a system that you understand, be it alphabetical, numerical or cross-referenced, on paper or computer. You should have files for specific projects and files of general-interest items. A separate file for pictures and another for newspaper cuttings. Files of character ideas and files of storyline jottings.

If your project is a non-fiction or educational one, you might want to subdivide your work into topic or chapter headings, and store information that way.

Remember, careful planning at this stage will save you a lot of trouble in the long run. Some well-considered work up-front is going to help you out no end when you come to actually sit down and get the project started.

Exercise 12

You've gathered some ideas, you've had some thoughts. One author told us that to get ideas, he often turns common situations on their heads, or headlines from newspapers or television back to front. For example, a newspaper headline, 'Lottery hoaxer fools family' becomes 'Family fools lottery hoaxer', and a storyline is born. Open a page – newspaper, book or internet, and randomly pick a word or phrase. Do the same again for another word or phrase. Keep going until you have something that fires your imagination. 'Power to the Grandparents', 'Grim tales at Bedtime', both are newspaper headlines as we type this. Can you slot your two ideas together? Can you turn an idea around? Or you could juggle those fridge-magnet words until something interesting emerges. Write out some of your own ideas (fiction or non-fiction) or cut out headlines, chop them up into word-sized chunks and juggle them around. This is an excellent activity if you have a creative block. If an idea emerges, sketch it out now, before you read on.

10 THINGS TO REMEMBER

1 *Remember to note all your ideas down as soon as they come to you. You will forget otherwise.*

2 *Gather together all the tools you will need for the writing trade, e.g. pen and paper/typewriter/computer.*

3 *Understand the importance of correct spelling and grammar if your work is to aid a child's literacy and education (and impress an editor).*

4 *Learn to type properly – even if you have to go back to basics – to avoid RSI later on.*

5 *Discover that computers and the internet are a modern writer's best friends.*

6 *Make sure you have access to essential reference books.*

7 *If you need to, think about how you can raise funds for your writing needs.*

8 *Look at your diary and see how you can realistically make time or fit in real time for your writing.*

9 *Organize your working space in a logical and ergonomic manner for your style.*

10 *If stuck, plan where you can go to find inspiration.*

4

....

What to write and who to write for

In this chapter you will learn:
- *how to choose the genre of writing best suited to your talents and aspiration*
- *how to shape your work for the market*
- *how to organize your work.*

You may already have very definite thoughts about the areas in which you want to write. You may have specific ideas for the fiction market: an intergalactic octopus which crash-lands in your hero's bedroom; girls from witch-school who use magic to spy for their country; a gritty urban update of *Little Women* or *Winnie the Pooh*. You may want to write a factual book that explains the human respiratory system in words and pictures; or possibly an exciting pop-up book on glass-blowing as a leisure activity. Whatever your reasons for choosing a particular field of writing work, there must have been some initial spark that made you realize you wanted to write. The task before you now is to nurture that initial spark and to turn it into a blazing bonfire of controlled creativity.

Let's take a look at the diversity of the children's market. You'll already know the most obvious split – the one between fiction and non-fiction – but there are many more divisions you may not know about.

Fiction

What is fiction? One renowned author was asked by some intellectuals to define 'the novel'. They were probably hoping for some obscure observations that they could take away with them to ponder at length. However, the author thought for a moment and then came back with the comment, 'It's telling a story.' The great thing about this response is that it pricks pomposity as well as nailing the truth.

The point of fiction is to tell a story, any story, in a way that will hold the attention of the audience. Storytelling is as old as humanity itself. No matter how far back you research into human history, you will always discover the relics of storytelling, from the aboriginal cave paintings in Australia to the hieroglyphs on the walls of Egyptian tombs.

In many cultures the tale-bearer was an important person. In ancient Rome, poets would be hired to tell tales of the behaviour and misbehaviour of gods and goddesses, as well as recounting, in verse, the deeds of more earthly heroes. In those days, oratory was a great skill, especially in cultures where the average person didn't read or write. These stories were part of the glue that held societies together. You know the kind of thing: whoever we are, slave or senator, we're all subject to the caprices of the same gods.

The earliest stories, as far as we know, were usually attempts at explaining how the natural world worked. In a way, they were like early science-fiction – tales intended to make sense of a world full of inexplicable events and phenomena. How do the seasons change, and why? What forces are at work changing the shape of the moon? What are earthquakes? Who tows the sun across the sky and where does it go at night? If you sail beyond the horizon, what will happen to you? What wonders or terrors lie beyond the sealed doors of death?

On the white, outer edges of old maps were written the words 'Here be dragons', but someone somewhere first had to invent the idea of dragons, just as someone somewhere created the idea of flying horses, magic rings and gorgons with serpents for hair. Equally, someone else invented androids and 'warp-drive' and little grey aliens who abduct people and experiment on them in interstellar spaceships. You never know – maybe you'll invent something that will fascinate readers 500 years from now. After all, someone has to come up with this generation's marvels. If there's one thing in this world that flies beyond all boundaries, it's the human imagination.

It would be useful at this point to take a look at the difference between 'fact' and 'truth' in fiction. A myth or legend about the goings-on of Greek gods may not be factual, but it can contain an enormous amount of truth. In many ancient religions the gods and goddesses frequently behave in ways that are recognizably human. They are capable of being devious, brutal, aggressive, compassionate, arrogant, loving, angry, stupid, thoughtful, selfish, brave and cowardly.

Myths, legends, parables and fables all have a similar root: they seek to enlighten while entertaining. And the more an audience is *entertained* the easier it is for them to latch onto the truth at the heart of a barnstorming story. This balance between enlightenment and entertainment leads us neatly on to an important point about writing for children: the best way to convey a message is to give the impression that no message is being conveyed.

There's an episode in *The Simpsons* cartoon series where Ned Flanders is having a yard sale. A bunch of kids is fascinated by a collection of picture cards he has for sale, until he tells them they show figures from the Bible and that by buying the cards they may learn something. The kids immediately run for the hills. If he'd told them they were characters from a computer game, he could have made some money and the kids would still have accidentally taken some knowledge on board. Bad call, Ned.

What about you? Are you worried about the environment? Do you want to warn kids away from drugs? Or do you just think a little morality might make out-of-control children behave better? If you try to shove these kind of issues in children's faces they'll act like the kids in *The Simpsons* – they'll be gone. You'd be amazed how quickly children will disappear when presented with something that's 'good for them'.

On the other hand, a story can be worthwhile, even if it contains no social message or moral at all. It can be valuable as pure escapism. It can simply be fun. Of course, reading is part of a child's education, but that doesn't mean children can't read just for entertainment. After all, even if the story is just a piece of escapist lunacy, the child will still be absorbing aspects of grammar, punctuation and syntax.

Anything can spark an idea. A conversation with a child, an item on the news, a random 'what if?' thought, a dream …

The unexpected coming-together in the same place or at the same time of a number of things that I feel strongly about, or that I find particularly fascinating.

Useful plot starters are folk and fairy tales, legends and stories of old.

The great thing about myths, legends and fairy tales is that they speak to everyone. This means they can be constantly reinvented to suit the demands and tastes of each new generation. (For how this works with a modern myth, take a look at the *Batman* movie franchise over the decades. It was all comic-book capers in the 1960s with Adam Ward; gothic weirdness in the 1990s with Tim Burton and Michael Keating; and then the back-to-basics Dark Knight approach with Christian Bale for the new millennium.) Similarly, ghost stories have lost none of their impact despite the attempts of science and physics to prove (or disprove) their existence. In past days, ghosts haunted the wild woods or distant, crumbling towers; these days, they lurk in office buildings and drive spectral cars down twilight streets.

In brief, the business of fiction is to present an audience with something that is 'truthful' (that is, believable or at least capable of creating a willing suspension of disbelief), but not based on fact. The Greeks had Ulysses; the Norsemen had Beowulf; the Anglo-Saxons had Robin Hood – mythic heroes all. The twenty-first century has the reinvention of favourite modern characters such as Batman, James Bond and Doctor Who, and favourite stories such as *Star Wars I, II* and *III*, *The Lord of the Rings*, *Sin City*, *Wolverine*, *Warriors* and *Twilight*.

CATEGORIES OF FICTION

Fiction breaks down into several categories. Publishers are always on the look-out for writers with a good sense of humour. If you can tell a tale that makes people laugh, your chances of getting published are healthier than for some other children's writing areas. The funny books are the most popular with young readers, and if you can make the 12-year-olds+ laugh, publishers will beat a path to your door.

Then there's fantasy, sword-and-sorcery, horror, scary/ghost stories and science fiction. The common thread in these areas is that they take the audience outside the accepted laws of nature, to an elfin city, a wizard's chamber, a werewolf's lair or a desert planet beyond Betelgeuse. These stories are continually popular, but do understand before you set out on your own fantasy trilogy that there is a lot of competition already out there. In fantasy you may want to create an entire world, but you'll need to be consistent – so if your characters are using chalk to write on cave walls, don't later on show them with mobile phones. Whichever of these areas appeals, try to keep the place and character names memorable and readable. Children lose interest if they can't pronounce complex and obscure names from your own imagination. You will need to come up with something exceptionally original if you're going to find an interested publisher in this genre.

Historical fiction is another category of fiction, but think twice before embarking on yet another telling of the legend of King Arthur – most angles have probably been covered. A story of children caught up, say, in the American Civil War will need to be heavily researched and very accurate. Even then, the most meticulously researched and presented story may not find a publisher for such a specific area unless you can create some compelling characters through whose eyes the history can be viewed. But if children at school are studying the area of history you have chosen, your chances of interesting a publisher increase. In all historical fiction the story must come first. The text should not read like a documentary with the addition of token fictional characters. Find out what areas of history are being studied, and look for a period or historical characters which have not been over-written about.

Romantic fiction can draw a large young-adult audience, as can thrillers and crime stories. Research your market, looking at different publishers and their series, and read the books to get a sense of the range of acceptable styles and limitations. Romance can range from growing friendship to potential parenthood, from historical to contemporary settings. But in a book that includes thrills and chills, or involves gangsters and criminals – you will need to know how far you can take the risk factor and what level of violence and gore is allowed.

Books with a school setting have always been very popular – children can readily identify with such instantly recognizable surroundings, empathizing with characters as they encounter everyday problems presented in a page-turning way. Similarly, books following the adventures and misadventures of a group of friends always go down well – although once again you will need to come up with a compelling new angle if you are to hold a publisher's attention.

Publishers are also always on the look-out for 'series' ideas (that is, an idea in which a regular cast of characters will appear in a succession of books). There are enduring favourites such as the Beatrix Potter tales, Flower Fairies, and Mister Men books. Now Rainbow Magic, Lemony Snicket, Twilight and many more series such as Beast Quest sell a lot of books by allowing an audience to follow the ongoing exploits of well-known or established characters.

Series books give the public what they want, by coming up with variations on particular themes. Such books can safely be bought in the knowledge that they will involve characters the reader gets to know and love in known situations.

There is also a call for poetry and plays for use in schools, as well as themed poetry collections for the general trade market. Poetry has never been an easy area for new authors to make their mark, or to earn money. You may need to establish yourself on the poetry scene first, via competitions, readings, poetry circles, online groups, etc. Yes we know children enjoy poetry and rhyme – but your market will most likely be limited to those countries who speak the same language.

In the young-adult market you will find a certain amount of issue fiction, in which contemporary social issues are explored. In this and other areas you will sometimes bump up hard against political correctness (PC). A fine line needs to be walked on this issue – you may agree that some topics and areas of behaviour are clearly and reasonably 'non-PC' – such as a book where the main child characters are smoking, doing drugs or getting drunk and sleeping around. The other end of PC is explored interestingly in an episode of *Desperate Housewives*, (Season 1: Running To Stand Still) where the character Lynette headbutts the woman who runs the play committee in her local school, and who wants to present a performance of 'Little Red Riding Hood' where the wolf is rehabilitated rather than killed, thus, in Lynette's eyes, ruining the story and neutering the play's natural and traditional ending.

> **Insight**
> Everyone in the writing, publishing and book-buying world will have their own thoughts on what is PC acceptable and what isn't, and to a certain extent you will need to write within the agreed social boundaries of the country in which you live.

Non-fiction

The range for non-fiction work is enormous: it can cover anything from a short piece in a magazine to a multi-volume encyclopaedia, to research writing for websites. Non-fiction books cover a vast range of subjects too – from educational studies and revision guides, to self-esteem and lifestyle, to activity books, to hobbies and interests. If this area appeals to you, then research what's out there, who is publishing it, and who might be buying the books – children, adults, schools?

Maybe your own children are interested in watching tadpoles transform into frogs. You decide to write a piece explaining the various stages of the transformation and outlining the best ways of looking after them. Add some information on amphibians in general, a few thoughts on their dietary habits and the environment they prefer; mix in a series of diagrams, illustrations and photographs, and you are well on the way to developing one of those 'How To Look After Your First ...' books that are found in bookshops, supermarkets, libraries and pet stores everywhere.

On the other hand, you may be an expert juggler. A short book on the subject may be a great way to pass on your skills and knowledge. And then you could put juggling into a wider context – the performing arts, for instance. Your piece on juggling could become a single chapter in a book about street theatre or the circus. A skilful juggling mathematician could even incorporate juggling into an explanation of the laws of probability and calculus. A biologist could use juggling to introduce a work on how it is that the human body is capable of such dexterity.

Every activity you can think of is capable of generating its own non-fiction guide. How to play football. How to use face-paints. How to make cookies. How to find bugs and where to keep them. How mobile phones work and how to use one. How to build a magic castle out of empty toilet rolls and discarded egg-boxes. How to cope with flu and why you became ill in the first place.

HISTORY

Who built the great pyramids of Egypt? Who invented gunpowder? What sparked the American Civil War? When did men first travel to the moon and back? In 2009 a Norwegian publisher produced a picture book entitled *The First Man to Pee on The Moon*. Going back to our PC thoughts, this title may work for Norway, but not necessarily for other countries – but the idea is one which would certainly make children we know read a book about space that they might otherwise overlook.

GEOGRAPHY

Where is Egypt and why did its ancient peoples rely so heavily on the annual flooding of the Nile? What is the Great Wall of China and why was it built? What happens when an agricultural society clashes with an industrial one? If you build houses on floodplains or nature reserves, what could be the outcome? Why do earthquakes happen?

SCIENCE

How were the pyramids built by a society that had not even invented the wheel? What is cement made of and how does it hold buildings together? How did people manage to get a rocket to the moon? Is global warming something humans have created, or is the changing climate due to a natural cycle? What will happen if icebergs melt or a species becomes extinct?

Non-fiction subjects can be approached in many different ways, and each approach will give an enquiring author a fresh angle from which to go about their research (be that person a teacher, an interested parent, an expert, or just someone who wants to find something out for themselves and then share their knowledge with others). The most successful non-fiction books for the general market will be those which have elements of fun. All of us learn and absorb information more easily, if we're enjoying what we are reading or investigating.

First ask yourself: do you have any qualifications, training, or accreditations in a particular area you could write about for non-fiction? Do you belong to any societies or organizations because you are enthusiastic about a particular topic or leisure interest? Do you, or have you worked in an area which has aspects which you could draw from? What do you know and how could your writing of the subject convince a publisher that you are the right person for the job?

Exercise 13

This exercise could be an ongoing project: Pick a topic you feel you know a lot about, or enjoy discovering and taking part in yourself. That could be sport, music, film, conservation, knitting, psychology, maths, fundraising, model planes, health – anything at all.

Now research what is published out there – look for the same theme, and the book styles which you would enjoy writing for. Include websites – someone had to write that information. What is the competition? What age-range would you choose to write for?

As a starting point, make a list of ten chapter headings for the book on your chosen subject. Consider what else you may need to research to make the book accurate and as up to date as possible. Could someone with no knowledge get a basic understanding? Would a child with some knowledge learn something new?

Lastly, what could you bring in which could make your book stand out from the crowd, and can you turn the idea on its head in some way to make it different or fun?

It's said that most creative writing starts off with the phrase, 'What if ...' What if there was a book for children explaining DNA (deoxyribonucleic acid – the building blocks of life) in an entertaining, amusing and informative way? Is there? Go check it out. If not, do you feel fired-up to research and write one?

AREAS OF NON-FICTION

It's too soon to go into details of how the publishing world works, but it won't hurt for you to understand that non-fiction divides into two main areas: trade non-fiction and educational non-fiction. You must research both markets before you start work on any project, as they have quite different and separate requirements.

Trade non-fiction includes all books and magazines ranging from pony, ballet world, comics, collectable partworks, and TV show fanzines, to music, fashion and lifestyle for teens and everything that you or a child might buy in the high street or online for themselves. Trade non-fiction includes everything from pictorial language learning books and *Maths Made Easy* to the hugely successful, fun non-fiction titles of the *Flaming Olympics* and *Horrible History* variety. Trade non-fiction will appeal to the general buying market and school purchasers.

Educational non-fiction books are primarily bought by schools and colleges for educational purposes. These can range from reading schemes to classroom textbooks to foreign language workbooks. These books will have been commissioned with the school curriculum needs specifically in mind. If you write a maths book that fits the curriculum and sells to practically every school in the country, you could make a lot of money – but don't try this without researching who is publishing what, as you will need to target those publishers, and create something which will suit their styles and the curriculum needs.

Faction

As this hybrid word suggests, 'faction' is mixing fiction and non-fiction together. You'll already have seen versions of this in movies or television mini-series which dramatize the opening days of the Gulf War, or the lives, loves, divorces and beheadings of Henry VIII's six wives. Anything which seeks to shed light on a historical character or event in a dramatized form is actually 'faction' (and on TV would be called 'drama-documentary') be it the life of Gandhi, D-Day, or the story of a forgotten midwife in Victorian Britain.

Books in the faction area include historical 'I was there'-type works in which the author 'sees' great events through contemporary eyes. Your hero or heroine could be the nephew of an adult who was there, or be an apprentice whether to a gladiator or an architect of the Industrial Revolution. This can be a very effective way of bringing historical subjects to life, although, as with all non-fiction areas, thorough research is vital.

Dramatized biographies can also bring past lives into sharp focus, as can dramatized versions of catastrophes or extraordinary events: the Black Death, the Asian Tsunami Disaster or the life story of the inventor of the jet engine can all be made more real to young people by giving them a contemporary, dramatized voice – although beware of writing a fictionalized account of a recent disaster or you may be accused of exploiting the suffering of others. A book for very young children about going into hospital, starting school, ballet lessons or learning to swim, can benefit from the faction approach.

And as if all the topics mentioned above weren't enough for you to take on board, give a moment's thought to the following: comics, activity books, computer games, and websites. An internet search of 'websites for children', or 'things to do' will bring you dozens of organizations and sites where writers may be needed for the content.

Suiting the language to the child

So you think you know kids? Okay, try this. You're seven years old and your pals have seen you reading a book clearly labelled 'For readers aged 5 and 6'. They fall about laughing. What do you do? It's a no-brainer, isn't it? You dump the book. It's just as likely that the modern seven-year-old will steer clear of anything aimed at their age-range and will head instead for books where the main characters are a few years older. It's cool to read about ten-year-olds when you're seven – it's lame to read about six-year-olds.

A lot of publishers divide their children's lists into very specific reading and interest ages, particularly those aimed at the younger readers. They do this in a variety of ways, from the deliberate inclusion of a specific target age on the cover to colour-coding or age-coding labels on the jackets, all of which are intended to act as a guide to their product. Whether this type of categorization is a good idea or not is under debate, with determined opinions on both sides, but while such methods are being employed, it's important for an author to understand what is going on.

The main reading age-groups have often been divided by publishers in this way: 0–2, 2–5, 6–8, 7–9, 10–12, 12+. Some publishers may take a more broadly defined colour-coding or series jacket design approach that will give a strong clue to the buyer as to the intended readership. As times and trends shift and change, these divisions and approaches are altered, abandoned, re-thought and then picked up again by publishers – whatever they get up to, you'll need to follow the trends as they change.

Children throughout the world learn to read at different times, at varying speeds and in different ways. A book written and published in England could easily end up being read in Russia, Belgium, Korea, Bolivia or Zimbabwe. The majority of children start full-time schooling around the age of five and will usually be reading alone and silently by the age of seven. But children's education and reading abilities vary enormously for many reasons, and something which one seven-year-old will discard as too simple may well cause problems for a child of a similar age but of a different reading level. You need to aim your work right in the middle of the age-range you've chosen. There are more publishers publishing low reading ability/high interest books – say books aimed at 11+ but with a reading age of eight, but these will generally follow specific briefs and guidelines.

Insight

What publishers want so far as language and word-count is concerned varies so widely that you're going to have to look how publishers publish, and read books in the area which appeals to you before you start writing.

A picture book for the very young may consist only of 12 words. Further up the reading scale, an illustrated storybook may consist of 2,500 words, and a book aimed at the young adult market could be up to 80,000 words. There are exceptions to this rule, but it makes no sense to offer a publisher a picture storybook for the very young of 4,000 words or a novel aimed at 12-year-olds that comes in at 250,000 words.

Insight

To repeat: children like to read about people slightly older than themselves. So, whatever age-range you want to write for, make sure the leading characters are either at the top end of that group, or slightly above it.

For readers aged 8–12, the age of your heroes should be 12+, and a book aimed at 7–10 year-olds should have characters aged mainly between 9 and 11. This is simple psychology and no more demanding than choosing a birthday present that is just a little older than the child for whom it is intended. Young-adult magazines appearing to target an audience in its mid-to-late teens are actually aimed at and read by children as young as ten, in much the same way as television programmes with a primary adult target audience are watched by children.

Fluent readers are going to devour everything from picture books, sometimes with a very adult subtext, to books that would generally be thought beyond their ability or interest. C. S. Lewis, the author of the Narnia series, said that his childhood was spent in a house teeming with books of every type, form and nature, some intended for children, and some emphatically not, but that he was denied access to nothing. Given half a chance, an inquisitive eight-year-old could have a field day with a copy of *Bridget Jones's Diary* in much the same way that an 80-year-old might still enjoy the exploits of Ratty, Mole and Mr Toad.

Exercise 14

As they grow older, children learn more words and are able to understand more complex grammatical structures. Writers need to tune in to these changes, and to know what words and sentence structures will work for what age groups. Find out how well you understand this.

Write a series of letters/emails, all of them on the same topic, but each of them aimed at a different age-range. Pick whatever subject you like, but make it something that you think would interest a child of any age. A description of an up-coming pop concert, a holiday trip to a theme park, or some crazy antics by wildlife you have recently witnessed.

First write your letter so it can be read to a pre-school child by a parent or some other adult.

Next, write the same letter for an eight-year-old.

Now write it for a 13-year-old.

Finally, try writing it for a 17-year-old pen-pal from another country whose first language is not your own.

Points to note:

▶ *Try not to 'talk down' to your audience. A 13-year-old isn't going to appreciate being written to as if they were only eight, and a 17-year-old, despite any limits on grammatical comprehension, will expect to be treated as an adult. Similarly, something which may be great fun for an eight-year-old (a new assault course at your local children's play area) is unlikely to mean a whole lot to a four-year-old.*
▶ *Your use of language should alter, from being simple and lucid for the youngest audience to more advanced and complex for the older readers. At the same time, your terms of reference must shift in perspective to suit the reader's interest level (amazing ice cream and finger-painting for five-year-olds; getting a backstage access all areas concert ticket for the teens, and possibly ice cream too).*
▶ *If you can, show your letters to a parent or teacher, or even better, to children of the appropriate age. Teachers or parents should be able to tell you whether you're using the right kind of language, and the kids will certainly let you know if you've hit the mark. Listen to what they say and take note of what you're told and then try the same exercise again, using a different topic but obeying the same rules.*

Did you do better the second time around? If not, why not – weren't you listening? Try again. If you've improved, well done – you've just had your first taste of 'constructive criticism'. You're on your way to being a professional writer.

Styles

He often changed his residence: and during his various
travels, while he visited the most celebrated parts of the
south of Europe, his admirers in England were indulged
with the productions of his powerful and versatile muse:
sometimes proudly soaring into the pure regions of taste,
breathing noble sentiments and chivalric feelings: at other
times, descending into impure voluptuousness, or grovelling
in sheer vulgarity.

This extract is a quote about Lord Byron taken from a book of
biographies published in 1845. How can you tell it was written
over 150 years ago? Well, the sentence goes on forever, for a
start. This author was producing work for an educated minority
readership for which the style of the description is as important
as the information being conveyed. There is also a very particular
moral tone being struck.

We spoke to one author who described being buttonholed by the
chairman of a school's board of governors (and would-be author)
who mouthed off about how bad it was that semicolons didn't
seem to get used much anymore. He blamed it on publishers,
but what he didn't get was that modern publishers need to keep
the interest of a modern audience, and you don't do that with
sentences ten yards long.

Two thoughts:

▶ *always keep your audience in plain sight*
▶ *brevity is the soul of wit.*

Your job is to communicate, plain and simple. Say what you
want to say as lucidly and briefly as you can, while still keeping
it lively and interesting. Telling a good story in 800 words is a
whole lot harder than stretching out the same story over 30,000
words.

Exercise 15

Try an exercise in brevity.

Describe your immediate surroundings in ten words. Not nine, not 12 – but exactly ten words. Show this to someone else and see if you've managed to convey a real feel for the place.

It's a little like constructing a Haiku – and it's not as easy as it sounds. You might need to try a number of different approaches before you really nail it.

The Lord Byron sentence we quoted was very much of its time. How might a modern, thumbnail biography approach the same subject?

He travelled widely in southern Europe, house-hopping continuously and pausing only to send back his latest works to his English admirers. These works ranged from the lofty and noble to the decidedly earthy.

The above modernization retains all the information of the original and manages it without a single colon or semicolon, while halving the length of the original.

A children's author has to keep an eye on how language changes. You need to speak directly to a modern audience – but you need to do it without falling into some of the more obvious traps.

These traps take on two main forms. First, there's the use of contemporary slang. Be careful – cool slang expressions are abandoned with surprising speed. A character saying, 'See you later, alligator' may have sounded very hip in 1962, but today it just sounds weird (and a few years ago, we might have written 'odd'!). For some time children have used the word 'loser' to describe anyone they despise or pity – or indeed, anyone they wish to insult ('What a *loser*') – and a casually tossed-off 'whatever' is a great way of expressing indifference or boredom. As we write, they are saying 'safe' to mean good and 'fit' to mean attractive, but are these phrases still being used as you read this book and if they've gone out of favour, what words have replaced them? You need to find out. Think carefully about this before you fill your book with slang that may well have an early sell-by date on it. Your book still needs to make sense in five years' time.

A lot of hot air is being generated right now in the debate about what harm texting, emailing and chat-room shorthand are doing to the literacy levels of modern children. It's an interesting question, and one that you should think about. The knee-jerk reaction of older people is to worry that the way words and sentences are telescoped and abbreviated is eroding children's vocabularies and grammatical expertise away to virtually nothing.

The bottom line is that in a modern society people have a tendency to want to get their point across as briefly and succinctly as possible. In the hit movie *Pirates of the Caribbean: The Curse of the Black Pearl* there is a pertinent exchange. Will Turner accuses (pirate) Captain Jack Sparrow of cheating in a sword fight. Captain Jack just looks quizzically at him and says 'Pirate!' Everyone watching the movie knows what this one word means – it means: 'Of course I cheated – I'm a pirate!' So, ask yourself – does this reduce language to rubble, or is it just a quick and neat way of getting your point across?

In other words, are texting, emailing and chat-rooming creating huge problems for language skills – or are they just quick ways for a perfectly literate child to communicate with friends? As a writer, you need to get involved in this debate, because your books will form part of the educational matrix of these children's lives. OMG! R U up 4 it – or do you deplore the paucity of semicolons in modern children's literature?

The second trap to avoid when writing is to presume that the moral climate in which you are living is the only acceptable one from which to view events. The biographer of Lord Byron did just that. Take another look at how pompous those words sound to today's reader.

You don't have to go as far back as the nineteenth century to see how social opinion has changed. Take a look at a few children's books written in the two or three decades after the Second World War. Pay attention to how boys and girls and men and women behave in these classic books. Women and girls cook and clean, while the men and boys fight enemies, aliens and hit burglars with spades.

Times have changed, but how often do you read an adventure story in which the hero is in a wheelchair? Or a story where one of the main characters is deaf, not deaf because the deafness is integral to the plot, but simply deaf in the way that people are in real life? It may not be everyone's idea of PC, but the way differently abled kids are depicted in the cartoon series *South Park* is very interesting. The character Jimmy Vulmer requires crutches to walk and has a pronounced stammer – but his overriding character-trait is that he is a budding stand-up comedian. He just happens to be – as he describes it – 'handi-capable'. And the character Timmy, both mentally and physically handicapped, was once voted the most popular disabled character on TV – in a poll where disabled voters outnumbered everyone else. In fact, quadriplegic *Seattle Times* columnist Jeff Shannon has described both these characters as 'goodwill ambassadors' by challenging preconceptions and confronting taboos head-on.

Organizing your work

For an amateur writer, having a good idea, coming up with a few characters and heading off into the unknown is all part of the creative process. It's fun not to know what's going to happen next.

Well, up to a point it is. But for most professional writers, heading for the horizon without much idea of what will happen when you get there is pretty much a waste of time. You need to put a plot together. You need to know where you're going and what will be there when you arrive.

Even if you get a publisher's attention with your initial 'Hi there, I'm a writer' letter, the next thing they're going to ask for is a detailed synopsis ('chapter breakdown') of your book, along with some sample chapters. This is fine if you've already written the book – although it may mean you scrambling together a hastily written synopsis after the event, and possibly finding that when the plot is laid out like this, a whole bunch of problems you hadn't noticed will suddenly become glaringly obvious. (Uncle George couldn't have met the kids at the railway station that day – he was on an aeroplane over Antarctica at the time.) On the other hand, if you are floating a concept for a book you haven't written yet, you'll need to be able to show where it's going. You can't simply say: 'Pat, George and Freda are teenaged friends who have a whole lot of great adventures, but come out of it OK.' You'll have to be a whole lot more specific than that.

> *When I was still an unpublished author, I heard Nina Bawden say that the only difference between a published writer and someone who can write a decent letter was persistent motivation.*

Forget publishers and editors for the moment – you don't want to waste your time with a book that stays on track for the first two months of writing, but which then does a spectacular nose-dive off a cliff because the creative rails have suddenly run out. Putting together a synopsis would have saved you a lot of wasted time and effort – and will possibly have shown you up-front how a few simple changes could have prevented the train-wreck of your story. And anyway, it'll really help you with your storytelling skills if you sit and write out point by point exactly what's going to happen through the book. It will help you to clarify ideas and highlight any plot-holes before you get started.

Your synopsis for a book could be as simple as a page or two of bullet points, outlining the main events in the story in the right order; or it could stretch to a detailed chapter breakdown, set out scene by scene and chapter by chapter, including not only the main story-threads, but also bits of planned dialogue, character and plot back-stories for your own benefit – and alternative possibilities which may or may not come to life once the actual writing gets going.

Many full-time authors are invited ('commissioned') to produce particular works; that is, they are paid a sum of money (an 'advance') on signature of a contract in which they agree to write a specific book (or a number of books) usually on a particular topic for a particular readership and of a particular length. Obviously a publisher will want to know what they are getting; so the author will usually be asked first to submit a proposal and then more detailed outlines of character and intent.

Following this, a publisher will usually ask for a full synopsis of the story so they can see exactly what the author intends to write, and so they can make editorial comments early on, thus preventing the problem of a major rewrite at a later stage.

Synopses are not only useful to publishers. You know by now that books in all age groups have quite tight word limits. It doesn't make much sense for a writer to start a book for 11-year-olds without knowing what's going to happen, but hoping that whatever happens will happen within the word limit. A professional author has to have a pretty good idea of where a piece of work is going, if only to make sure it gets to its conclusion at the right time and not 2,000 words short or 5,000 words over the acceptable length of the book.

Always go back and revise what you've already written. You can never do that too often anyway, and it may well set off a new stream of ideas – or changes. If you write consecutively, as I do, skip a couple of chapters, write a future bit and later join it up – alter/junk as needed.

Some authors sit down in a locked room and write and write until the story is all there in front of them. Some write thumbnail sketches then wander off for a while to let their ideas simmer and stew. Others use the 'tumble drier' approach, in which the plot is allowed to rumble around in their heads until it resolves itself.

Still others take a long walk to thrash out complicated plot lines. Others use the 'orienteering' approach, in which individual ideas are run up mental flagpoles in a more-or-less straight line from chapter 1 to chapter whatever; the task then being to map-read your way from flagpole to flagpole.

Then again, the plot may come to an author piecemeal and out of order, starting life as a heap of scraps that need to be sorted out before a pattern emerges. A plot may kick-off when you see something that clicks with an idea that has been in your Ideas File for months. Marry them up and see what happens.

A synopsis presented to a publisher is not written in stone, and plots can be altered as you progress if better ways forward present themselves. Don't be afraid to make changes if second thoughts turn out to be better thoughts. And be prepared to have to rewrite existing chapters if a brilliant idea suddenly hits you halfway through a book but requires 'seeding' earlier on. (A computer makes this sort of rewriting a total breeze!) But bear in mind that if you've been commissioned to write a book on honeybees, presenting the publisher with a book on hosepipes isn't going to go down very well. Changes should stick to the spirit of the original plot, and it might even be a good idea to keep your publisher informed of what's going on, just to prevent problems later on down the line.

Insight

Some authors use their friends, family or partners as sounding boards or alternative brains when they're putting plots together. Just talking things through out loud is sometimes enough to help unravel tangled plotlines or release log-jams in the story.

If you have no children of your own, then the children of a friend could be a useful source of ideas. A half hour with a child can produce better results than six months of staring at a blank sheet of paper or an empty computer screen.

Some authors like to keep their synopsizing to a minimum, simply sketching out the plot and leaving the details for the full writing journey process. Others will write detailed, scene-by-scene, chapter-by-chapter outlines that leave nothing to chance.

There is no right or wrong way – you will find out what works for you – and you should be prepared for major reworking if new and better ideas hit you mid-way through. Very few authors really know exactly how they plan on getting from A to Z: after all, the journey is all part of the pleasure. We will cover this more fully in the next chapter, when we discuss plot structures.

Exercise 16

Write a short synopsis of the most recent book you have read from what you remember. Does it tell the basics of the story? What was memorable?

Write a blurb – the words used to describe or praise the book on the back jacket cover. These can be anything from a couple of sentences to a paragraph. Do not look at the real book's blurb first, compare your piece of writing afterwards. How did they compare?

Take a look at the book again now if you need to, and write a review. Why not add it to the reviews section of an online bookstore or book group? See how your thoughts compare with others.

10 THINGS TO REMEMBER

1 Focus on your targeted market by knowing what's already been published.

2 Work out how to tailor your good ideas to your audience, through establishing ages of characters, proposed length, language and style etc.

3 Read more books for your intended age group to make sure your language suits the expected age of reader.

4 Edit and hone your work until it fits the word limit to the planned age-range.

5 Practise writing synopses until the content and pace look enticing.

6 Take out anything which you have doubts about and could potentially upset the current PC trends.

7 Be cautious when using slang and transient idioms to keep your work 'timeless'.

8 Aim your work at the average reading ability of your potential readers.

9 Don't forget to pitch the ages of your main characters at the top end of the age-range you're writing for.

10 Brevity is the soul of wit, so keep to the point and don't waffle.

5

The basics of writing fiction

In this chapter you will learn:
- *the essentials of storytelling: storylines, plotting, character and situation, structure and narrative voice*
- *how to hone your style and create a publishable work of fiction*
- *how to revise your work and overcome writer's block.*

You don't need to be a mechanic to drive a car.

Meaning what, exactly? Theatre critic Kenneth Tynan made the comment that a critic was a person who knew the way but didn't know how to drive.

The point is that a good writer doesn't necessarily need to know every detail and nuance of the 'mechanics' of the language in which they are writing. You're not going to need a Master's Degree in English to write a readable book. What you do need is a good ear for language and the ability to put words on the page in a way that engages and entertains people. What you don't need to know is why a pluperfect is a pluperfect or why the plural of 'foot' is not 'foots'. A highly academic knowledge of your language may help you to produce a very polished piece of work – but that doesn't mean anyone is going to enjoy reading it.

As long as you have a good grip on the basics of your language, you'll pick up the rest as you go along. By looking, listening and reading, you'll soon get a handle on what works and what doesn't. In the end, you're selling *yourself* through the printed word – even if your story is a first-person narrative by a ten-year-old girl and you're actually a 40-year-old man. Your job is to make the reader believe in the world or worlds you are creating, to care about the characters and to want to know what comes next. To do this you need to 'be in the moment' – to make your *audience* believe and care, first of all *you* have to believe and care. The world of children's literature is no place for post-modernist irony or cynical sub-text.

Storylines

Some people say there are only three basic plots in fiction, split into seven classic plot lines that probably came down to us from the Ancient Greeks via Shakespeare and suchlike. We decided to check this out by asking people we thought might know the truth.

Here are some of the responses we got.

1 *Cinderella (rags to riches).*
2 *Faust (the debt has to be repaid).*
3 *Achilles (the fatal flaw).*
4 *The eternal triangle (man plus woman plus X).*
5 *The spider and the fly (good versus evil).*
6 *Romeo and Juliet – a tragedy (boy meets girl, boy loses girl, boy gets girl back).*
7 *The great 'romance' (X meets Y, they hate each other, then they fall in love, then they live happily ever after).*
8 *The twister – at the end of the book, you realize nothing was quite what it seemed.*

Some people said there were up to 36 different dramatic situations and gave us lists to prove it, but we thought eight would be enough for you to be getting on with.

It really doesn't matter how many archetypal plots there are – one publisher boiled it down to this: 'There is a problem. The problem develops. The problem is solved.' In other words, the 'beginning', the 'middle' and the 'end'.

It may occur to you that in movies like *Pulp Fiction* and books such as William Burroughs' *The Naked Lunch*, these three divisions of storytelling have been kicked all over the ball park, and it's true that some liberties can be taken with the way the narrative flows – but for the time being you need to learn to write stories that start at the beginning, to quote *Alice in Wonderland*, and then go on until they get to the end. In that order. Beginning. Middle. End.

You also need to learn how to spread the flow of the story evenly over these three phases. You don't want the beginning to drag on till three-quarters of the way through the book, then the middle and the end to be crammed in at breakneck speed in the final few chapters. One author we spoke to remembered reading an unsolicited manuscript where the bulk of the story involved introducing a whole lot of friends and family of the main character – only to have them all drop out of the plot when the character went abroad and started to have the adventure that was at the heart of the story. And then, just as things were getting interesting, the book stopped. Bad writing!

Publishers and agents often receive manuscripts with 50-page introductions or very promising picture book stories that fall apart when the author tries to wrap the plot up in the final couple of sentences. This kind of thing happens when an inexperienced author dives head-first into writing a novel without giving much thought to where they're going with the story or why they're going there. This is where plotting in advance pays dividends. This is where things start to get professional.

Writing for a living is hard. Hard because you put your heart and soul into it, only to have work either rejected or, more rarely, accepted by a publisher – at which point an editor will probably tear it apart and make you write it all over again. It is, of course, for the best, but that doesn't make it easier. So if you want to write, write a story you will enjoy working on again and again, a story that is fun or satisfying for you to tell.

It's time to ask yourself a few questions, before you pick up a pen or sit at your keyboard or typewriter to begin writing.

WHAT DO YOU WANT TO SAY, AND WHY DO YOU WANT TO SAY IT?

A work of fiction must be inspired by something. Even if the idea seems to have popped into your head out of nowhere, you can bet your life it has been gestating away in there for a while – inspired possibly by some snippet or scrap in your Ideas File. Having brilliant ideas, though, is only the first part. Now you need to get your brilliant ideas into shape.

There are a couple of good reasons for doing this. First of all, you need to know if your idea has 'legs' – meaning is it strong enough to run the length of the book you are planning. Secondly, you have to find out exactly how passionate you are about turning this idea into a book – especially if the book is intended to be many thousand words long.

If the thought of painstakingly working through your story and writing it out a few times in synopsis form, and then tinkering, tweaking the plot and changing things that don't quite work sounds like a total turn-off, then you might ask yourself whether you're really so fired-up about writing the book in the first place.

> **Insight**
> Everything you will ever see for sale has been researched, tested, trialled, re-designed and tweaked hundreds of times over before it hit the shelves or the website. Books are no different.

STORY LENGTHS

Remember what we told you about the way publishers approach their market? Books for young adults are generally longer than books for the 'middle fiction' range. These are, in turn, longer than storybooks, and storybooks are longer than picture books. In other words, if you're thinking of writing for the young-adult audience (12+), you need a plot that you can sustain over 50,000 words or more. If you're aiming at a ten- to 12-year-old audience then you're looking at approximately 40,000 words – and so on down the age-range.

You may think that 50,000 words sounds like a lot, and you might think to yourself you can slow things down a bit or add some 'off the ball' scenes to pad it out – but remember these days that you have to compete for the attention of a 14-year-old with a whole lot of other distractions. The plots of longer books can be more involved and complex, but in the end the average reader has to understand what is going on.

PLOTTING

If you're writing a thriller or a mystery where you want to keep readers guessing, don't fall into the trap of mixing up 'intriguing' with 'confusing'. It's fine to string a reader along with clues and red herrings, but in the end everything has to make sense. When someone gets to the end of a crime thriller or mystery story, they have to be able to think back over the book and wonder how they were so dumb as to not spot all the clues they were given about who stole the diamonds and how.

Murder/mystery/crime-type books need to be very carefully thought out. For example, the usual method of plotting crime stories is to start with the 'event' (murder, theft or other crime), then jump to the 'resolution'. With both ends of the story in place, you can then get busy figuring out how to get from place 'A' to place 'Z'.

A MURDER MYSTERY

Here's your 'event'. Professor X is found dead in her study with an axe in her skull. The point of the story is to find out who wielded the axe and why.

Your hero or heroine will be the person who unmasks the murderer, and who explains at the end how the crime was committed and who did it.

Exercise 17

You are writing a detective novel. Your lead characters are a girl and a boy aged about 12. A theft has taken place at their school: the charity box has been raided.

The two youngsters have a pretty good idea who the thief is. Come up with thoughts on the following:

1 *Who stole the money and why?*
2 *Why do the youngsters suspect the thief?*
3 *Why do they seek to solve the crime themselves rather than pass on the information to the authorities?*

Here are some obvious answers:

1 *The money was stolen by the headteacher to feed a secret gambling habit.*
2 *The youngsters saw the headteacher coming out of the room where the money was kept only a few minutes before the theft was reported.*
3 *They dare not tell anyone because who would believe the word of two students against that of their headteacher?*

So as not to make things too easy for yourself, now come up with three different ways of setting up that plot without the headteacher being the villain.

Your hero doesn't need to be particularly smart, or young, or sighted. So long as readers like him, the hero can be a well-meaning idiot who stumbles over the truth by accident. Your heroine could be the caretaker's six-year-old daughter who saw something odd on the morning of the theft but who isn't taken seriously – leaving her no alternative but to solve the crime herself. The story outline idea in the exercise could also be developed to fit in a fantasy genre, issue fiction, or a humour genre, and for different age groups. The headteacher could be a werewolf or a shapeshifting alien, or the gambling habit is an obsessive compulsive disorder, or the headteacher is addicted to collecting china frogs. These are the imaginative possibilities of putting ideas together.

One of the problems with thrillers or crime stories where children or young people are the lead characters is that the writer has to come up with plausible reasons why adults don't take over the investigation. If you're writing a detective series, you'll have to think of a whole bunch of different reasons why this is the case. Why don't the kids tell an adult? Why do they put themselves in danger? How come these days, when the crook corners them, don't they just get on the mobile phone and call for help?

Another style of storytelling is the 'twist ending' – where a reader's assumptions about the book they have been reading can be totally upended by some unexpected revelation at the end. Books of this type that you might like to investigate would be *The Turbulent Term of Tyke Tyler* by Gene Kemp or *First Day Jitters* by Julie Dannenberg and Judith Dufour Love. If you'd like to investigate an adult novel that totally undermines at the end everything you assumed was happening, try Iris Murdoch's *The Black Prince*. Children can derive a lot of fun from finding that their preconceptions were all wrong – but this kind of storytelling needs to be done with great subtlety and skill if it's going to work – and bear in mind that if you hope for a second reading, there will need to be more to your book than a sneaky ending.

Characters and situations

Let's get back to the original questions of 'what' and 'why'.

WHAT ARE YOU WRITING?

Have you dreamed up a winning character? Someone whose life and whose adventures you just know people are going to go crazy over? A character as memorable as Toad of Toad Hall from *The Wind in the Willows*. A. A. Milne's Piglet from the *Winnie the Pooh* stories, Long John Silver, Pippi Longstocking, Lemony Snicket and Artemis Fowl? These characters are so strong, rounded and well defined that most have survived for decades and the books that feature them are still being reprinted and read today. But as well as being great characters, they all have something else in common: they are all attached to an engaging plot.

STRONG CHARACTERS IN INTERESTING SITUATIONS

Have you come up with an amazingly good plot? Does it have helicopters? Dangerous underground caverns? Explosions? Car chases? Spaceships careering into the heart of the sun? Are the heroes in constant danger of being killed on every other page? That's all fine – but no matter how thrilling it is, and no matter what kind of break-neck speed the plot storms along at, it needs one other thing. It needs characters that the readers care about.

If, as sometimes happens in plot-driven stories, the characters are fairly two-dimensional, then they need to be in a situation where their actions are important on a wider scale. For example, animal rights warriors have released thousands of infected and mutated rats from a mad professor's lab. Josh Blank and his team must recapture all the rats before they infect the whole population, and millions of lives are lost. The individual characters of Josh and his gang might be a bit sketchy in a book like that, but what they do will be hugely important.

Here are some basic equations:

Characters without a plot = nice people – shame they've got nothing to do. Yawn.

Plot without characters = plenty of action, no involvement. Where's my Wii Fit®?

Write nothing that doesn't push on the story, develop a character, or strengthen the atmosphere. Imagine the scenes like a play – get the stage set absolutely clearly in your mind, as on a stage, but only use the details you actually need.

Try mixing the real with the unreal. Pick a group of friends or family and put them in a backdrop of one of those disaster movies you've seen and see how it plays out. You'll know your characters well enough to have them respond realistically.

In blockbuster disaster movies, there will be a major or series of catastrophes and lots of noise and amazing visual effects to give sight and sound realism. But what happens at the start of the movie? You get introduced to the characters that are going to get caught up in the disaster. This is really important, because without an emotional engagement in the story, all you're left with is a whole bunch of pyrotechnics. Amazing to look at, but so what? Take the movie *Titanic*. It was awful that so many people drowned when the ship went down, but the people you really want to survive are Kate and Leo. Take another movie like *Pearl Harbour* – while the visual effects were amazing, a lot of people thought the characters were unrealistic, and that the film had no real emotional depth.

Far too many scripts arrive on publishers' and agents' desks with covering letters that say the book has 'something for everyone'. For 'something for everyone' you can usually read 'a big rambling mess of the wrong length, for no specific age group written by someone who doesn't know the first thing about the publishing market.'

DIFFERENT APPROACHES

Different types of fiction need different approaches. For instance, a thriller should end most chapters with a cliffhanger, so that the reader wants to find out what happens next. A character-led book should have chapters that end with some dilemma facing one or other of the characters, again so that the reader is forced to start a new chapter in order to find out how the problem is resolved. Think about how television soap series end each programme.

Short chapters are generally a good idea. A reader may see a five-page chapter and think, 'I'll just read one more before I put the light out,' whereas they would put the book down for the day if they saw that the next chapter was 25 pages long. Psychologically, bite-size chapters can easily draw a reader into racing through more of the book than they intended. They finish the book at breakneck speed and need to go out and buy your next novel, or go onto your website to find out when the next one is being published. This is going to be so good for your career.

Chapters don't need to be the same length, although it's probably a good idea to keep them at a similar word-count just for balance. A chapter should include a scene or a run of linked scenes that are put together for some reason. The last page of a chapter should leave something unresolved so the reader is drawn into reading the next one. And the next chapter should also end on a cliffhanger – and so on right through the book.

Dialogue has the effect of breaking the page up and of avoiding big blocks of narrative. Have your characters do most of the talking, if possible, and limit your narrative asides to scene-setting and to important explanations.

If your book follows several characters all doing different things at the same time, you could leave Tania hanging off a cliff for an entire chapter while you show what her pal Eddie is up to. Then you can drop a piano out of a window beneath which Eddie is standing and then leave him about to be flattened into the sidewalk while you go back to see how Tania is getting on, still clinging to her cliff-edge.

WHY ARE YOU WRITING THIS STORY?

You've had an amazing story idea. Other people should be allowed to read what you have spent so long writing. You owe it to humanity to get it out there. Your problem now is to put your story in front of an appreciative audience. You need to find a publisher. As with most things, first impressions are vital. Most agents and publishers will tell you that they can spot a 'winner' within the first paragraph or, at worst, within the first three pages.

So, how do you get them on your side?

In a work of fiction you need to introduce your characters, put them in some sort of context, and give some idea of what sort of book this is going to be. You can't do all this on page one. First, you have to grab your public by the lapels and force them to keep reading. Much of the background detail can be added later on.

The book can begin with a knock on a door by person A. The door is opened by person B. Talk between the two characters makes it obvious that B knows A, but is shocked by their unexpected arrival.

The first chapter can continue by describing the reaction of the various people inside the house to the arrival of A; and during these exchanges the relationships of the various characters can be sorted out. The chapter can end with a decision having been made as to whether A is allowed to stay in the house or is thrown out again. (The unexpected visitor could be a delinquent teenager returning to the family home after an unexplained absence of several days/weeks/months.)

With the situation and the main characters now in place, the second chapter could take a look back at how A got into trouble in the first place, and why the rest of the people in the house have a problem with him/her.

START WITH A BANG

Start your book with a bang – an effect often called the 'crash-start', and explain the reason for the bang later on. Look at how action/thriller movies get into gear. These movies often start with the main character involved in some unexplained action. (Check out *Raiders of the Lost Ark* or *Star Wars IV* for perfect examples of this.) The action may not even include the main characters at all – for instance, the movie *The Fellowship of the Ring* kick-starts with a huge battle between good and evil that took place thousands of years before Frodo and Sam were even born. This is a great way of grabbing an audience's attention from the very start, and also allows for a more slow-paced scene to follow, where the main characters can be introduced while the audience recovers from the big bang. If the action is gripping, the reader will be prepared to wait a while to find out more on who, what, why and where. If you are looking for ways to give your chapters a nail-biting end, watch those last few minutes of television soap operas that will give you ideas of how to construct mind-blowing cliffhangers.

You don't always have to set the scene before the action starts, and in a lot of cases, it's better to leave the explanations until later. If the plot centres on one big scene, then maybe a flash-forward could be used as a teaser. For a book involving an earthquake, you could always start the book with a few pages describing the first few minutes of the quake, before going back into real time and covering the days leading up to the quake (and introducing those all-important interesting characters).

Flashbacks can serve a similar function as flash-forwards. The book could start with the seventeenth-century burning of a witch, then fast-forward to the present day and the lives of people living in the same village, and how the echoes of that ancient event affects their lives.

Exercise 18

Write the opening paragraph for a book, and work on it until you have one that will grab the reader and invite them to read on.

Your opening lines should be more interesting than 'Once upon a time' or 'It was a dark and stormy night.' Something intriguing might include:

▶ *(For a picture book.) The duck crashed through the window and landed in Gemma's breakfast cereal. 'Hi,' said the duck, 'I'm kind of lost. Can you point the way south?'*
▶ *(For middle fiction.) On his way home from school one day, Barney was picked up and carried off by a space ship piloted by an intergalactic octopus with a bad head cold.*
▶ *(For young adult fiction.) Mum was always saying, 'Wear clean underwear. You never know when you might get hit by a bus.' As I lay on the hospital trolley, I didn't know which worried me more: my mum, my underwear, or the fact that my ten-year-old brother, Simon, had been driving the bus!*

QUESTION YOUR MOTIVES

Insight

Why do you want your work to be published? Is it because you're desperate to entertain people? Do you want to share some information or knowledge, or do you just want to be rich and famous?

Do you have an idea for a series or sequence of books? Bottom line, your chances of hitting on a perfect idea or formula without a lot of experience and research are pretty limited. You may have read one book of a successful series and thought to yourself, 'I could do that.' Too late! Someone else has already done it. You need to come up with an entirely new idea, and it's going to need plenty of 'legs' if it's going to turn into a series of six or 12 or 24 books.

The gap from being an aspiring writer to being the author of a successful series is a huge one. But don't trashcan those brilliant series ideas – just be prepared to be patient. Publishers aren't likely to commission an unknown author to produce a series, but the situation may well be very different for an author with a few published works under his/her belt. The thing you must remember with series books, is that each one must stand alone, and make perfect sense. It's no good you thinking: 'I'll explain that in the next book', treat each book as a one-off, even if your characters, location or themes will stay pretty much the same.

What other motives could you have? Maybe you're trying to work your way through some personal problems via the printed word; maybe you have an autobiographical tale to tell; or maybe you have a moral point to make. All well and good, so long as the end-product is entertaining. Tales of personal angst, no matter how universal the cause, still need to be 'page turners' (and you need to remember that publishers have their own motives and criteria). Here are some of the questions that may run through a commissioning editor's mind once they've read your story:

- ▶ *Will it be profitable/inexpensive to produce?*
- ▶ *What are the views of the editorial, sales and marketing departments?*
- ▶ *Will it sell and who to?*
- ▶ *Is it complementary to our list?*
- ▶ *Do I have a slot for it in my publishing schedule?*
- ▶ *Is it a new approach to a subject?*
- ▶ *Who is the author, and what are they like? Will they be good at publicity, interviews etc, and are there any other marketing angles?*

These considerations shouldn't dictate what you write, but you should have an idea of what will go through the mind of a publisher who likes your work.

There's more. Fashions are always changing in the book industry. The passion for graphic novels comes and goes, so does the interest for fantasy. A topic which publishers may be falling over themselves to buy one year may flatline two years later. Part of being a successful author is to write work that means something to you, which you enjoy writing, and will have a chance of surviving in the current marketplace.

Chase the market. I like fantasy, but when I was starting out, fantasy was anathema – so I got rid of the fantasy. This pragmatic approach worked, and once the wheel turned and fantasy was back in fashion, I was a full-time writer and in a position to write and get published the fantasy books I'd always wanted to write ...

Finding your voice

Is your book going to be written in the first person, or the third person? Is it going to use past tense or present tense? Is it going to include the thought processes of your characters and, if so, how many minds are you planning on giving the reader access to?

Let's look at these things one at a time.

FIRST PERSON

First person is where the entire story is narrated by one (or more) of the characters in the book – usually a single, dominant character. In this format, you, as the 'author' don't get to say anything. You, as the 'character' have to say it all. All the events in the story must be revealed via the thoughts and the voice of this character. The reader can only know and experience things that the main character knows and experiences.

You need a strong, well-thought-out and rounded character for this technique to work. The author of a first-person book has to make sure that everything thought and said by the character fits. A ten-year-old boy will have to perceive events like a real ten-year-old boy would. He can't think like a 50-year-old woman. A 16-year-old girl has to think like a real 16-year-old, even if the author is 65.

Let's put this in context.

There's been some horseplay between ten-year-old kids that ends with a valuable vase being broken. Imagine how the children themselves would see this. Then think of the reaction of the adult who hears the vase go crash and who comes to see what's happened. Try writing this scene in the first person, initially from the child's point of view, and then from an adult perspective.

Here's a start for you:

> *Child: We were only playing. I mean, a person is entitled to play, aren't they? And if that vase is so totally priceless, then Mum was a bit daft to leave it there in the first place ...*

> *Adult: I've told and told you until I'm blue in the face: don't horse around in the living room, you might break something! The moment I heard that crash I knew what had happened.*

How about adding a third voice? An older brother or sister who has been left in charge of the children? How would they react to the incident?

A problem with writing in the first person is that it can be a little tricky to include information that is vital for the plot, but that the narrator doesn't know. In first-person stories, the reader knows only what the narrator tells them (although devices such as, 'I didn't know this until later, but what happened was ...' can help out in some cases). You'll also have problems when the story involves several different characters all doing different things. The reader can only learn what has been going when the main character either witnesses something (by observation or overhearing) or is told about it. One way to deal with this is to pass the information on as a conversation between the main character and his or her friend.

It's also possible for a first-person book to be narrated by someone who is not directly involved in the action: 'I'd like to tell you about something that happened to some friends of mine ...' In this format, a story can be put together in which the opinion of the narrator may not be the same as the opinions of other characters in the book. The courting activities and rituals of a bunch of 13-year-old girls and boys could be amusingly narrated by a younger sister or brother: 'Don't ask me what my 13-year-old big brother Matt sees in her, but he's started getting really stupid over the girl who delivers our morning newspaper.' The great thing about doing it this way is that it 'personalizes' a story. The narrator speaks *directly* to the reader, rather than through the voice of the author. In this way, readers will feel as if a real friend is telling them the story.

THIRD PERSON

The third-person set-up is where the narrator of the story is separated from the action, and the word 'I' does not appear except in dialogue. The reader is one step removed from the characters in the book, and events are related by a 'storyteller'.

This kind of storytelling goes back to the days of oral mythology, when poets and bards would chronicle the activities of the gods and the immortals for their audience. The third-person format is useful when a story involves several elements all occurring simultaneously, and when the narrative needs to shift constantly from one set of characters to another. It's easy to switch from perspective to perspective in a third-person narrative. For example, one character could be held captive by the villain of the story while the other characters could be searching for him or her. The third-person format allows the narrative to shift its perspective rapidly from character to character and event to event in a way that would be much more difficult if the book were written in the first person.

Third-person narratives also make space for a broader overview of what is going on at any given time. A character being chased across moors by a maniac (or across other lands by enemy groups of aliens) won't have time to describe their environment. But within such an urgent setting, the author through the third-person narrator, will be able to snatch a few moments to set the scene, and perhaps even to give a voice to the maniac. In some cases it may be vital for the reader to know the reason behind the chase, even though the character being chased doesn't. This style allows the author to tell the readers things that the leading characters in the book may not know. In a suspense thriller, it adds a lot of tension if the reader knows there is a dangerous maniac in the closet that the innocent lead character is about to open.

The problem with the third-person format is that it can separate the reader from the characters. That said, it's fine for a third-person narrated book to include the private thoughts of as many characters as the author wants. Presenting the 'thoughts' of a character can be a useful device, but you need to be careful over exactly how many brains the reader gets to look into. It won't take long for the reader to work out who the villain is in a 'whodunit' story if they learn the thoughts of all the characters, or all characters bar one. It's usually best to limit the reader's access to one or two lead characters, and use the 'thinking' device only when there is no one for these characters to speak to. Dialogue is always more lively than narrative, so when using the third-person format, be sure to allow your characters to 'talk' the plot along as much as possible.

The advantage of the third person is that the author is able to narrate events in their 'own' voice (or in the voice of a disinterested and unbiased third party). It allows for the motives of several different characters to be explored and for a number of simultaneous plot strands to be followed in a way that a first-person narrator would find very difficult.

Exercise 19

Try writing the scene with the broken vase again, this time in the third person. Write it first in the context of a children's book and, therefore, from a child's view, and then from an adult perspective. The two versions should come out quite differently. Explore the differences and think about what you have learned from this exercise.

MULTIPLE NARRATIVES

You can also write a book narrated by two or more first-person characters, but be wary of including too many voices as this will just get confusing – or of giving your voices unequal 'talking time' in the book – or of adding a voice halfway through which disappears again without explanation.

A simple device for this sort of multi-voice storytelling is for successive chapters to be headed with the name of the character whose voice is being heard or for different characters to be introduced using different typefaces. In this way, you could describe a romance between two teenagers and how characters react to the same events with no authorial overview at all. An evening at the movies for Justin and Sarah might be seen as a great success by Justin. He may tell the reader what a great time he had, how he held Sarah's hand all through the movie and how he is looking forward to their next date. Sarah might have a totally different story to tell. She might tell the reader how utterly bored she was, point out that Justin wore aftershave which was overpowering and had clammy hands, and make it quite clear that she has no intention of ever dating Justin again. The following chapters could then chronicle the 'romance' from those two sides, with neither of the characters actually having much idea of what is going through the mind of the other while the reader knows *everything*. You might be able to shake it up a little if you work it so Sarah gradually realizes her first impressions were wrong and that she really likes Justin after all. And what if Justin, fed up with Sarah's rejections of his advances, decides she is not worth the effort and stops asking her out on the very day that Sarah decides she will finally agree to a date? A story like that could easily be written in the third person, but think how much more lively and immediate it becomes when the only voices being heard are those of Justin and Sarah.

A favourite first-person format is the *diary*. A number of very successful books have been written in this style, so you'd need to come up with something quite new and exciting. A particular problem with telling a story in diary format is that it is virtually impossible for events to be given anything other than an immediate perspective. The writer of a diary is not going to be in a position to explain events of immediate relevance if they don't find out about them for a few days. In some types of story it doesn't matter that the reader only knows what the narrator knows; in others, this lack of an overview, or at least of hindsight, will make the story virtually impossible to write in any way that makes sense.

A story can also be written so that it shifts between the third person and the first person. One way of doing this is by including letters from one character to another within the general third-person framework. This can help to present the opinions and attitudes of a particular character in a way that would otherwise be less vivid. Returning to the Sarah and Justin story, the date could be described in the third person and without any particular insight into how the two characters felt. This could be followed up by Sarah emailing an internet chat room pal, describing her feelings, and Justin texting a friend to tell him how it all went (or at least how he thought it went). The story could even be given a further twist: Sarah could be emailing a male friend, in which case the reader will have to decide whether the things that Sarah writes describe how she really feels or only how she wants her friend to *think* she feels. You could write the story so that the reader only *thinks* the emails were written by Sarah, because they had her name at the bottom, but finds out later on that they were not written by Sarah, but by Justin for his own amusement, and were just him fantasizing over how Sarah might be feeling. In fact, he may never have asked Sarah out at all, and the whole 'romance' could be going on in his head and on his computer and between him and a long-distance friend who lives too far away to know the truth. There's the twist ending we mentioned earlier. And how about twisting the twist? What if Sarah gets access to Justin's computer and finds these bogus emails? How does she feel about that? She could go ape – or she might think it's really sweet and ask Justin to go out with her. Either way works storywise. When using diary, letter, text or email styles, you will need to understand your character's voice and style and know the difference. Emails are usually more immediate – like a phone conversation – and contain less detail and description.

By now you should be realizing that giving a book a voice and format is as complex and open-ended as everything else in the writing world.

Books can also include time shifts. For instance, the first chapter could be set in the present day, but the second goes back six months to follow a different plot strand, or to explain how the present-day plot strand came about. In fact, the entire book could time-hop right through – with you keeping the audience up to speed by starting each new scene with a date and time in which the events that are to follow take place.

As part of your ongoing research, approach books, TV, radio drama and popular movies in a more analytical way: check out how these media use multi-layer viewpoints – revealing the same events from different perspectives. For instance, in *Harry Potter and the Prisoner of Azkaban*, the action towards the end is a puzzle until both the characters and the reader/viewer realize that a magical time-slippage has occurred and the three friends are in two places at the same time.

NON-HUMAN VOICES

Up until now, we have really been discussing formats for different human voices. But it's possible to write books in voices that are not human. How about these two examples:

Aliens
Say you decide to write a story from the perspective of a creature from another planet. If your chosen creature is a messy green blob from Mars, then you may have difficulty in rounding out the character, but something reasonably humanoid or at least with a reasonably human attitude may allow for a whole sequence of entertaining incidents based on misunderstandings between species. An alien race may land on Earth whose method of communicating is via hitting each other over the heads with saucepans. How would this go down among humans?

> *The silvery spaceship comes to ground in the park and a door panel slides silently open. A being appears, clutching a saucepan. The creature proceeds to spell out 'Hello, how*

are you, my name is Ftunnng' by whacking the leader of the welcoming committee over the head with the saucepan.

A word of warning: success in this format is very difficult to achieve, and you will very likely hit up against the 'get rid of the guy with the pointed ears' attitude, so called because that was the verdict of a high-ranking TV executive when shown the pilot to the original *Star Trek* television series – he wanted Spock dumped because he didn't think watchers would be able to empathize with an alien. The point being missed was that human behaviour can often be thrown into sharp focus when viewed by an 'alien', and Spock turned out to be the hit of the show!

Animals
Anthropomorphism means giving animals human thoughts, motives and rationalities. Think long and hard about this before you get working. Unless you're planning on turning yourself into an animal, you'll have to stretch your imagination to its limits if you're going to present a book in a first-person animal voice. Really, it is best not to try unless you are absolutely certain of your market.

The one exception to this rule involves picture books. In this context, publishers can find it very useful to have the main characters appearing in animal form, especially in co-edition books (books that are commissioned and published in several languages/countries at once) where, for instance, the obvious nationality of the main characters and the location setting may limit the saleability of a highly illustrated book which is going to be published in France, Senegal and China.

Several very successful books have been written in the third person, chronicling the adventures and activities of animals or groups of animals. Richard Adams's *Watership Down* is one – he did an enormous amount of research work on the way rabbits behave in real life in order to give his book a semblance of 'reality'. He had to humanize the thinking processes of these animals, but their day-to-day lives were depicted in the same way as an average rabbit's. As an aside, the other classic tale about this famous book is the number of times it was turned down by publishers before finally finding a home.

Sometimes publishers want stories of talking animals who wear clothes and who are really just furry, hairy, spiky or scaly humans. Sometimes they like it, sometimes they don't. This can change all the time, and without much warning, so you're going to have to keep a close eye on current trends before you set about trying to talk a publisher into the 'Adventures of Harry Hedgehog'. A clever, well-written animal story can be a real winner, but have a good look around the marketplace to assess the competition before you get to work.

While we're on the subject of non-human voices, there's one area that all the publishers we contacted totally hated. They really, really don't like inanimate objects that think, talk and walk about on their own.

It's true that there have been some successes in this field, but generally publishers will run a mile when confronted by 'Fiona the Friendly Frankfurter' or 'Terrance the Talking Table'. The following titles are from a list of stories submitted to a publisher and, to make things worse, handwritten on lined paper torn from a shorthand notebook:

▶ *Greg the Gnome*
▶ *Simon the Sea Gull*
▶ *Carly the Cat*
▶ *Bluey the Budgie*
▶ *Charlie the Chimney*
▶ *Betty in Bunnytown*
▶ *Violet the Vacuum Cleaner*

Don't go down that path – it doesn't lead anywhere.

Exercise 20

While we're on about names, have you had any thoughts about the names you might give your characters or have always wanted to use when writing? Do a little

(Contd)

research – from those names books for parents-to-be, or the 'history of popular names' books, and from your personal memory.

Think of four characters and give them twenty-first-century names – names that are not dated, and not presently overused in children's books you have read recently. Then do some more research and give four characters names from your favourite historical period that would sound authentic. Now think of four made-up fantastic names for a sci-fi or fantasy story. Have you chosen names that will read easily, be memorable and suit the characters and situation?

Past, present or future

Past tense, present tense and future tense. Yet more ways to format your story.

PAST AND PRESENT TENSE

The past tense is the usual way in which to tell a story.

He ran across the road. She followed him, dodging the traffic as she tried to keep him in sight.

The storyteller is writing about events that have already taken place, and putting them in that context by using past tense.

People will fall naturally into using the past tense when telling stories, although in some cases, a kind of urgency or immediacy can be added by the use of the present tense:

'So I say to him, I say, you come one step closer to me with that gherkin, and I'll have the law on you, so help me, I will. And he looks at me with his eyes all kind of narrowed-up,

and I think: he's going to do it. And then he comes for me,
and I run down the street, yelling my head off, and he chases
me, waving his gherkin and shouting, Stop! Stop!!'

Or:

'So I'm saying to him, I'm saying, you come one step closer
to me with that gherkin, and I'll have the law on you, so
help me, I will. And he's looking at me with his eyes all kind
of narrowed-up, and I'm thinking: he's going to do it. And
then he's coming for me, and I'm running down the street,
yelling my head off, and he's chasing me, waving his gherkin
and shouting, Stop! Stop!!'

Now let us try it again in the past tense:

'So I said to him, I said, you come one step closer to me with
that gherkin, and I'll have the law on you, so help me, I will.
And he looked at me with his eyes all kind of narrowed-up,
and I thought: he's going to do it. And then he came for
me, and I ran down the street, yelling my head off, and he
chased me, waving his gherkin and shouting, Stop! Stop!!'

Or a different sort of past tense:

'So I was saying to him, I was saying, you come one step
closer to me with that gherkin, and I'll have the law on you,
so help me, I will. And he was looking at me with his eyes
all kind of narrowed-up, and I was thinking: he's going to
do it. And then he was coming for me, and I was running
down the street, yelling my head off, and he was chasing me,
waving his gherkin and shouting, Stop! Stop!!'

So you can see how both present and past tenses can be used in
different ways to create different effects. And that is not only true
for first-person narratives:

'You come one step closer to me with that gherkin,' she said,
'and I'll have the law on you, so help me I will.'

He looked at her with narrowed eyes and she realized he was about to pounce.

She ran down the street, yelling for help while he chased after her, brandishing the deadly gherkin and shouting, 'Stop! Stop!!'

Present tense:

'You come one step closer to me with that gherkin,' she says, 'and I'll have the law on you, so help me I will.'

He looks at her with narrowed eyes and she realizes he is about to pounce.

She runs down the street, yelling for help while he chases after her, brandishing the deadly gherkin and shouting, 'Stop! Stop!!'

Using the present tense cranks up the urgency of the piece. It creates the illusion that the reader is actually there while the event is taking place.

The big problem with using present tense is that it's a little unnatural, and you'll need to keep focused to make sure you don't slip back into the more normal past tense. Also consider that you can create bigger problems for yourself – especially if using first-person present tense. Your reader can never know anything that the narrator doesn't know, and there's no way of covering simultaneous action by other characters or explaining other events.

Exercise 21

Using the above examples as guidelines – but maybe without the gherkins – write a page-long piece in the past tense on any topic you like, and then rewrite it using the present tense.

Check out how using different tenses changes the story –
and pay particular attention to any difficulties or problems
that arise.

List a few examples of the sort of stories that you think
would work best in past tense, and those that would benefit
from the immediacy of present tense.

Conversation

Picture a scene of rolling countryside. A man and a woman stand
on the brow of a hill. It is a block-busting generation-spanning tale
of love, revenge, sex, money, hatred, money, wealth, sex, power
and money, but not necessarily in that order, written by someone
called Sapphire Diamond or Jack Ironstone. A rider approaches on
a black stallion. The woman speaks.

> *'Oh! Can it be?' Elvira gasped breathlessly. 'Yes, it's Tyler,*
> *my adopted half-brother whom Father found in the gutter*
> *and brought home to share our good fortune despite what*
> *the old gypsy woman said about him being a black-hearted*
> *devil. But why is he here? Father sent him to manage the*
> *New York office of our multi-national kippering firm and*
> *not to return unless something terrible happened. I have not*
> *had word from him these past two years, although we were*
> *loving playmates as children and in my innocence I always*
> *thought we would be married one day.'*

As exaggerated as that speech may be, it highlights a common
problem with dialogue: translating conversations into readable
and realistic dialogue on the page while conveying all the necessary
information.

How do people speak to one another? You're not going to find out
about real speech from the TV or radio or movies. Get out there!

Go where you'll be able to overhear people talking to one another. Listen to how they speak and try to analyse what's going on. This could be a party, a meeting or anywhere two or more people are gathered in conversation. Think about how most people speak in different situations – with their family, on the phone, to a teacher, among friends, when nervous and when confident. Children play dozens of dialogue roles to suit the situation and company.

Poor dialogue will let a good story down badly: you have to get it right. There is a big difference between real conversations and conversations as they appear on television or in books. In real life, people will start a sentence, then change tack suddenly, stammer over certain words, repeat themselves, digress, stop midway through saying one thing to say something completely different, leave observations hanging in mid-air, half-say things, contradict themselves, be interrupted, and talk over one another.

What you have to do is to make sense of this chaos and present it on paper so it can easily be understood. You don't want to sanitize your dialogue too much. 'Real' conversation may not work on paper, but obviously 'made-up' unrealistic conversation is no better.

Insight

A reader has to believe in the characters you invent, and a major part of that belief will hang on your ability to make those characters speak in a natural and unaffected way.

A good rule of thumb is to speak dialogue out loud. Your family and friends may think you've gone crazy when they hear you arguing with yourself behind closed doors, but the fact is that the only way to check whether a line of dialogue or an exchange between characters really 'works' is to hear it spoken out loud or acted out.

As stressed in the last chapter, avoid using the fleeting idioms of the present day. You want your book to be read in 20 years' time, so unless the plot has to be anchored in a particular time-frame, you will want your characters to sound fresh and contemporary to future audiences. Street slang should largely be avoided. In real life, a person may say 'know what I mean?' or 'dude' at the end of every sentence, but on paper this affectation will just become annoying.

An aggressive person picking a fight may repeat the same bullet-hard phrase over and over to gain attention. 'You talking to me? You talking to me? You talking to me? You talking to me?' Children will often swear for no particular reason and without aggression, simply because such words are considered a normal part of 'playground' conversation among their friends. Swearing and bad language are not automatically removed from books for young adults (although they would obviously be inappropriate for younger age-groups), but you should think carefully before having one teenager character tell another to 'f*** off'. This has little to do with the moral standards of publishers and editors, and plenty to do with selling books: adults do not necessarily want less socially acceptable language to be seen to be authorized by having it presented to their children in the pages of a book. If you want to write a down-to-earth, nitty-gritty, urban-realism type book filled with drug fiends, teenage thieves and social outcasts, then go right ahead – but be prepared for the fall-out and don't be surprised if hardly any publishers want to take it on. If your dialogue is strong and direct, the reader will understand the impact, without the need to include profanities.

In real life most conversation is ephemeral and of limited importance. A lot of it is anecdotal. It involves telling your friends or family what you've been doing, talking over something funny or outrageous or strange; repeating a tale told by a work colleague or school friend; asking for the salt to be passed; wanting to know when dinner will be ready or where your favourite trainers are. You know the sort of conversation we mean. That's fine for real life, but you need to reduce it down to the essentials, and think carefully about it before you include it in your book. No one wants to read pages of irrelevant dialogue which does not further the storyline.

All written dialogue has one of two possible purposes: either it's there to move the plot along, or it's there to deepen the understanding of the characters who are speaking and their relationship to one another. Keep dialogue short and to the point. Avoid bogging down important dialogue by including mundane and irrelevant activities on the part of one or another of the people speaking. On TV or in a movie, having characters doing things while they speak makes for more interesting viewing – but on the page, this description just gets in the way and slows the pace down.

It is important when you are writing your conversations to show the different ways people express themselves. What you don't want, is every character using the same voice. Different ages will use different words. People from different backgrounds will use different styles. Someone with a strong accent may use different phrases and expressions.

A shy person, for example, with important information to convey will express themselves in a different way from someone with a loud, outgoing personality. A single character will use several different modes of speech depending upon their audience. If one of your characters is from another part of the country, or another country, a city or a country village, you may want to differentiate their voice for the reader's imagination. 'Zat ees good,' said the French student. 'Och nae,' said the Scotsman. But be subtle. Do include a few hints of accent when you first introduce your character. After that, keep the accent or style clues to a minimum. Endless literal or phonetic translations are just hard work to read and can become tiresome. If introduced well, your reader will imagine the character's voice, and hear it themselves each time they speak. That subtlety will also give your character more life and depth – making them real and identifiable.

How are you going to frame your dialogue? What's wrong with the following?

Jeanette came running into the room.

'I've seen him!' she gasped breathlessly.

'Who?' Sasha enquired excitedly, leaping up.

'Alvin Darkside!' exclaimed Jeanette impatiently.

'What?' Gladys broke in urgently. 'The Alvin Darkside?
The pop star?' Her face was alive with excitement.

'Exactly!' Jeanette stated sighingly. 'Alvin Darkside. My hero!'

'I like him better than you do!' wailed Sasha groaningly.
'And now I'm going to miss him because Mum won't let me
go out.'

'Your mum won't know if you sneak out,' Gladys
proclaimed whisperingly. 'Who's to tell her?'

'Him!' Sasha complained despairingly, pointing to the
20-stone guard who clutched the other end of the chain
which her mother had attached to her ankle.

'Don't worry about me,' the guard observed smilingly.
'I'm Alvin Darkside's biggest fan.'

'Hoorah!' Jeanette whooped exultantly. 'Now we can all go
and see Alvin!'

And without further ado the four of them raced pantingly
for the door.

Horrible, isn't it? This is what is known in the trade as 'adverbitis'.
It's a similar disease to 'adjectivitis'. The chief symptom is an
author's inability to leave nouns or verbs alone. Why write 'she
said' when you can add 'sadly' or 'gladly' or 'effusively'? Why
use 'said' when you could put 'exclaimed', 'ranted', 'quipped',
'declared', 'opined', 'effused' or 'remarked'? There's nothing wrong
with these words, but get a grip! If someone is breathless, then say
so; if a person shouts – make it clear that shouting is going on, but
don't insult your reader and labour the point.

To keep your storyline moving forwards, keep interjections between dialogue to a minimum. There is nothing wrong with a simple 'he said' and 'she said'.

If the dialogue is between two people and is relatively straightforward, you could even leave the speech entirely to its own devices and give only a guiding 'she said' and 'he said' here and there as reference points. Be careful if you have three or more characters in conversation: a reader can quickly lose track of what is going on if the author does not reference each comment back to its source. It is no good if, halfway down a long chunk of dialogue, a reader has to count his/her way back to the top of the page in order to figure out who is saying what.

While we're on the subject of dialogue between several characters, if there are four people in a scene, for instance, you should make sure each of them gets to say something at some point. Readers can't 'see' a character who isn't mentioned or who doesn't talk. If a character in a scene neither speaks nor does anything, you might as well get rid of them. This is especially pertinent when you have a 'gang' who all meet together. Ensure in any ensemble scenes that everyone gets at least one line to say.

Sharing dialogue around has an additional function, especially in stories that require set-piece explanations (such as a mystery story or a crime thriller). A long monologue by one character can be improved if it's shared between two or three others, or if it takes the form of a question and answer session. There's a reason why Batman is teamed with Robin, why Sherlock Holmes hangs out with Dr Watson, and why human companions travel with Doctor Who. They're there, at least in part, to draw out explanations and to break up what would otherwise become boring soliloquies.

Another problem with dialogue can occur when an author is very obviously out of touch with young people and the way they express themselves. If you don't have regular contact with the age-group you're writing for, then you need to get some – or at the very least start watching children's television. TV isn't the best way of finding out how modern kids talk to one another, but in the early days it will give you a general idea of what's going on out there. And if you watch kids' dramas and soaps, you'll also be seeing how other writers handle dialogue.

Exercise 22

Rewrite the exchange about Alvin Darkside with an eye to removing all the unnecessary adverbs and adjectives. As with the example of the Lord Byron biography, keep the meaning and interest of the piece while dumping all the rest.

Once you've done that, why not practise the same discipline on your own dialogue? It's probably sensible to keep it down to two characters for now (you can worry about convincingly written crowd scenes later on). Set up a scene where two characters are having an argument, pick your own topic, and give the two characters totally opposing points of view. Write a page-long piece of dialogue.

Use only the word 'said' when you are indicating who is speaking. No 'retorts' or 'declareds' or 'proclaimeds'; use just plain old 'saids'. If you can, don't even put 'she said' every time one of the characters speaks. (But remember, never let a reader lose track of who is speaking.)

Read the conversation aloud to yourself – or even act it out. Could a real person actually have said the words you put into your characters' mouths? Is the sentence structure correct, or would a person run out of breath halfway through? If you have a recording device, use it to listen back to your dialogue. Does it sound realistic? Can you believe that real people would say such things? If not, why not? Where are you going wrong? Does your dialogue come across as being too heavily written? Does it sound like it comes from a page rather than straight out of a real person's mouth?

(Contd)

Once you feel comfortable with your page of dialogue, push yourself a little further by placing two characters in a different situation so that you have to take account of their surroundings as they speak. They could be walking along a street, hurrying through a busy park or out canoeing together. Try to incorporate their movements into an unobtrusive, sympathetic narrative as they argue.

Now take the whole piece to another level by adding a third character with yet another point of view. Add a parent who tells the two children to stop arguing. Include the reaction of the children to this interruption. Add a younger child. Add several more characters. See what effect these people have on the argument.

The aim of this exercise is to take you one step closer to that point where, like the novice dancer who suddenly realizes she has stopped counting out the rhythm, you find your invented characters taking over and speaking with their own voices.

Grammar

We've already explained that you need a good working knowledge of the grammar of the language you're writing in. So now let's take a swing at one of the more common grammatical errors that drives publishers out of their minds.

Apostrophes cause people an awful lot of trouble. Its? It's? Its'? It is pretty straightforward, and you really ought to try to remember it:

- ▶ It's *is short for* 'It is': *'It's time you went home.'*
- ▶ Its *without the apostrophe is used when you want to say something like* 'The boat skimmed the waves, its sails

billowing in the wind.' Its *refers back to the preceding
direct object to denote the noun's possession of the
following noun:* 'the sails of it [the boat] billowing in
the wind.'

▶ Its' *does not exist at all (although that fact does not stop
people sticking their apostrophes in the strangest places).*
▶ Do'nt. *Wrong!!* It is 'don't', *a contraction of do not. The
apostrophe in this case denotes a missing letter,* 'o'.
▶ Can't: *same thing – a contraction of cannot.*
▶ *Likewise* shan't *(shall not),* won't *(will not),* isn't *(is not)
and so on.*

Also be careful when using apostrophes with plurals:

▶ Children's books *(books of the children): the plural, children
does not end in s, therefore the apostrophe appears before the
s denoting 'of the'.*
▶ The boy's book: *one boy, owning one book.*
▶ The boys' book. *More than one boy, collectively owning one
book. The apostrophe appears after the s, thereby showing
that the book belongs to more than one boy.*

There are some great books out there – like *Eats Shoots & Leaves*
by Lynne Truss which are fun guides to punctuation.

Some style cautions

Watch out for language that is obviously dated or archaic.
Whatever time period your story is set in, you are writing for
children of today. Phrases such as, *'For he thought he was right'*
and, *'Algernon was one of those people for whom dancing was
easy'* read as if the author has been dead for 50 years.

Avoid descriptions that are blatantly unrealistic. *His eyes flashed
like daggers in the red neon lights. Her eyes reflected the sunset of
her soul.*

Don't introduce a superior adult voice into a first person narrative, e.g. 'So, dear reader...'; no one likes to be talked down to.

Research, search the internet, or ask friends what the phrase 'purple prose' means. Listen, read, understand, remember – and don't fall into the trap of over-describing anything, especially when writing for the vivid imaginations of impatient younger people.

> *'I glanced in the mirror, seeing my long blonde hair, and the baby-blue eyes that made me look younger than my real age of 14.' I don't care what the creative writing course said: people do not make a complete objective inventory of themselves every time they look at a reflective surface, and that is not a convincing way to describe a character.*

> *There's a temptation to keep fiddling with the purple prose as you go along, but I think I'd go completely potty if I fretted over every sentence. For young readers (probably all readers) it's the story that matters, so keep the creative engine driving towards the reason you wanted to write the story in the first place. Feel the passion foremost. When it's done, go back and polish. You'll find it a much prettier shade of purple by then.*

> *The lazy repetition of individual words is my pet hate. It implies that the author doesn't know better, or hasn't taken the time to read and polish it – either which is less than impressive to an editor. 'The infuriated editor marched through the office. Wailing and gnashing his teeth as he marched along' would be an example. It would be so easy to substitute the word 'raced' for 'marched' in either instance.*

Insight

Read a wide variety of books and examine the different styles. Ask yourself what you like and why. Use a thesaurus or word finder to avoid repetition and to enrich your style.

Everything is about balance. You don't want to put off your reader by using words way beyond your reader's comprehension, so that the prose becomes dense and difficult. But also, don't be afraid to occasionally use words which may be beyond the expected understanding of the age of the reader. If a word is used in context, then it will make sense. And if it's interesting, or has a lovely sound or spelling, your reader may want to find out for themselves what its definition is. Find a style that you enjoy writing, and is your own voice.

Beginning, middle and end

We've already told you the importance of balancing your story across the three areas of plotting. You have to get the reader hooked by an attention-grabbing opening chapter, then you can ease the pace a little to fill in the background and put the characters and the action in context. You'll have your synopsis to hand – probably setting out everything that has to happen in order to get from the start to the finish.

We included 'probably' there on purpose, because in the process of writing, things may change in ways you could never have foreseen. This is fine, unless you've been commissioned to write a book with a fixed plot, in which case changes will have to be authorized by the commissioning editor. On the other hand, if there's no book contract and your story is taking you off into unexpected places, be prepared to go with the flow, so long as that flow doesn't leave you stranded on a mudflat in the middle of nowhere. Keep your planned finale in mind. Rewrite your synopsis, taking the changes into account – plot your new way through to the end. Perhaps the book is telling you that there's a better way to go than you originally thought.

Here are two different ways of presenting a story.

THE SURPRISE ENDING

As we have already mentioned, this is also known as the 'twist' or the 'sting'. A surprise ending makes the reader follow the characters through a series of events without knowing how things are going to work out. Will they all survive? Will someone die? Who? How? When?

In stories of this type, the tension and interest is kept up by adding unexpected twists in the tail of the plot, false endings, shocks and astonishing last-page revelations.

But don't pull your twist out of nowhere. It's not okay for all the murders to have been committed by Oscar's younger half-sister who has lived all her life in Ulan Batur and who is never mentioned until the detective drags her from a hiding place behind the potted palm. If you're planning great revelations, you have to foreshadow them in some way. It's your job to put in plenty of clues about Oscar's half-sister, otherwise the reader feels cheated and it looks suspiciously like you made her up at the last minute because you couldn't think of anything better.

Clues and 'hooks' need to be carefully thought out and skillfully seeded throughout the story. The 'hook' is the means by which the 'hero' escapes certain death. An author needs to insert the 'hook' into the narrative in such a way that the reader is aware of its existence, but unaware of how important it will become later on.

An example
Somewhere early in your book, you show that your main character has some skills with a rope. Don't make a big thing out of it – maybe another character comments on a row of Golden Rope awards on the shelf in his room.

Your hero gets himself caught up in a big international diamond-smuggling conspiracy and, towards the end of the book, he's set adrift in a boat heading for the edge of a 200-metre-high waterfall. He's pretty much doomed.

You'll also need to mention, again in passing, that there's a length of rope in the boat. A long mooring rope, maybe? Perhaps the villains who cast the hero adrift threw the mooring rope in his face as the boat floated away from the jetty.

Now you need one final 'hook' in the shape of a tree stump, pointed hunk of rock or something at the very lip of the waterfall.

One amazing escape coming up.

He grabs the rope. He fashions a lasso. He hurls the lasso at the tree stump. It misses! Gasp! He has time for one final throw before plunging to his death. The lasso catches on the stump just as the boat careers over the edge of the waterfall. He swings through the waterfall on the end of his rope. He is saved!

Why stop there? Why not include a map of where the diamonds are hidden? A vague map which says the diamonds are 'under water'. Your hero swings right through the waterfall on the end of his rope and finds himself in a secret cavern behind the waterfall. And in the secret cavern he finds the lost jewels. He has not only saved himself from certain death, but he has solved the mystery of the cryptic clue.

The trick when coming up with death-defying escapes is to have made the reader aware of potential escape devices in advance but without being too obvious.

Hooks are relevant not only to adventures: all plots need their share of clues and hooks if the climax is going to make sense.

THE KNOWN ENDING

Another way of writing a book is to let the reader know from the beginning, exactly what happens at the end.

Ragnar Ironhand lies dead, shot by an arrow in the Sinister Castle of Grimmwold.

Now go back six months and show Ragnar coming to Castle Grimmwold. The reader is now hooked on finding out which of the characters Ragnar meets in Grimmwold will kill him. Will it be Eliza Goldenheart, the half-human half-elf maiden who secretly loves Ragnar? Or was it Earl Mordred, the brooding Lord of

Grimmwold? Or Filafel, the green-skinned water-nymph from the Great Dark Forest. Or Lord Adrin from the mountain realm of Gar, torn apart by his unrequited love for Eliza Goldenheart? The only way to find out is to read the book.

You have all your hooks and clues in place, and you have plotted your hero's way to a brilliant climax. But you've still got to avoid the 'one leap and she was free' pitfall. Loose ends must be tied up, good must prevail and evil be punished, but not all in the final paragraph. The end of your book needs to be planned as carefully as the beginning.

In a particularly gruelling or draining book, it might be as well to add a comic or soothing scene to the final chapter. We're not saying that all books need a happy ending, but most publishers and readers like to experience a 'feel-good factor' somewhere in the story.

High drama or fraught emotion can benefit greatly from moments of calm or comedy. Shakespeare knew this, often throwing 'crowd-pleasing' comic sketches in among all the bloodletting and mayhem. Scenes like this don't only relieve the tension, but they can also help to throw the more serious elements into sharp relief. Many successful television series and feature films have adopted the comedy-drama format, and many heroes are now heard to wisecrack relentlessly in even the uttermost extremity. But if you go this way, be careful not to turn it into a gimmick – it can get annoying quite quickly. There are only so many times a hero can slice off the head of his opponent with an axe and then say, 'That's going to hurt in the morning.'

'Issue' fiction can deal with traumatic and upsetting real-life situations, by showing how someone else dealt with tragedy and giving a 'you are not alone' message to kids facing the same problem. But kids won't want to read relentlessly depressing material without a glimmer of hope or humour. Even tragedy can contain elements of farce.

This leads us to another topic of particular relevance to children's writing. It's usually better for a hero to outwit or outsmart a villain than to whack the villain over the head with a large rock. Children like plenty of action; they want the plot to take off like an express train and hurtle along to a breathtaking climax, but it's part of your job as a responsible author to make sure that any violence is put firmly in context. The more down-to-earth the setting of your story, the more important it is to show violence as a painful aberration and one to be avoided if at all possible.

If your story is reliant on some level of violence, then bear in mind that there is a big difference between 'cartoon' violence and real-life violence. Be sure to show the consequences of violent acts, not just in terms of immediate pain, but in a wider context of long-term physical and psychological damage. Whether your work is aimed at the middle fiction or young adult audience, check other books of a similar nature to see how other published authors have dealt with potentially controversial areas such as violence, swearing and sex. *Forever* by Judy Blume is an interesting case in point. Her graphic portrayal of teenage sex in this book caused all kinds of controversy when it was first published, although it is now seen by many as a classic.

Revising

Insight

Your story is not going to work perfectly the first time you write it. You need to get used to the idea of revising. Don't be precious – be prepared to chuck out stuff, change, adapt and edit. Learning to write well is all about letting go of bits you love but which just aren't working in the book you are writing.

Revising? I find it helps to leave a piece of writing for a week or two after finishing it. You can then come to it fresh and read it more objectively. Even more helpful is reading a story aloud to a child … you can gauge if your pacing and plot are good by the child's reaction!

Even the brightest diamond benefits from a good polish.

Authors frequently spot sections in their published books that could have been improved. It happens all the time. You just have to get over it and move on. An author commissioned to produce a book will be given a deadline by which that book must be handed over. That deadline dictates the point where revising has to stop.

How do you create your own revision cut-off point? There's no simple answer to this one. Some authors will simply mark a date in their diary and keep to that.

> *Writing is work. Set a deadline if one hasn't been set for you and live like a hermit!*

> *It helps to arrange a date to show it to a friend.*

You have to find your own balance with this. On one hand, you don't want to present a publisher with something that looks half-finished. But on the other hand, editors have a role to play and a particular editor may well have an entirely different view on how your book should be tidied up.

You could easily spend months and months fine-tuning your book until it is a lovely thing to behold, but how are you going to feel when a publisher says, 'We quite like it, but it needs polishing'?

The response is to revise and revise until the book says what you wanted it to say, and says it in as grammatically accurate a way as you can manage. And then remember that no book ever gets published without some editorial alterations. One author said:

> *Revision offers the opportunity of looking at your complete work from a totally different angle. All the groundwork has already been done so you can concentrate on a hard edit. Always take the comments and advice of a professional editor. They are editors for a reason.*

Not every writer we approached had such a forgiving and positive attitude to the editors they have encountered in their career, but the bottom line is that *publishers* will certainly agree with it – so you need to bear this in mind.

If your book tells a good story in a professional manner and grabs the attention of a publisher, you'll be given plenty of opportunity to revise it later.

Editors will always adopt a 'hands-on' approach to your book once it has been accepted. It's not unusual for an author to be told their book will be accepted so long as they are prepared to rewrite large sections of it. What this means is that the editor has seen that certain appealing 'something' in the book, but feels you haven't exploited that 'something' properly. At this point you're entitled to decline the editor's suggestions, but a more professional approach is to give very careful consideration to what you are being told. After all, as a new author you must be prepared to listen and bow to professional advice if you want to get published.

> *Editor: I've read your book, and there's a lot in it that I like. Would you be prepared to completely rewrite it for us?*
>
> *Author (thrilled): Of course!*
>
> *(Six months later)*
>
> *Editor: Well, I've had a chance to read your revised manuscript and I think it's much improved. Now, would you like to go away and rewrite the final two-thirds of it?*
>
> *Author: (teeth gritted): Yes.*
>
> *(Six months later)*
>
> *Editor: You're almost there. I've made six pages of comments about the areas I think you need to reconsider, but on the whole I really like it.*
>
> *Author: (with fixed grin and maniacal stare): No problem!*

(Six months later)

Editor: Well done. We'll take it. There, that wasn't so difficult, was it?

REVISION METHODS

How you go about revising your work will depend on how you approach your writing in the first place.

If you're still working in longhand, then hopefully you'll have taken our advice and left every other line blank and given yourself wide margins. This will give you some space for alterations. If you find you need to insert entire scenes, say, in the middle of page 11, then write the scene on separate sheets and number them 11a, 11b and so on, as well as making yourself very clear, highlighted notes on the original manuscript to remind yourself of where the scenes are to be inserted. Never ever assume you will remember these things. Always leave yourself coherent notes. For all you know, you may not have the chance to go over this work again for months, and by then you may have forgotten those great extra ideas.

Using a computer makes the task of revision so much easier – it will allow you to do all the editing you could wish before a hard copy (printed paper copy) is produced. And it will allow you to keep every previous draft of your book on file – just in case you find that a scene edited out along the way, suddenly needs to be popped back in. A computer will also allow you to shift entire sections of the book around at will and effortlessly insert, delete and correct your book until it is just right.

You may be two-thirds through revising a book when a new idea occurs to you. The problem is that you're going to have to backtrack through parts of the book already written in order to seed the idea properly. If you are on a creative roll you may not want to go back over these points straight away. Make notes in your synopsis of the changes you've come up with and go back to them when you have finished the entire book – you may find that even more ideas will have come to you by then.

Try to be consistent. If you said in Chapter 13 that the electricity has been cut off in the house, you can't let a character switch a light on in Chapter 14. If you decide to have a discarded inhaler as a clue, make sure that the person who discarded it has been shown to be an asthmatic earlier in the book. Some authors will make up a card index or filing system for each character and scene. Details will include physical aspects of characters – brown eyes, black hair and so on – and sketches perhaps of the layout of significant buildings along with descriptions. Children have a great eye for minor detail, and will quickly spot any mistakes.

Insight

Always reread your work with an alert mind and in one sitting if you can – if you are only half-awake or if you try to read it over several days, you may miss something glaringly obvious.

Check for inaccuracies yourself. Was so-and-so at work on the day of the arson attack, or were they off sick? Does everything make sense? Does it all flow? Might it work better if the scene between Kevin and Dolores took place after the scene where Peter is discovered lurking under the bed in Mr Ponsonby's house?

Sometimes you may find that the simple effort of shifting scenes around will work wonders. Be brave, and be prepared to jettison much-loved scenes if it turns out that they are irrelevant to the main thrust of the story. Nothing need ever be wasted, keep the relevant pages or keep it on a separate computer file – a scene which does not work in one story might well prove successful in another story later on.

Hitting publishers' preferred word-targets takes experience, so the chances are that you will need to add to or take away from your story before it will approach the approved length (not that you should feel that you are chained to a specific length if your book has other ideas). Let the story unwind itself naturally, and leave concerns over precise word-targets to the publisher. A good novel will not be rejected because it is a few thousand words over or under a publisher's preferred target.

Say you have the whole thing plotted out in synopsis form: there are no glaring contradictions, no gaps, no problems. It all flows seamlessly. Or does it? One of the problems for an author is that you can sometimes be too close to your book to spot plot-holes which, to a fresh eye, are horribly obvious.

This is where joining an authors' group will come in handy, or you could show your manuscript to a trusted friend. An objective eye may see things that you've missed. On the other hand, putting the script away, rather than rushing to the postbox immediately can also help. Forget about it for a few days (or longer), and then read it again. You may know exactly what happens in your book; after all, you have got the whole thing nicely sorted out in your synopsis. But unless you tell the story clearly on the page, you may find a reader unable to take that 'obvious' step from A to C, for the simple reason that you never actually explained B. Once an agent asked an author, 'How did the diamond ring get in the river?' to which the author replied, 'The swan in the High Street swallowed it!' 'I see,' said the agent, 'but it doesn't say that in the book.'

Exercise 23

Pick a topic, any topic – a recent day out, a description of your home, a birthday party. Anything you like. Now, with the aid of a watch, egg-timer or whatever, write on this subject for five minutes. Don't get rid of anything. Try not to pause for thought. Imagine this as a kind of 'stream of consciousness' exercise. Just go for it!

Now forget all about it until the following day, or at very least, much later the same day. Look at it again and reread what you have written. Spend ten minutes revising it. Note the ways in which the original has been improved. Is it longer or shorter? In either event, examine what you have done and think about why it is better.

Writer's block

What is writer's block? It is that day when you sit down to write and find yourself, several hours later, still staring blankly at an unspoilt sheet of paper or an empty computer screen.

Writer's block can be caused by a lot of different factors. Sometimes outside stress can trigger it. If your life is in some major turmoil, the chances are that you are not going to be able to concentrate on your writing.

The first question to ask yourself is whether these external stresses can be removed? If the gas company has decided to spend a couple of weeks digging up the road outside your writing place, can you set yourself up somewhere else until they have finished?

Might the problem be overcome if you altered your writing routine? Are you trying to write too often? Theoretically you might be able to write for 15 hours at a stretch, but if the creative part of your brain works only for two hours before needing a rest to recharge, then the other 13 hours will be a waste of your time. Two authors made the following comments:

> *If I get bogged down in a storyline, then I sometimes just leave it and switch to working on something else for a while. I go and make a cup of tea, go and talk to my kids, get away from my desk for half an hour and then come back and start on something else. The coming back bit is really important! And sometimes, if I'm writing and I think, this isn't very good, this isn't really working, then I force myself to keep going, and keep churning the words out just to get through that particular section of plot. You can always go back and revise and edit. Just keep writing. It doesn't have to come out perfectly first time.*

> *Going back over what I've already written helps. I usually allow a 'block' to take its course; sometimes things just*

need to settle down. The waiting can allow for some other developments and insights to emerge from the depths of your imagination or memory.

You could be stuck in mid-plot with no idea of where to go next. Don't worry, you're in good company. By his own admission, while writing *The Lord of the Rings*, J. R. R. Tolkien was stuck in the caverns of Moria for an entire year before coming up with a way forward for his characters. Write a single line if that's all you can manage, or put away the work you are stuck on and write something entirely different. An angry letter of complaint to the gas board, or getting in touch by email to someone you've been meaning to catch up with might be all you need to unlock your creativity.

As one of the authors mentioned above, the 'block' may not be in your imagination, but just as frustratingly, in your inability to get the words down in a satisfactory way. If this is your problem, you might find that just getting the scene finished in a badly written form will be enough. Tomorrow, you can come back to it and work it up into something that you will be pleased with – but if you walk away from it now – the block may still be there the next day.

I find that getting out of one scene and into another can be a nightmare – searching for an elegant and pleasing way of leaving one piece of action and then introducing another can be very frustrating! I generally find that these transitional pieces of writing benefit from being left 'ragged' and then cleaned up later. A book can be like a shark – if it stops moving, it's dead in the water!

If your imagination is blocked, how about taking some time out to look through your Ideas File. Perhaps there's a way forward hidden in there somewhere. Discuss the plot with a friend or with a group of children: as we said before, a fresh eye can work wonders, and a fresh mind may come up with a solution that might never have occurred to you. Brainstorming sessions can throw up all manner of intriguing ideas.

Of course, if you've taken our advice and worked out your synopsis in advance and in detail, then your creative storytelling 'block' will come at an early plotting stage, and will not mess up the actual writing of the story. If you are truly blocked on a project, it is perfectly okay to put it to one side, and begin something else. You can return to the first piece at any time you feel re-inspired. Many published authors have unfinished works, or ones they are just not happy with. Sometimes the timing is just not right. Be brave, don't punish yourself by going over and over it. Let it go, for now.

One word of advice. When brainstorming with someone, don't instantly dismiss their ideas, no matter how feeble you may privately consider them. Friends may very quickly clam up if they get the feeling that you think they're talking rubbish and, you never know, their forty-third idea may be just the one you've been searching for, or it may give you a potential springboard for a better idea that you would never have come up with solo.

Another approach could be to open a dictionary or newspaper or website at random until an inspirational word or thought emerges. This may sound a little strange, but we have been told that it really does work.

On the other hand, you may find that putting the work aside for a few days will do the trick. Have a change of scene, do something new, go for a long walk. Redundant as this advice may sound, the best bet is to stop worrying.

As one editor put it to us, 'We're not exactly dealing with brain surgery here. It's not *that* important!'

10 THINGS TO REMEMBER

1 Be sure you now know how to devise basic plots and storylines. Very simply, for fiction your script should tell the story in thirds: one third beginning, one third middle, one third ending.

2 Appreciate the importance of good characters and strong stories. If you can't empathize with your hero, then why would you want to read on? If the heroine is great, but the story sluggish, what do you need to do to give it page turnability?

3 Start a story with an exciting bang and experiment ending chapters on TV soap series-style cliffhangers.

4 Avoid over-writing. If in doubt, leave the extraneous detail out!

5 Find your voice and style, don't think you have to emulate others. Be unique, be yourself!

6 Make sure you understand the use of tenses, and which are easier and which more difficult to convey stories.

7 Create realistic dialogue with pace and punch.

8 Grammatical troubleshooting – know your faults and don't trust your computer spell-checker.

9 Know the importance of revising and tweaking until you are really happy with your work. If you think it's 'OK-ish', chances are a potential editor will not.

10 If you've got writer's block, do what works for you to unblock it, or try something you've never tried – whether going to an ice hockey match or a local youth band gig. Look, listen, and learn from the young people you meet and see there.

6

....

Illustrations and picture books

In this chapter you will learn:
* *how to work with illustrated books, both fiction and non-fiction.*

Overview

In this chapter we're going to be taking a look at the skills you will need if you're planning on working with both words and pictures. Your first challenge is to find the balance between words and illustrations. On the whole, books for younger readers will have fewer words and more pictures, and as you work your way up the age-ranges, this balance will shift until pages with words on will far outweigh illustrated pages.

Some books, especially those aimed at the middle fiction age-range (eight to 12-year-olds), may have occasional illustrations, say, at the beginning or the end of chapters, or a few pictures scattered throughout the text, just to brighten the book up.

In graphic novels and Manga (and sometimes in works of non-fiction), the entire story is set out in comic-strip form. Plenty of adults read this kind of book, and more and more titles are being aimed directly at a non-child audience. In some European countries – France for instance – Manga has a huge market and there are graphic novels to be found in large sections in many supermarkets as well as in specialist bookstores, displaying comic strip versions of everything from Mickey Mouse to Marcel Proust. As we write, the market for this kind of book is growing in America, but UK publishers we have spoken to are still reluctant to take it on, so remember to research the market before you get going on a Manga or graphic novel subject – you may have trouble placing it.

If you're planning on writing a book that needs pictures, then you're going to want to get some advice or ideas from an illustrator. Maybe you only need a few line drawings dotted around the book, or possibly you have come up with an idea that will involve fully illustrated colour pictures on every page. Either way, a professional illustrator will eventually be involved, maybe only at the end, or possibly all the way through.

Illustrated books

Books for the very youngest children start off with plastic bath-time books, board books or cloth books. These are deliberately chewable, soakable, scrunch-up-able and constructed to survive everything a small child might do to them. At their simplest, these books may have pictures and no text at all, bound together to be looked at or sucked as the mood takes. A basic alphabet book could come next, with each letter illustrated by a big, bright picture: 'A for Apple', 'B for Boat', 'C for Cat', and so on. But bear in mind that these books only make sense in one language. An English 'A for Apple' book is not going to work in China or Argentina, unless it is used for bi-lingual education purposes.

Following on from simple alphabet books are those books where the pictures are accompanied by a single word: 'House', 'Cat', 'Boat', 'Dog', 'Tree', 'Flower', 'Car', 'Cow' – and there's an eight-page book already. Writing and having one of these books published is nowhere near as simple as it may seem. For a start, these books will mostly be made up 'in-house'; the ideas will be developed almost entirely by people within the publishing house, or concocted solely by the illustrator – after all, it does not take a particularly brilliant writer to add the word 'cat' to a picture of a cat. For slightly older readers, the wording might be 'The cat sat on the mat in a hat' – and so on up the age-range: 'Puzzledust the wizard's cat wore a pointed hat when she helped her master weave his wonderful spells.' These different texts could all be used to accompany exactly the same picture.

Unless you can come up with something very original, you're going to have problems in finding a publisher for this sort of book. Most ideas in this line have already been thought of, worked out and published. You really need to research the marketplace very thoroughly before spending any time on these types of book.

Once children have passed the 'chew-it-and-see' stage at, say, three years old, we get to what is known as the '32-page picture book'. These picture books contain a simple story in 32 pages which the child will be able to follow with the help of anyone old enough to read it to them. Despite their apparent simplicity, these 400-or-so-word books are actually very difficult to write. Books of this type usually have a full-page coloured picture on each page, accompanied by a small block of large-print text.

Exercise 24

Economy of writing is one of the keys to any heavily illustrated book.

To this end, take a piece of writing you already have to hand. It doesn't matter how long it is. Now reduce the word count by half, while keeping the plot coherent and the story interesting.

Now reduce it by half again. (You may be able to do this by simply removing all adjectives and adverbs – try it out.)

You will be surprised how much is retained even with such drastic pruning.

Illustration fashions and tastes change over time. Check out some older picture books and you'll see this straight away. Pictures that may have been all the rage 20 years ago may nowadays seem quite old-fashioned. Similarly, the type of story that might have interested publishers a decade ago may no longer be of interest today. Or it might be that something that fell out of favour suddenly becomes popular again as the industry recycles itself. Either way, time moves quickly on, and no publisher wants to be left behind. Go and look at some recently published works to find out what's in and what's out. Also, bear in mind that different countries have widely differing tastes for illustration styles and for text lengths.

PRINTING AND BINDING

If you're particularly interested in writing for picture books, you will find it useful to read and research the more technical side of the production and publishing and printing process. The entire publishing, printing and sales process is probably far more complex and time consuming than you knew.

Very briefly, all books are printed in 'signatures' or multiples of eight (hence the name 32-page picture books: 32 being 8 × 4). Eight pages are printed at one time on one large sheet of paper which is folded, trimmed, and bound into book form. If you look at the spine of a hardback book, you'll see how these signatures are bound together by being sewn into multiples and then fitted together between thick card covers. The most economical way of printing is in multiples of 16 and, as we know, the economics drive industry.

Hardbacks are more expensive to produce than paperbacks. But, in the picture book market, the fact that hardbacks last a lot longer than paperbacks do means that publishers are prepared to produce picture books in both forms. The sewing together of the signatures also increases the strength and durability of a hardback. The more a paperback picture book is used, the sooner it will fall apart, while the more rugged hardback will survive a lot longer.

On the whole, picture books are larger than books intended for older readers. This takes into account the importance of the size of illustrations. A small child will probably spend much longer looking at the pictures than they will listening to the text being read, and the larger the format of the book, the easier it is for the child to pick out and point to things, especially in detailed illustrations, which interest them.

Insight

Bookshops often display picture books face-out to entice people to buy them. From the author's point of view, this is great. A face-out picture book is going to take up plenty of space on a book shelf in a store, which means it will draw the attention of people who are browsing for something to buy.

Books intended for beginner readers (that is, those children who are able to read simple things for themselves) will tend have longer texts than picture books, but still in the multiple-of-eight format (48, 64, 96 pages) until it heads into middle fiction territory (eight- to 12-year-olds) of 144, 160, 176 pages and upwards. Once again – research you home territory publishers for market requirements.

A modern paperback book is bound in a quite different way from hardback books. The printed and folded sheets are ground flat at the spine and glued into the covers. These days the glue used to hold paperbacks together is intended to keep the book in one piece for over 20 years – and glue technology is improving all the time. Even if it's dropped in the bath, a paperback should not come apart. Something to think about before you rush out to buy a digital e-reader.

PUBLISHERS' TIME

Something that often bugs writers is why their picture book takes so long to get printed and published. Their frustration is understandable, but they need to realize that publishers tend to plan entire years ahead. For example, an editor might call you in the New Year to say that your book will be published in

January. But the editor is not talking about this January; they are projecting into next year – or more likely, the year after. We call this 'publishers' time' and it is something you will need to get used to. An 18-month to two-year wait between acceptance of a book and its publication is not unusual.

Why is that? Well, for a start, a lot of editorial and production processes have to be completed, from jacket ideas to text design and all these various elements co-ordinated. Your publisher will probably need to have page proofs ('finished' pages) printed to send out to foreign publishers in order to attract interest and money for co-editions. (Remember this term? It refers to a book simultaneously published in two or more countries at once.) A totally different company from the one that is printing and folding the pages may print the cover of a hardback book. These two things need to be brought together for binding either at the printers or by a separate binder. Add to that the fact that these companies may well be in entirely different countries, and you'll get an idea of why so much time is passing. Book buyers need to be given advance information about new books. How many they then say they will order, could influence how many books a publisher will print on their first print run.

Until now we've been concentrating on simple picture books, but a quick browse in a bookshop will show you other kinds. There are pop-up books, where cut-out sections are pulled up to create a three-dimensional effect when a page is turned. There are books that incorporate sounds, smells and different touch sensations. There are also lift-the-flap books and books where the child pulls a tag or turns a fitted card wheel to reveal hidden pictures. Cut-out books sell well, as do 'paper engineering' books in which older readers are shown how to make trains or houses or whatever out of pre-pressed-out and coloured shapes.

Again, think hard and take a good look around the market before you get going on ideas for these markets. Many of these books are conceived in-house by the publishers. Although successful 'activity' and interactive books sell well, they are very expensive to produce and a publisher will need to be convinced that a large audience exists before to make the book a viable product.

COLOUR PRINTING AND CO-EDITIONS

Colour printing is a very expensive process and publishers are going to be careful about what they take on. To try and keep costs down, they will often show samples of text and some illustration layouts or spreads to foreign publishers and international book fairs in the hope of bringing out one or more co-editions (that is, a joint publication) funded between two or more companies.

It's important to understand the significance of these co-editions. It's all to do with keeping 'unit costs' down. The more books a publisher can print in one run, the cheaper each book will be to produce (the unit cost). It's exactly the same process that allows supermarkets to sell things more cheaply than a corner shop. They buy in bulk at a discounted price, and the saving is passed on to the consumer.

In exactly the same way, if a publisher can be sure of good international sales for an expensive-to-produce book, then they'll be prepared to print a large number while keeping their costs down. Co-editions guarantee a market in at least one other country, and could mean doubling the initial print-run of a book. If a publisher can find a foreign company to come in with them, then translations can be made, and the books for both countries can be printed together by the same printer. The finished copies can then be sold and shipped to the publisher ready to go straight into the shops in that country.

Full-colour printing (traditionally 'four-colour printing', because virtually any colour can be produced from a combination of four basic colours) is expensive, especially on the sort of good-quality, glossy paper that does justice to the illustrations. A publisher will need to be totally convinced that your picture book idea has co-edition potential and is going to make money before they'll go ahead with the project.

TEXT FOR PICTURE BOOKS

If you still think you have what it takes to break into the picture book market, then you're going to need to know what kind of text lengths are required. A 32-page picture book can have as few as 14 words, up to 800 words – but there are wide variables regarding intended age-group and individual publisher's requirements.

Here's an example of a 32-page spread. This gives you 12 double-page spreads in which to tell your story, once you've discounted the end-papers, the page with publisher's information on it and the title page. So, as you can see, in a 32-page picture book, your story probably will not begin until page 6, and might have to be wrapped up by page 29 if there is a repeated end-paper. Your narrative will have to be spaced fairly evenly through these 12 spreads. Normally, you wouldn't have a big chunk of prose on one spread followed by only a couple of words on the next. The story needs to balance out, and this takes study and practice.

Your text can appear on these spreads either in a block in some 'empty' space (space deliberately left by the illustrator) or along the top of the spread, or along the bottom. It can even appear in two blocks, one on each page of the spread, or entirely on one page with the illustration filling the other. (Check out the design layouts of popular, and/or award-winning picture books.) It's easier for children who are learning to read, or those with sight or learning difficulties, to read typeface printed on a white surface, rather than type which is overlaid on a coloured background.

All these things will need to be thought through when you put your story together, although once your initial idea has been accepted by a publisher they'll have someone work with you and the illustrator on the general design of the book.

The illustration shows a sequence of book spreads labelled, in order: Front Cover (1.), End-papers (2.), Publishing Details (3.), Title Page (4.), the beginning, 1st Spread (5., 6.), 2nd Spread (7., 8.), 3rd Spread (9., 10.), 4th Spread (11., 12.), 5th Spread (13., 14.), 6th Spread (15., 16.), the middle, 7th Spread (17., 18.), 8th Spread (19., 20.), the end, 9th Spread (21., 22.), 10th Spread (23., 24.), 11th Spread (25., 26.), 12th Spread (27., 28.), End (29., 30.), End Papers (31., 32.), Back Cover.

THINK VISUALLY

Insight

You must start thinking in pictures. Anything that can be seen by the child doesn't need to appear in words. You don't need to describe characters, scenery or action that is going to appear in picture form.

Pictures, no matter how action-packed, are always snap-shots. They can only capture a single moment. Your task as the author is to link those moments together into a flowing story. Use your words to push the story on and to explain to the reader how they get from picture A to picture B and so on. A successful author thinks visually.

You will probably have ideas about what your characters look like or how their surroundings should be shown. These details can be explained separately. Write down all this kind of information and hand it over with the manuscript. You may also have ideas about the layout and type of pictures you would like, but be prepared for a publisher to have their own opinions about this.

Then again you may have no idea at all of how the illustrations will fit with the text. This isn't a problem: an illustrator's job is to put your words into pictures. But you still need to keep your eyes on the beginning-middle-end balancing act.

On the whole, the middle of your story should take up as much space as the beginning and the end put together, if not slightly more. In a 32-page book, this would mean the beginning should take two or three spreads, the middle would take six to eight spreads, and the end another two to three. These are only guidelines, but it does give you an idea of the sort of balance you should be aiming for. Another thing to avoid is the gabbled ending, where the story suddenly goes into overdrive because the author hasn't left enough word room to bring it to a well-rounded conclusion.

Balance has to be achieved through the pacing of the text as well as the pacing of the story being told. In a 400-word, 12-spread book, you should try to accompany each spread with about 30 to 40 words.

Picture book stories need plenty of movement. There's no room for long static conversations between characters. We told you in Chapter 5 about the importance of ending chapters with cliff-hangers; in a picture book every spread has to be a cliff-hanger in its own right.

The most successful picture books manage to include, as well as the basic story to entertain a child, a kind of 'subtext' that attracts and amuses adult readers. Ask friends or family what bedtime picture books make the favourite reads, and take a look at why they have such longevity. If an adult is going to have to read the same picture book over and over to their child for weeks on end, the successful ones will be those with glorious illustrations, and/or storylines which continue to appeal to their audience. They may also have a poetic style (but not be in poem form), and comforting storylines. The same picture book classics may come up as favourites over and over again. When bookstores, book clubs or newspapers and so forth makes lists of 'Favourite Books For Children', which picture book titles reoccur, and what is it that they've got which works so enduringly? Read some, ask others' opinions, and find out what you think makes them work so well.

Where picture books are concerned, the only way to do any serious research is by going to a bookstore or a library and actually handling the things.

When I was researching a picture book, I picked out some bestsellers to examine. I'd use a sheet of paper to cover the pictures first, so I could judge how well the story worked without the illustrations. Then I'd do the opposite, and block out the words.

VARYING THE SCENERY

In a picture book, the view needs to keep changing. Your book can't be set in a single room, for instance, unless some fascinating *visual* changes are going to take place in that room. Each turned page has to show something new and exciting. The best way of learning how to do this is to read published picture books. Check out how texts and illustrations work together in these books. Or try a different approach: block out the text with your hand or a sheet of paper, and see how much of the plot you can follow simply by looking at the pictures.

In a well-plotted picture book, the pictures should almost tell the story on their own. The same kind of effect can be achieved by turning the sound down on a television while watching cartoons.

See how much of the story is carried by the pictures. Your text only needs to carry about 50 per cent of the story; let the illustrations do the rest. That's what they're there for.

Example
    Text: Mum was late!

    Picture: Harassed-looking mum with gaping handbag, open coat and hair all over the place is pulling child out of house. The child is fully dressed, but Mum is still in her nighty and slippers. By the expression on the child's face, Mum clearly does not usually take him out in her night-clothes.

The effect of this on the reader is to make them wonder what is going on, and make them turn the page to find out. Why is the mum late? Why does she have a nighty on out of doors? What happens when she realizes how she is dressed? Will the little boy tell her that she has forgotten to get dressed, or leave her to realize on her own? Where are they going?

All conveyed by three words and an intriguing illustration.

Or the same picture could be accompanied by something quite different:

    Kevin had the feeling that this wasn't going to be just another ordinary day.

This example shows a more complex text, intended for an older reader. Now you've got your reader hooked, you need to get going with the story. If the book revolves around one character, then that character needs to appear on the first page.

In a ghost story, the first picture may be of Martha in her haunted bedroom. This establishes her as the heroine. On the other hand, the ghost may be the hero, whose private space Martha is invading. A story like that could begin with the ghost peacefully lying on the bed and reading, and continue with the ghost being disturbed by

Martha charging in wearing hobnailed boots, swinging a football rattle over her head and shouting loudly. The reader would instantly sympathize with the ghost and would appreciate that the story was to be told from the disturbed ghost's point of view.

A mouse, living in the skirting-board, has its life made a misery by the endless conflict between a well-established ghost and a young ghost-hunter. The story would then revolve around the mouse's attempts to get rid of both the ghost and the ghost-hunter – or possibly to come up with some way of convincing them to live peacefully together.

Exercise 25

Write a text for a 12-spread story in as few words as possible. Your challenge for this exercise is to have the story begin in one place and end in that same place: it could be a garden, in a submarine, beside the dinosaur display in a museum, or wherever. The other spreads must each contain a different scene to keep things interesting. Your aim is to create a coherent story, which moves along nicely, as well as keeping to the beginning-middle-end structure.

It's not easy to do this well, as you'll find out. But on the bright side, a successful picture book text could earn an advance as large as that of a 40,000-word novel!

Important points

VOICE OF THE NARRATOR

When writing for the youngest age-groups, it's best to keep the voice of the narrator (meaning *you*!) well out of the way. This is the kind of thing to avoid: 'Can you guess what happens next?' or 'Can you see where Squishy the Squid is hiding?' Small children find this kind of text very difficult to understand, especially those still learning to read.

TENSE

Avoid complicated use of tenses. Keep the story in a single tense and keep the sentences short and to the point. There are some very poetic picture books out there, but they are generally aimed at older readers. In picture books especially, adjectives and adverbs should not be necessary – the illustrations will deal with that kind of detail. If a heroine is wearing her favourite red scarf, the only comment needed in the text is that it is a favourite, and not that it is red. If a hero is entering a building with a sign outside saying 'Swimming Pool', then there is no need to write: 'Zac was going to the swimming baths for a swim.'

INTERNATIONALITY

Remember the importance of the international market for these books. Publishers may be reluctant to take on a book which has no international context. A book published in the UK may not work in other countries if it is filled with very British elements such as people delivering milk to the house, police officers in traditional domed helmets, red post boxes or animals such as hedgehogs or polecats. Things like that may not travel well to other countries. On the other hand, a bright red double-decker bus might work outside the UK because this is such a universally understood image.

Likewise, in the UK the *post* is generally delivered through a front-door letterbox by a postman/woman, but in the USA the *mail* is more usually left in an external mailbox by the mailman/woman. Similarly, acceptable phrases, words, jokes, homilies and superstitions in one country, may be meaningless or even misunderstood in another. A black cat that crosses your path in the UK is considered a lucky omen. In Italy it is seen as a very unlucky omen. In the UK, 'washing up' means cleaning cutlery and dishes after a meal; in America it means washing your hands and face. An English person in America offering to help someone 'wash up' is going to get some very strange looks. However, stories like Babette Cole's picture book *The Trouble with Mum* has a universally understood subject – parenthood! There are many other exceptional picture books which have travelled worldwide: Eric Carle's *The Very Hungry Caterpillar*, *Guess How Much I Love You* by Sam McBratney and Anita Jeram. *The Gruffalo* by Julia Donaldson and Axel Scheffler, although completely in rhyme, was liked so much by foreign publishers that they translated the text – and it has become a bestseller.

These problems work both ways, and a UK publisher might reject a foreign picture book that deals with things that make little sense outside the country where it was written, or because the illustration style is not popular in the UK at present. The thing to keep in mind when writing your story is that it should not be too parochial. A child on the other side of the world should be able to understand it just as well as a child who lives two streets away from you.

FASHION TRENDS

Fashions and trends of acceptability change, and you need to do some research to find out what you can and can't do in a picture book. Violence, sex, gore and general mayhem are obvious taboos, but these days there is also a reluctance to publish books where the boys go out doing adventurous things while the girls stay at home with their mother preparing lunch, in between washing dolly's clothes and vacuuming the house.

Fashions for witches, dragons, dinosaurs, mice and fairies for example come and go. Look at what has been published this year, and if you see a glut of similar creatures or themes, be careful – in a couple of years something else will be the flavour of the year.

Setting the text

PRESENTING YOUR PICTURE BOOK TO THE PUBLISHER

A picture book is not the same as a storybook. A picture book has narrative illustrations; a storybook has an illustrated text and is intended for older readers. Do you get the difference? A storybook story could be read and understood without the illustrations, whereas a picture book story probably wouldn't work if there were no pictures. But, the chances are that with both these examples the text will need to have 'read-aloud' qualities: meaning that the style and rhythm and patterns of the text will have to work when read *to* a child as well as read *by* a child. The easiest way to check on this is to read your script out loud – and maybe make a recording of it so you can listen to it over and over and figure out which bits work and which don't.

PICTURE BOOKS

Insight

As far as illustrations are concerned, unless you're a professional artist with experience of illustrating children's books, the best advice we can give you is to leave illustrations well alone. It's another whole area, with lots of practical and style concepts to think about.

There are various ways to present the text of a picture book story. Some authors merely type out 'Page 1', followed by the line(s) of text, and then use a fresh sheet of paper for page 2. Others will present as follows:

Page 1
Mum was late!
(Illustration of harassed-looking mum ...
and so on)

If you have specific ideas for what things should look like, then you could include some stick-person images or written instructions to explain what you'd like to see. You can even suggest perspectives and other potential ideas. But don't be surprised if the editor, art director, design department and/or publisher has other thoughts.

When an editor reads a submission, they may be looking for a story to suit artists they already have in mind. In this case, your story will need to fit into a particular visual style that already exists. At other times, an editor will look for an appropriate illustrator and may consult you for your opinion as to the final choice. It's fairly unlikely that you could ever enter an editor's office with your picture book idea fully formed and be allowed to say, 'I want it exactly like this, thanks.'

Publishers will have contact with a whole host of illustrators and artists whose work they are familiar with. Like with everything else, publishers will tend to go with artists whose work has been successful in the past. As an unknown writer, you're only making things harder for yourself, if you are also trying to sell yourself as an unknown illustrator at the same time.

Be really wary of inviting an artistic friend to do the illustrations for you. How are they going to feel if your story is accepted, but a publisher who wants to use an established book illustrator dumps their pictures?

Even a great draughtsman with plenty of experience in other fields may well fall into some of the more obvious traps when they try to illustrate a book. For instance: a face drawn across a double-page spread will look very odd when the nose vanishes into the cleft between the pages. There are other important techniques and limitations, ranging from depth and variety of colour to where the text should sit, that an illustrator should know about when working on picture books. Leave the artwork to the professionals. In general, don't take advantage of friends who you think can draw, and don't submit your own artwork unless you really know the business of illustrating children's books.

STORYBOOKS

While picture books spread the workload equally between words and pictures, storybooks have more than twice the text, are usually smaller in size, and rely much less heavily on the artist's input. An average storybook text length starts at around 2,500 words. The story will be split into several chapters and spaced out with plenty of illustrations.

As with picture books, the story should be well balanced and full of interest and movement, but the balancing act between words and pictures doesn't need to be quite so precise. The 2,500 plus word-length allows much more room for dialogue and for brief descriptions of things that will also appear in picture form.

Some storybooks are illustrated in colour throughout; some are part-colour, part-black-and-white line illustration; and others are black-and-white line only. Check 'beginner reader's' series for styles. This is one time when you really do need to leave the internet and go out into the real world. A brief trawl through your library will show you the range of illustrations used in storybooks, from the meticulously detailed and highly realistic full-colour works to the kind of cartoons that are so fluent that they look really easy – until you try it.

Let's say you've submitted a beginner reader storybook text. The editor is interested but wants you to make alterations before they take it on. These alterations may be intended to clarify or brighten the plot, or to spread the action out a little (especially if your story takes a little while to get off the ground and then ends all in a rush on the last page). Or the editor may think you have included some piece of grammar that is too complex for the intended readership, or a word or two that needs to be exchanged with something more simple.

By now you should understand the style and the kind of words you need to use to hit your target audience, but an editor may still suggest alterations which change your original phrase 'inharmonious discord' to 'terrible noise' without losing its sense.

Once a text has been accepted, the publisher will work finding an appropriate artist. Generally the publisher will choose the illustrator and an in-house design team will work on the layout. You may well not have much of an input at this stage, apart from being kept in the loop about which artist the publisher has chosen and being sent examples of their work.

Next you may be sent proofs of the text set out as it will appear in the finished book, with gaps left for the illustrations. Around the same time, you should get to see some roughs (usually loosely sketched drawings) of the artwork. Sometimes the first thing you will see are colour photocopies of the finished pictures. Hopefully (but not always), you will be asked for your opinion at the rough artwork stage, so that you can add your ideas, or point out any errors. We have seen picture books where one character had a moustache which appeared and disappeared, and another where a character's sweatshirt changed colour and style throughout the book.

Detailed illustrations could take an artist weeks or months to complete, so this process will take some time.

Moving on up the age-range from storybooks, you will discover middle fiction books with, say, ten or so line drawings and maybe small vignettes at the beginning or end of chapters. As with picture and storybooks, you'll be kept informed of what's happening with the illustrations, but on the whole, scenes to be illustrated and the placing of illustrations will be out of your hands. (Don't feel too left out of it – chances are the illustrator will also be told exactly what the publisher wants drawn – it's not often an illustrator will be told: here's the book – go illustrate it.)

Like we said, the older the reader, the fewer pictures their books will generally have. Of course, there are exceptions to this, one of which is the graphic novel style, intended to attract an older readership. Text for graphic novels has to follow the same style as that for photo-stories in teen magazines. It is almost a comic cartoon format and written mostly in dialogue with only very brief explanations. If this area appeals, do your research, study the layouts, and write and ask publishers for any briefs they may have for their series.

Book covers

A lot of your publisher's time, thought and effort ought to go into deciding what should appear on the cover of a book. The audience for which the book is intended needs to be considered carefully and the cover design aimed specifically at grabbing their attention. In a perfect world, your book should shout out from the shelves to be picked up and bought – but unfortunately, in the real world, constraints of both time and finances can cause problems with this process and unfortunately you will really only be a bystander as this takes place.

The look of a book cover is created from several elements. If it is part of a series, then there has to be a series title somewhere. Then the title of the individual book and the author's name, followed by a picture, photograph, or montage intended to sell the books to the target audience.

If you have specific ideas for the cover of your book, then by all means let your editor or publisher know, but keep in mind that there are design and marketing teams whom you would hope know a lot more about the intended market than you do. The people who sell the books often have the final word – and sometimes that authority is extended to a major book store buyer. Your opinion should be sought and hopefully you will be kept informed at every step but, to be honest, as one editor told us in a moment of weakness, if you were to express disapproval of a cover at a late stage, the chances of you being able to make any changes at that point are limited, not least because the artist will already be under commission and money will have been spent.

Nevertheless, as an author to whom we spoke testified, it is possible to effect changes, and it's certainly easier with the progress in technology. He was shown a 'finished' cover painting for one of his books, only to spot that the cat in the picture was an entirely different colour from the one described in the book. The next time he saw the picture, the cat had been recoloured.

In other words, if your comments are concerned with inaccuracies, you may be able to effect changes, but if you just plain don't like the design or the pictures chosen for the cover of your book, you may well simply have to live with it.

If you are lucky enough to have written a book with crossover potential, then it may be published in two editions – one for the children's market and one for the adult market – and the jacket designs of these two editions will naturally reflect the different age-groups being targeted.

Illustrated non-fiction

Most of the same rules apply to illustrated non-fiction as they do for illustrated fiction. However, non-fiction books are far more design-led than fiction, as the text and illustrations are integrated across the pages. It is really important that you, as the author, see the rough artwork before it is approved for completion. Presumably you will have researched your subject and know what's right and what isn't. If your topic is the internal combustion engine, then obviously any drawn illustrations (as opposed to photographs) have to be absolutely technically correct.

Photographs, too, must be of the right subject, taken from the appropriate angle and preferably one which won't date too quickly if the non-fiction work is about a topical subject. A non-fiction work will probably have a great deal more editorial input and author guidance than a work of fiction. You may also have much more control over the suggested kind of illustrations and/or photographs to be used, unless you are writing for a series that already has a clearly defined style.

10 THINGS TO REMEMBER

1 *Learn to think visually to get the right balance between text and pictures.*

2 *Look at different areas and options: from bath-time books to web pages to Manga.*

3 *Appreciate the different picture book formats and word-counts for different age-groups.*

4 *Understand the technical side of the publishing process and why there is so much time between submission of a proposal and publication day.*

5 *Understand why co-editions are so important for the international market success of a book.*

6 *Think about what you need to do to make your book have international appeal.*

7 *Think about what your story needs to have to make it stand out from the crowd.*

8 *Keep up to date with the changes in fashion and style by researching the latest picture book publications and the ones that get prize winning attention.*

9 *Think about why the prize-winning books won and how you can present your idea to make it stand out.*

10 *Experiment with different approaches and lengths for your text and judge what works out best for your theme and style.*

7

Markets for fiction

In this chapter you will learn:
- *about the breadth and diversity of the fiction market*
- *how your work should fit into that market.*

Who writes?

People who want to write for a living, or for part of their living, fall into four main categories. They are:

▶ **Ink junkies:** *the obsessives, who write because they can't help it; putting words onto paper is the way they express themselves and the way they make sense of the outside world. They can be prolific letter and email writers and can also be found posting frequent reviews of books and movies they love or hate on sites such as Amazon, or creating writing websites on the internet and submitting fan fiction to pre-existing sites. If they get published, it's often through sheer persistence, dedication and determination.*

I started off writing stories about characters in books that I had read. I think that kind of thing is called 'fanfiction' these days, and it can be found everywhere on the net. It was only after several years that I started creating my own characters.

▶ **Firecrackers:** *these are people fizzing and popping with ideas; they want to get these ideas out into the world and* *the only obvious way of doing that is by writing them down. Sometimes this character type will flit from one good idea to another without ever actually researching or completing anything. If they can discipline themselves to write an entire story, they can do very well for themselves.*

My biggest problem was always following through. I found myself coming up with pages and pages of great two-line ideas – but it took a lot of self-discipline and work to turn a 'great' idea into a full story.

▶ **Drifters:** *these are people who already have contact on some level with the publishing world or with the media and who slip into writing for children because it seems like a good career move. Sometimes their knowledge of publishing and their writing skills click, sometimes not.*

I worked for several years as an editor in a large publishing house, so when I started my family and was unable to work full time anymore, I found my knowledge of the world of children's books came in very handy when it came to pitching storybook ideas. Writing became a very family-friendly career move.

▶ **Wannabees:** *these are people who think that writing for children is easy, and that they can come up in their sleep with better stuff than they see in the bookstores. They also think it's an easy way of making a lot of money. They will either get a very quick wake-up call, or they'll spend their lives muttering about conspiracies because none of their sure-fire hit books has ever been published.*

You probably fit in there somewhere. To be honest, each of the above categories has a reasonable chance of success just so long as they have something new and original to say, and so long as they are prepared to obey the rules of the marketplace. Sure, you could be a maverick – but you'd better be a genius with plenty of luck along with it, or no one in the publishing world is going to take you seriously.

ASSESSING YOURSELF

This chapter covers the way you're going to sell your work, so it's time for you to take a good hard look at what you've written so far.

You're halfway through this book, so if you've been reading it in chapter order, you should have done several things by now. If you've been skimming and chapter-hopping, you might consider going back to the beginning to pick up some of the tips you may have missed. At this point, you should have your Ideas File up and running. You should have done plenty of research on the internet and in bookshops and libraries. You should have gone out into the world for first-hand inspiration. You may even have visited schools and/or book fairs. That's a lot of 'shoulds', but they need tackling.

The time has come for you to figure out whether there's a market out there for your work. This book is all about getting published – about turning your raw talent into something that opens the doors of publishing houses and gets your book into the stores.

So, what were you working on that made you pick this book up? Have you changed it at all since you started reading? Does your story have a beginning and middle and an end now? If not, why not? Have you plotted the whole story through, whether it's for a picture book or a young adult fantasy trilogy? Have you spotted plot-holes? Unnecessary characters? Scenes written in the wrong order? Have you checked grammar and spelling?

Be honest with yourself now. Do you think you're close to the mark, but not quite there yet? Perhaps it just needs a few plot-tweaks here and there, a nip and tuck to trim up flabby scenes, or does it seem like you haven't quite pitched it to the right audience? Are there too many long words and complex, multi-clause sentences? Or isn't it sophisticated enough for your young adult audience?

The suggestions we've given you so far should already be helping you to address these problems. Perhaps during your research, you've found out that your great idea is already out there. Don't panic! Maybe you can look at the same idea from a different point of view.

Remember there are no 'new' ideas. The best you can do is to update or amalgamate old ideas and add your own personality to the mix.

Every writer has their obsessions and their interests – the writer's job is to universalize the personal, to plough the furrow of their own minds and turn up fresh material that will hold the attention of their readership.

Your idea may still have legs even though someone else has taken it for a run before you. After all, that writer is a quite different person from you. Use your individuality to create something new.

By now you should also have a fairly good idea of how the publishing world operates. You should know which publishers are most likely to be interested in the piece of work you have created. You're going to save yourself a lot of wasted time and postage by targeting the right publishers or literary agents.

In Chapter 9 we're going to cover the practicalities of submitting your work in detail, so we won't go into that here. But it is time to take a look in more detail at the different kinds of publishers that exist.

Who publishes?

There are a whole lot of publishers on the lookout for picture books, illustrated books, and longer, text-only fiction. At the top end of the market are the major trade publishers whose products can be found in most high-street bookstores, and in libraries, school book clubs, supermarkets, mail-order clubs, online booksellers, overseas and so on. These are mostly large corporations with their main offices in capital cities, which may be owned by overseas corporations, and they may have swallowed up lots of smaller publishers and lists over time.

These large conglomerate publishers are not the whole story. There are also plenty of smaller trade publishers (who often specialize in niche markets), which include family-run businesses and regional publishers who concentrate on producing a small number of high-quality books. In these days of desktop publishing and freelancers, small companies like these can be run from a laptop and are worth investigating. Both types of companies have points for and against. The big corporations have plenty of sales and distribution clout in the marketplace, and the ability to make sure your book gets sold throughout the world. On the other hand, a smaller company may be able to give you more personal attention. With these smaller publishers you're less likely to get chewed up and spat out in corporate meetings where every book or series has to go through a stringent series of tests specifically aimed at dumping anything that isn't certain to make big bucks.

Smaller, independent publishers can often do very well in their less muscular way, offering you a dedicated team who will work hard on your book and who prefer quality to overt commerciality. These companies are respected for the quality of their products, and will gain the attention of reviewers and book-award assessors, simply because of the high standard they regularly achieve. Major publishers with their sales and distribution power are often outgunned by some of the excellent sales figures these independents achieve.

With both of the above types of publisher, title-specific websites are often produced to give their product a high profile on the net. Check out *Warriors*, *Artemis Fowl* and *Beast Quest* – all bestselling series with interactive websites.

By the way, the good news is that both of the above types of trade publisher will normally pay advances and royalties.

Exercise 26

Look on the internet for websites dedicated to bestselling children's books. Make notes of how they draw potential and established readers in.

Can readers send messages? Are there quizzes and competitions?

Is the site user-friendly; is it animated?

Using this research, see if you can create on paper the outlines for a website for something you have written.

PACKAGERS

Another type of publisher in the marketplace is the 'packager' or 'packager–publisher'. These companies will often develop an idea on their own and then approach one of the major trade publishers with the completed product, the point being that all the major publisher has to do is pay the packager, add the book(s) to their list and set about the distribution. Packagers might approach a 'major' with anything from a single picture book to a series of books. These are also the people who may design technically complicated products which have glossy artwork, holograms, cut-outs, and so on. They may even present the publisher with merchandising spin-offs such as boxed sets of books which may include mugs, T-shirts, cuddly toys, bookmarks or an interactive computer game.

Products like this are often seen in the bargain or remainder bookshops, toy shops, high street chain stores as well as the more usual outlets. There are publishers allied to film and TV companies who solely sell books related to programmes, brands and licensed characters. To get an idea of how spin-off merchandising works, wait for the next Hollywood animated feature film to come out and then check out how quickly the stores fill up with the books and merchandise.

Packagers are not generally geared to accepting unsolicited projects (an original idea by you), but a good idea suited to a particular company's style is well worth submitting. Such well-thought-out proposals, targeted appropriately, do not waste anyone's time and, even if your idea is not picked up this time, the company may well add your name to their author files and come back to you when they need someone for a particular project suited to your talents.

Packagers often only pay originators or contributors a flat fee or one-off payment, and also claim the copyright. We'll go into this later, but bear in mind that your flat fee may look a little sick if the product you helped develop shoots off to become a major financial success.

I have worked with packagers for several years now. Their editorial demands can be very harsh, and you have to work within very specific parameters and to strict deadlines, but I find this provides excellent training for the 'real world' of publishing, and teaches you not to be so precious about your work. And it also gives me a steady income that comes in very handy to fill the gaps between royalties for my own books.

OVERSEAS PUBLISHERS

Stores these days are full of cheap products of varying quality from a lot of different countries. Children's books are no exception, and the material from some places is not always up to the standard of the major trade publishers. If you do place some work with a foreign publisher, your payment will often not be very high, and you'll have the added problem of how to check the accounting procedures of these companies if they're on the other side of the world.

First contact

AIM FOR THE TOP

Go for the major publishers first, but make sure that the work you plan on submitting to them is something that they will find interesting. All publishers have their own 'lists' and your book will have to fit. The best way of finding out what kind of books a particular publisher deals is to check out their websites, or write/email and ask for a copy of their most recent catalogue. You will also be able to pick these up at book fairs. Your local book shop or library may have copies of catalogues and sales material too which they can let you look at or keep.

Be prepared to change your work to fit the requirements of an individual publisher. You'll have better chances of being published – especially at the start of your career – if you submit work that exactly suits the publisher you have chosen. In the real world, a busy commissioning editor may well choose something that slots easily into their catalogue, rather than something that will only fit after a lot of editorial hard work. Your story could be great, but if it's twice the length it should be, then an equally good book with the correct word-count may win out, simply because it requires less effort from the editor. We call this a 'rookie mistake' and it's one you should know how to avoid by now.

What every publisher has in common, is that as a business they need to make money. There is nothing new about this. Over 100 years ago two publishers said this about manuscripts they were considering:

> *It is beautifully written from a literary point of view, but it is not sufficiently exciting for the class of readers which publishers, unfortunately, have to cater for at the present.*

Two thoroughly competent readers find in it literary qualities of a high order, but both hesitate to recommend it for publication when the commercial question arises, Will it pay?

The Author 1909

BRIEFS

Some publishers are willing to supply 'briefs' that will give you an idea of their specific requirements, especially where a series is concerned. These are usually single-page outlines that detail word-count, style and content specifications. After all, if you're submitting a young adult romance, it's handy to know in advance whether kissing is allowed, whether the courting characters are permitted beyond the bedroom door, or whether they're only allowed to hold hands.

Publishers' websites, or possibly the publisher's phone receptionist may give you the name of the commissioning editor of the series you'd like to write for. Send them a letter accompanied by a stamped, self-addressed envelope for their reply, asking if they would please send you a brief. As we mentioned before, all personalized initial enquiries should be in letter form, not emails or phone calls. Your email will just be one of dozens and dozens on their computer, and your phone call, if it's even answered by the person you want to speak to, (unlikely in these days of voicemail) will be intrusive and possibly annoying. And the last thing you need right now is an annoyed editor.

Insight

So, the rule is – communicate on paper, or via the publisher's website, and if you want a reply, send a self-addressed and stamped envelope with your letter – remember you're only one of hundreds who write letters like this every month and the postage costs to the publisher soon add up.

Editors will appreciate it if you approach them in a professional manner, and they may remember you even if the particular piece of work you have submitted is rejected. Check the publisher's website – they'll probably have a section outlining the best way of submitting work to them. If it does, follow every single request before going to the post office.

LONGER FICTION

If your first piece of work is a young-adult novel, a trilogy or a sequence of linked novels, you're not going to find a whole lot of publishers willing to look at it or them. This is for a number of reasons. For a start, a single book needs a lot of publicity if it's going to get noticed. Publishers will generally take the route of least resistance – an easy sell with plenty of money at the end. Publicity budgets, especially in the UK, are very tight and most of the money is going to be spent on books and authors with a proven track record. As a new writer, your book is unlikely to have a great deal of publicity money spent on it, and you may find that wonderful promotional ideas floated early on never actually materialize.

Young-adult fiction is taken on by a limited number of publishers, especially with one-off books, and these form only a small percentage of a market that is dominated by books for the younger age-ranges. This is partly because 'young adult' is quite a woolly term; and people in their early teens are as likely to be reading Jane Austen or Stephen King as they are to choose anything specifically targeted at their age-group.

CROSSOVER FICTION

Harry Potter is a phenomenon. As is Philip Pullman's *His Dark Materials* trilogy. Both authors wrote books aimed for a younger market, but managed to produce work that also fascinated older readers. This kind of double whammy is known as a 'crossover' – meaning that the product has crossed over from one intended market into another. You shouldn't try to write a crossover hit – there aren't specific lists or publishing imprints as such – the best you can do is to target your particular young audience and hope for the best.

Of course there have always been crossovers: adults have been buying children's books for their own entertainment for a long,

long time – think of *Alice in Wonderland*, *The Wind in the Willows* and the *Winnie the Pooh* books as classic instances of crossover. And in the late 1960s and early 1970s, it became quite the fashion accessory to be seen carrying Tolkien's *The Hobbit* around with you at college. (*The Lord of the Rings* is, of course, a crossover without parallel – to the point now where it is hardly possible to tell whether it really 'belongs' in the children's market or in the adult market.)

Many books aimed at young adults these days have sophisticated jacket designs, which can't be told apart from adult fiction. (There's an obvious reason for this. Remember what we told you a few chapters back about aiming for the top of the age-range? The top of young adult is... *adult*.) These books may appear in both the children's and the adult sales sections of bookshops.

Publishers will also repackage/rejacket/rebrand children's books that were first published a couple of years ago, as well as those published decades ago. They do this to keep the books in fashion for new readers. Older classics are sometimes published in a retrospective or facsimile style. One reason is that every couple of years brings a new age of reader – the nine-year-olds reach 11 and so forth, and secondly because books read and loved by a child will still retain their magic when that child is grown up. Parents will often buy books that were their favourite childhood reads, not only for their own children, but also to allow themselves briefly to bring back more innocent times. The Narnia books are a prime example of this – and you might like to check out an online bookstore to see how the covers evolve with each new publication so that they still work for their target audience. Modern hardback editions of Enid Blyton books from the 1940s and 1950s often have the original covers and are aimed very much at the nostalgia market.

More recently, books by Terry Pratchett and Mark Haddon have bridged the gulf between children and adults. Publishers have been quick to see the potential to exploit the crossover market, and will now simultaneously publish books in two distinct packages – one with a cover aimed at the children's market, and another geared towards drawing in as large an adult readership as possible. Also, the more sophisticated book jackets and covers will appeal to age-conscious teens who, while they would not be seen dead reading a kid's book, are very happy to have the adult version on display.

This concept of a crossover product has also resulted in genuine 'crossover' covers – where the images depicted are aimed at appealing to adults and children at the same time. Meg Rossof's book about Britain at war, *How I Live Now*, has such a cover – with girl-friendly butterflies and flowers, together with the darker elements of thorns and barbed wire.

Another kind of crossover is provided by authors whose work is generally aimed at adults, but who are able to step across into the children's market. On rare occasions this can be done by someone from an entirely different branch of the entertainment industry – the pop singer Madonna, for instance – who is famous enough to get their children's book published because it is hoped that they will carry with them a potentially large crossover market.

But like we said, don't try specifically to write a crossover novel (with the main characters aged 17 to 21 years for example). As the great screenwriter William Goldman once said – 'No one knows anything.' He was talking principally about the impossibility of guessing which movie would be a hit. The same goes for the publishing world. No one knows which book or books might cross over. Just write the book you want to write – and hope for the best.

SERIES FICTION

There's a huge demand for paperback series fiction for the simple fact that it's much easier to build a faithful readership and to sell a book in a successful series or imprint than it is to sell a one-off title. By 'imprint' we mean books with a recognizable collective logo or jacket design with an identity within a larger publishing group – as opposed to 'series' books which will usually follow the adventures of a particular set of characters, or contain stories of a specific nature – say, horror or crime. It's all to do with expectations – and if a branded series delivers good reads, then a buyer will know they can trust the series to deliver more good stories.

Insight

Before you decide to write for an existing series, find out whether more titles are being commissioned and get hold of a copy of the publisher's brief or guidelines. Follow the instructions before submitting a proposal or synopsis and three sample chapters – or whatever is requested.

For a series outline of your own, you would also need to submit further plots, so that the publisher is able to see that the idea has 'legs'. If it is a school-based series or a series concerning a gang of friends, bear in mind that there are already plenty of similar series out there, so you'll have to come up with something really special to attract a commissioning editor's attention.

Exercise 27

Create your own series.

Give it a context: a school, a youth club, a family house, etc.

Create four memorable characters – give them names and personality traits – and describe what they look like.

Why do these characters hang out together? What do they do?

Now come up with six single paragraph storylines that could form the basis of six books.

Was it easy to come up with these stories? Could you dream up another six? And another six?

If not, what was the problem?

Was the situation you created too limiting? Can you make it work better by changing things around a bit?

Now write a one page 'sales pitch' to explain your series to a potential publisher.

If you can't get your idea across in a single page, then the chances are it is too complicated. Remember, a potential reader has to be able to start off by buying any book in a series and immediately be able to understand what is going on.

EDUCATIONAL FICTION

There are publishers who specialize in producing fiction for the educational market. Their activities range from buying titles from trade publishers and producing their own editions mainly for schools and libraries, to creating 'in-house' reading schemes.

Educational publishers also produce a wide variety of original fiction material to suit many special needs. This can range from picture books to longer fiction introducing such themes as bereavement and divorce, as well as issues of concern for those with differing abilities or needs.

For children who find reading more of a challenge, high-interest but lower reading ability books, known as 'Hi-Lo readers' are produced. These books are for children and adults who may be learning to read but who are too old to be interested in 'Percy the Parrot' picture books. Hi-Lo readers are not as easy to write as you may think, as you'll need to keep to simple sentence structures and word use, but the publishers involved often have detailed guidelines on language and grammar.

There are also Quick Reads usually aimed at the older young adult and adult readers who have either lost the reading habit or find reading difficult. They are described on the quickreads website as 'short, sharp shots of entertainment', and are often condensations of well known books, or have been especially commissioned by publishers. It's a very interesting area, and one you should investigate.

Publishers' educational/schools reading schemes will have been thoroughly researched and planned as well as having been tested in schools and focus groups. Your enquiry about writing for such schemes will probably result in the arrival of a very long and detailed outline, and sometimes even a word-list from which your text has to be constructed. This is writing within very precise parameters and is not really intended for people without either published writing or language teaching experience.

Educational publishers often approach authors and illustrators directly, or commission teachers whom they know to be good writers, as they will have a working knowledge of the way children are taught to read. If you work in this area, you may already have the necessary knowledge and expertise that educational publishers require, but we've also found that being a good and enthusiastic teacher does not always give someone a head start on becoming a published author.

Insight

If you are interested in this area of publishing, then it's worth visiting school or educational exhibition fairs. You'll also find the appropriate publishers there and you'll be able to do some research before making your initial approach.

DUAL-LANGUAGE BOOKS

Dual-language books are published for those children whose first language is not that of the country in which they are living and being educated, or for those families who are or wish to be bilingual. These books are most often seen in picture book format, in which the text appears in two languages, and are most likely to have been bestsellers in their originating language. A few publishers seek original works in this area; if you are fluent and competent in other languages, then you may find this type of work interesting.

RELIGION

The religious publishing market has various publishers dedicated solely to the publication of religious or spiritual material. The numbers of publishers and books for children with these background themes have been on the decline in the UK. Those publishers still commissioning are on the lookout for work that fits their particular beliefs, but conveys the message in a subtle, perhaps wholesome, way without being didactic or 'preachy', particularly where the fiction area is concerned.

GRAPHIC NOVELS/COMIC BOOKS

When we use the term 'comic book' we're not talking about the *Beano* or *Fun-Time with Mickey Mouse*; comic books are the same as graphic novels, except that they are generally slimmer and are usually issued monthly – as with *The X-Men* or *The Fantastic Four*. Graphic novels or comic books are stories that are told in words and pictures in comic-strip form. These books have come a long way since they were aimed at the children's market; nowadays the graphic novel is also frequently used to tell very stark and harrowing tales, and although many are read by children, a lot are certainly not intended for a young market. For examples of this see *Persepolis* by Marjane Satrapi or *Watchmen* by Alan Moore.

In many countries, the fashion and passion for graphic novels has been growing steadily and continually, both with a children's and an adult audience – and frequently with both at the same time. The managers of many specialist European Manga stores will tell you that they have as many adult customers as children. Many Manga publishers, however, tend to license already published works and then get their staff editors and illustrators to work on the texts.

It is a visual and fast-paced way of telling a story, and you'll need to be able to write succinctly and with the artist in mind at all times. Many graphic novels or comic characters form the basis for children's (e.g. *Spiderman*) and adult (e.g. *A History of Violence*) films, television, computer games, merchandising and so forth.

There is a great deal of cross over in the world of graphic novels, notably with titles such as *Tank Girl* by Hewlett and Martin (which also became a film, T-shirt, etc.), Neil Gaiman's *Sandman* series, *Peacemaker* by Ennis and Dillon and *Aria* by Holguin and Haberlin. And this is not to mention the Japanese Anima and Manga graphic novels – many of which are startlingly graphic in their visuals and most definitely not for the children's market. As you will see from the above examples, these graphic novels are often co-written by the person who tells the story and the person who illustrates it.

In the adult world a notable graphic novel would be *King Lear* illustrated by Ian Pollock, although there are many other examples, including a graphic novel version of the movie *Serenity* by *Buffy the Vampire Slayer* creator Joss Whedon, as well as 'serious issue' works such as *Palestine* by Joe Sacco which uses the 'comic-strip' genre to explore the weighty problems of that region in the early 1990s, and of course Frank Miller's renowned *Sin City* novels, which now also exist as a movie.

As with all specialist fields, you would need to have a good working knowledge of the mechanics of the genre before you attempted to produce work of this type, and anything beyond an initial storyline would need to be seen by and discussed with an experienced illustrator before there was any point in you taking it further.

FILM, TELEVISION, RADIO AND THEATRE

Insight

If you're thinking of writing for film, television, radio and theatre, then really you need a book or learning course aimed at this specific craft. Each of these is a highly specialized market area that calls for very different and distinct skills.

Writers are frequently commissioned to write to order a script based on an idea, or within a framework, already chosen by a producer or director or script-editor. For instance, writers approached to write a story for the TV series *Dr Who* will obviously be expected to take on board all the established characters and characteristics of the series. Similarly, if you are asked to script the next James Bond movie, your work will need to conform to all the expectations of the genre in its 'rebooted' back-to-basics new mode.

Often a writer with a track record will be approached to adapt an existing novel or TV series for radio, or a classic novel for television. Most work will come in this form, and it's rare for an unknown writer to place a brand new piece of work. Recycling is all the rage at the moment, and many films and TV series and radio plays are based on pre-existing books or comic books, rather than on new and original material.

This is a very tough arena for a newcomer to fight their way into – not least because the media world likes to bet on winners, and winners are those with an established track record and proof of successful experience in the field. It's the old catch-22 situation again for anyone seeking employment in this world: commissions to write for broadcasting are rarely handed out to people who have not got a proven expertise in writing for broadcast.

As we said, different media require different skills. For instance, the plot of a film would need to be explained in a way that would make sense over one-and-a-half to two hours of screen-time. A movie has to be sold in two sentences, meaning you'd have to be able to say up-front: this is *Toy Story 4* meets *Twilight* in order to get enough attention to have someone even glance at your script.

On the other hand, television may require a story to be broken into two parts, or three or 13 any other variable. And even a single-episode story will probably have to be divided into two distinct chunks with a cliffhanger in the middle to help viewers jump the commercial break without changing channels. Episodes of *Doctor Who* are 50 minutes long despite airing first on the non-commercial BBC – this is because they want to sell it to foreign television companies who will want to insert commercial breaks.

These episodes also have cliffhangers placed at specific points to hit the commercial breaks.

On radio, everything you want to convey to the listener will need to be in the dialogue that the actors speak, or in sound effects, or, as in the case of the radio dramatization of the *Gormenghast* books by Mervyn Peake, by a separate narrator or storyteller.

Theatre will again have differing requirements to suit the limitations of a flat stage and scenery changes. Many scriptwriters and playwrights have previous, published book-writing experience, but writing for these areas calls for entirely different abilities. The jargon differs from the book world, too. What we have been calling a synopsis would be called a 'treatment' in the film and visual arts world. There will be a cast list that may include descriptions of un-named characters, such as: THIN SPOTTY TEENAGER. There are technical terms of direction, for example, 'FX' for sound effects, or 'beat' for a pause in the dialogue. Take a guess at what 'POV', 'Fade In' and 'Int' mean? (OK, 'POV' means 'point of view', meaning the angle from which a shot is taken; 'Fade In' is probably fairly obvious, and as for 'Int' – well, if you really want to know, do some research.)

You would also need to learn a quite different way of dealing with dialogue, punctuating a spoken piece with adjectival explanations. For instance:

> *BOY (Terrified) No way! No (beat) way!*

The 'slot-time' of a TV programme may be one hour, but with opening and end credits, as well as advertisement breaks, the actual dialogue of your script may run for less than 40 minutes of that hour – and that's without taking the big dialogue-free car-chase scene into account. These days an American TV series such as 24 is often under 40 minutes long all-in, and the length is gradually being eroded as time is sliced out of programmes to make room for more advertising revenue.

Part of the skill expected from the writer will involve understanding how to lay out a script and how much time the dialogue takes on a 'read through'. If your script for a TV show over-runs, things will be taken out whether you like it or not, so you need to time this virtually to the second or risk losing something important in the 'cut'.

You will also need to be able to think visually, and to describe coherently whole scenes of action where nothing is said. In other scenes, you might be able to set the scene very quickly: (Int. Kitchen. Day), but even then the subsequent dialogue will need to be full of physical and emotional pointers – as with the terrified boy mentioned earlier.

Exercise 28

Try re-writing a story of your own so that it would fit a ten-minute slot on television.

Now time it by reading the dialogue aloud, adding appropriate time-slots for action to take place.

Is it 12 minutes long?

Trim two minutes.

Is it eight minutes long?

Add two minutes.

Keep at it until your piece is exactly the right length.

There are many specialist books on the market for these writing areas (e.g. *Break into Screenwriting* by Ray Frensham) and there are courses on scriptwriting which will teach you how to set out a screenplay and point you towards finding work for film, television, radio and theatre. You should definitely seek out some kind of professional advice or tuition if you want to attempt writing for these areas.

You also need to realize that the children's slice of these markets is very small, and shrinking with some of the major broadcasters – with perhaps the exception of the younger age group's designated children's channels. Children's broadcasting air-time is also made up of many foreign series imports, so before you decide to adapt your young-adult novel for a television two-parter, you need to be very realistic, and have some understanding of time-slots and the type of programmes being put out by whichever channel you choose to approach. TV executives are not going to change things to suit you – it is you who must adapt your work in order to present them with something they might want.

Once you have gained the necessary scriptwriting skills, research will be your key. Unlike with publishing, in the media world who you know is as important as what you know. You can research the television and radio listings market for details of the programme producers to whom your work could be submitted, but it will be even more helpful if you know someone who knows that producer, or you have met them at a course, industry function or via a professional organization such as the Writers' Guild, or Radio Independents Group.

Media listings directories are published annually, both in print and online and these will give you a good idea of who's who in the media world, and where to approach them. There are also media magazines and annual festivals, although it would be a mistake to travel to Cannes or Sundance with a script under your arm. As with our advice for attending book fairs, a producer having a chat with friends at a party is unlikely to want to hear a half-hour 'pitch' from you detailing which A-list celebrities you think should star in your movie, and what SFX or VFX would work really well in scene 54.

Most films, television and radio programmes are produced independently of the broadcasting companies and they are often on the lookout for good ideas and new material. However, these independent companies have to research and raise interest, find a broadcaster or distribution, organize complex financing, clear rights, and get a draft screenplay written way before they can even begin to think of going into production. It's a deeply detailed area, with many different professions involved. Next time you are at the cinema or rent a DVD, take time to read the end credits and check out the range of people involved – from runners, to completion bond companies, to insect wranglers, to script advisors – all of whom have played a part in making the movie you have just watched.

This massive and complex procedure can easily take a couple of years for a television drama, and often much longer for films. For radio broadcasts, programming can be decided up to six or even 12 months in advance, and for stage plays, well, a theatre that has a slot to take your play, and one that the production can afford, will need to be pre-booked.

Some publishers do produce fiction plays and playlets for schools and religious markets, both for trade and non-trade outlets. Long-running series, children's soap operas and educational broadcasts frequently use different storyline writers, but you will need tenacity and luck to break into this market.

The market for live theatre, ballet and dance is very small, and tends to be confined to previously published or other well-known works. Fame can follow the success of small local productions, schools theatre groups and fringe or festival successes, but short of finding a wealthy producer who likes your work, your best approach may be to find a theatrical agent who specializes in selling to these markets.

Payments for television and radio generally work along specific guidelines, but they're quite complicated to the untrained eye, and include repeat fees, overseas sales and so on. Payment can also be based on the experience of the writer – so a new writer for television will usually be paid less than an experienced writer, even though you may think you have done the better job. Guidelines can be obtained from screenwriting societies, but if you get a job, you may want to find professional advice on your contract so that you don't lose out if your work is widely sold. If you're particularly interested in these areas then joining one of the appropriate organizations will provide you with plenty of regular information, guidance and news of the latest market developments and legal complexities via their magazines.

Payment in all of these media areas is not as large as the movie-type industry hype and extravagance might lead you to believe – not until you hit the big time, anyway. Few writers in these areas are given a profit percentage – however, if you wrote the original book for which dramatic rights have been bought and which has been turned into a blockbuster film, then enormous numbers of books may sell as a result.

ELECTRONIC COMMUNICATION

As the world of electronic communication expands and evolves, steady work can be found for computer-literate authors. This work tends to attract flat fees as you will probably be one of a large number of freelance writers and editors working on a particular project. Also, the copyright of the project will belong to the producer of the electronic work or other software being developed. Work in this area could include writing sections for encyclopaedias, adding to a game based on a bestselling series of children's fiction books or writing for educational websites. Type in 'educational websites for kids' and your search engine will bring up a host of ideas about whom approach.

There are plenty of conferences and shows you can attend, although some are expensive. Exhibitors tend to be hardware manufacturers and software developers, displaying their abilities and wares, with very few actual publishers in attendance. Check before you go so you know exactly what to expect from a conference or show.

Tracking down the original producer/creator of a software package in order to present an idea to them may be a difficult process, as they are often bought in by the publisher or especially commissioned from an independent firm. Computing and gaming magazines, shops and special supplements in educational newspapers will also help you to narrow down your search for writing areas which could interest you.

MAGAZINES AND COMICS

The UK comic market is very small these days and you would be hard-pressed to find much beyond the *Beano* and the *Dandy*, but there are a lot of children's magazines on the market, from those aimed at tiny tots such as *Sparkle World* (USA) or *CBeebies* (UK) through titles like *Girl Talk* and *Doctor Who Adventures*, to teen-zines such as *Kiss*, *Bliss*, *Sugar* and *Shout*. Much of the material for these markets is produced in-house, or bought in from other countries, thereby limiting your publishing chances even further. As ever, study the market and submit appropriate material for short stories, photo-stories, cartoons and so on.

Many of the magazines for younger readers are based on cartoon or well-known picture book characters. The magazine publishers license the right to use these characters from the owner (licensor). Authors are then employed to adapt or write suitable material involving these characters. The licensor then usually approves the work before it can be published, and this can mean rewriting work several times until it is judged fit for publication. Licensors can be very difficult to please. You will need patience.

If you are able to get into these markets, they can prove a steady source of income. Experience in these fields, the ability to work to tight schedules, and writing about characters not of your own creation can be valuable experience. Potential book publishers are impressed by an author who shows versatility. It is worthwhile developing a range of writing skills, especially if you aim to make a living.

COMPETITIONS

A lot of newspapers and magazines run competitions for short stories and poetry, and some even go for plays and novels. A number of organizations, societies and arts councils run annual competitions, so it's worth keeping your eyes open. Submit material that fits the competition regulations exactly, even if that means adapting something to suit. Writing to a specific order will be a useful experience and, while you may not win the big prize, you may well get to see your name and possibly your work in print – a good boost to your morale as well as a potential cash prize. Winning a competition or being published in almost any kind of format will draw the attention of a potential publisher, too. If the prize is to publish your work online, you must realize that you are then unlikely to be able to police what happens to it next, and any hope of keeping hold of the content and a right to be rewarded for further publication is lost.

ANTHOLOGIES

Some publishers regularly compile seasonal or themed anthologies of short stories or poetry.

It's too difficult to second-guess what these publishers might be looking for next, so find out who they are, and then ask them for information as to what is currently being commissioned. Often an independent editor or author is chosen to compile the anthology and they will have prepared a brief for their requirements. Once again, remember to write and enclose a large stamped, self-addressed envelope with all such enquiries; do not telephone or email, unless specifically asked to.

CONDENSATIONS

Yet another specialist market is for 'condensed' books – that is, shortened versions of 'classics' such as *Alice in Wonderland* or *Pride and Prejudice* and similar out-of-copyright books or licensed modern classics. These may be aimed at the educational market and writers with a teaching background often have the appropriate skills needed to turn a complexly written classic children's book from the nineteenth century into something that a modern audience will enjoy. Writing styles and social attitudes shift so quickly that even works from 50 years ago may need a modern makeover to appeal to today's children.

AND, FINALLY, BLOGS AND BITS AND PIECES

There's less call for filler items in the children's market, but they include jokes and letters, as well as humorous story and information slots in appropriate magazines and newspapers. Choose those publications that will pay for your material.

Insight

Blogs – creating an online diary – are definitely a way of bringing yourself, your ideas and perhaps your writing to a publisher's attention. Books have been developed from blogs; blogs can help publicize your published writing as can all sorts of social networking via e-technology.

What you don't want to do, is give your story away via the internet, have it abused, and make no money from it. The general public do not understand about copyright, and many do not recognize intellectual creations (whether music, books, photographs, art, or film) as anything other than a free entitlement.

10 THINGS TO REMEMBER

1 Think about what your favourite area of children's writing is.

2 Decide what you want to write, rather than what you think you should write. Experiment with different areas until you find the one you are most happy with.

3 Find out which publishers and producers might be interested in publishing your work. Look at those who most closely fit the work you are producing and tailor your book a little if necessary to fit their style.

4 Be professional about the way you approach a publisher.

5 Don't attempt to write crossover fiction – these books are successful by accident rather than design.

6 Read some series fiction, and notice how each stands alone with minimal introduction of the strong characters and settings.

7 If appropriate, find out what and where the market is for educational fiction.

8 Look into what opportunities there are for writing for children in comics and magazines.

9 If you want to write for the TV, radio, movies and theatre market, find out what other skills you would need to learn. Try adapting a couple of pages of something you have written for these other areas.

10 Be on the lookout all the time for other possible fiction outlets.

8

Non-fiction books

In this chapter you will learn:
* *the complexity of the non-fiction market*
* *the specific skills and knowledge you will need to enter the market.*

What's the difference?

What is the difference between 'fiction' and 'non-fiction'? It's the difference between 'truth' and 'facts'.

Everything you write has to come across as being *true*; that is, having an internal order and sense, no matter how unusual or strange that truth may be. Even the wildest cartoon or the most surreal comedy has to conform to its own inner logic, otherwise it's just a mess. It's this basic created structure that we refer to when we talk about truth. It's all to do with creating a willing *suspension of disbelief*.

Take a werewolf story. If a reader is going to accept that people can turn into werewolves on the nights of the full moon, you have to convince them that inside the world you have created on the page, this is 'true'. By the same token, if yours is a 'rags to riches' story where a penniless street urchin grows up to be President of the United States, you have to make the events that lead from one situation to the other seem believable – seem 'true'. These are the kind of truths that we deal with in fiction – but non-fiction relies far more heavily on facts.

Getting it right

Non-fiction calls for research on a much more rigorous level than fiction. Once you have your basics sorted in a fictional novel, you can fill the story with all the invented detail you like. This isn't the case with non-fiction.

Insight
Whatever subject or area you approach, if your book is non-fiction you will have to do a great deal of very thorough research.

Take a look in the back pages of almost any biography. There will be a bibliography – a whole list of other books the writer has referred to, as well as others which contain further reading material. Often, it has to work this way – getting information from things that other people have already written down. Say you want to write a new book about Napoleon's childhood. No one who knew him is alive. How else could you do the necessary research except by reading previous books, researching via the internet, and delving into archives of contemporary files and documents.

But first of all, ask yourself whether the world needs another biography of Napoleon. Maybe you've come up with a fresh angle by concentrating on his early years? Maybe you want to explore the way in which Napoleon's upbringing and religious orientation might have led to the conquest of Italy and allowed for the emancipation of indigenous Jews from the oppression of the Roman Catholic Church. Investigating this will involve working your way through scores of factual books and contemporary documents, gathering information, noting anomalies, joining the dots, and then fitting all this into your own 'take' on Napoleon.

Research of this kind is always vital if you decide to tackle a historical subject. Each of those previous books you read will probably have their own bibliography at the back – your work may well expand exponentially if you're going to do a thorough job. At the same time, bear in mind that going back to the original sources of all information may be vital. A mistake either of understanding or translation may have been copied down the centuries – and you might be the person to reveal that a long-held 'fact' is actually wrong.

Insight

An internet site created by an ill-researched or biased enthusiast may provide inaccurate information. Research from a variety of sources, and look for authenticity.

What if you want to write a book about the Amazon rainforests? You'll be able to pick up written and online information, but you might also want to consider a visit to the Amazon Basin for 'field research'. If you're considering the effect of the modern industrial world on the rainforests, then you'll need to ask a few local people for their opinions. It is no good just chatting to industrialists and government officials. You're going to have to head into the jungle and speak to the indigenous people, to see what they think of things. If you are planning to write about any country or culture, you need to have experienced it from all angles for it to be an accurate and objective piece of work.

Insight

Any non-fiction book is going to take time and money: your own time and the time of people you interview or observe; and your own money, unless you're lucky enough to get a bursary, sponsorship or a commission from a publisher.

You might think you're an expert in your chosen field, but you need to face the fact that there are going to be other experts out there who disagree with your findings. Even if you think they are entirely wrong, you'll have to pay attention to their opinions, even if it's only to shoot them down.

Faction

Faction is dramatized fact and there is a lot of it about. It can be something like: 'I was a drummer-boy at The Battle of Gettysburg' or 'My Diary as a Royalist child in the English Civil War' or even 'I, Clytemnestra – a child in the Court of Ancient Rome.'

Or it can take the form of a school play depicting important historical events:

> *The scene: the Atlantic Ocean in 1492:*
>
> *J. Tar (a sailor): Land ho!*
>
> *C. Columbus (an explorer): Wow, look everyone! America!*
>
> *Full Ship's Company (very hungry after weeks at sea):*
> *At last! Hamburgers!*

Faction can make it easier for young people to take information on board. And it can be sweetened even more by making it funny. Publishers are very keen on books that cover famous historical events or times in a jokey manner. Take a look around the bookshops to see what is fashionable in non-fiction.

> *Many of my books are based on historical events and/or set in other countries and cultures. Having roughed out a synopsis I do a great deal of research before I begin writing the book. Can I find enough information? Is there another book already out there with a similar storyline. I can't travel back in time, and I haven't always been able to visit the places I write about, so I always have my script read through by an expert before I deliver it. This could range from a museum archivist to a history professor or authority in the country where my story is based. I can usually find an expert who is willing to help.*

Another example of faction is the kind of picture book where a young child is taken for a tour of flora and fauna to be found on the seabed by a friendly and informative seahorse, crab or other character.

With children's non-fiction, the aim is always to find a new way of sneaking information into a child's head, whether it's as simple as a *What are Insects?* guide for very small readers or an objective factual guide to *Safe Sex* for young adults.

A factual book that looks informative but light-hearted is more likely to be picked from the shelves than a dull-looking, school-like tome. Which would you choose: *Extra Maths for Beginners* or *Let's Have SUM Fun?*

A good non-fiction author must be up for a lot of diligent research. You need to be accurate. Your publisher may not be an astronomy expert and needs to be able to trust that your inventive astronomical book is correct. Reviewers love finding errors in non-fiction books, and if an acknowledged expert trashes your book in a widely read review it could sink without trace. Also, your chances of ever getting another book past an editor will be zero if you locate Alpha Centauri in the wrong place, or if you get the size of the Sun wrong, etc.

Journalists or people with a background in research often make good non-fiction authors. Interestingly enough, we have also found that very good non-fiction authors do not always make good creative fiction authors and vice versa.

Laugh and learn

In children's non-fiction, you have to present your facts in an appealing way. 'Appealing' in this case has to cover several bases. A piece of work will have to appeal to teachers, librarians and parents or guardians, as well as to the child itself. It will need to be targeted accurately at the intended age group, with suitable language, interest and understanding levels, and it will need to deliver all the necessary information in as few pages as possible. Passing on information in a brief and entertaining way is a very special skill.

All authors should make sure that their book is a children's book, not a simple adult book in disguise. The text should also be carefully aimed at the publisher's needs.

Writing in a high-level, technical way is not appropriate. The experienced, perfect author writes few words with clarity and style – appropriate for what is required, not to impress.

The general trade market isn't interested in serious, studious, sleep-inducing books. 'Force-feeding' with fun is the way to go.

Illustrations

Most modern non-fiction books are full of illustrations. Information goes down better with photographs, pictures, cartoons or diagrams. Illustrators and designers are going to be deeply involved in the look of your non-fiction book right from the outset.

Your book may need photographs. There are picture libraries that keep vast collections and can probably provide a picture to go along with almost anything you might write.

Newspapers, magazines and websites will have their own pictorial archives that you may be able to use. Or you may need to approach museums, art galleries and private collections to find the exact source material you want. A designer will usually find the appropriate pictures, but there may be occasions where this time-consuming task falls to the author. You'll need to know from the start who pays for this, whether they need any copyright clearance, and will the photos you have chosen or suggested date quickly?

Copyright and getting permissions

'Copyright' is a property right that exists in virtually every kind of work (written, printed, electronic), as well as in the typographical arrangement of published editions, and in sound recordings, films, broadcasts or cable programmes. Copyright protection is automatic, giving control of the right of copying to the authors/creators or to their assignees/transferees, e.g. '© University of Reading'.

Exercise 29

Research the definitions of 'copyright', and 'intellectual property'. You could begin by looking at the British Copyright Council's and the World Intellectual Property Organization websites, and others like the University of Cambridge which has some very good advice on copyright and tracing rights holders. Investigate websites and perhaps register online to access further information. Books such as *The Writer's Handbook*, *Writers' and Artists' Yearbook* and *Inside Book Publishing* are invaluable sources of information for your writing career. Get the latest editions of these kinds of books, or research them at your local library. Also check out The Copyright Licensing Agency and The Authors' Collecting and Licensing Agency. Find out who they are and what they do.

Copyright can be a complex subject, because different creations have their own copyright terms, and different countries and territories have their own copyright laws. At its simplest level under UK law, any written works which you created from your own imagination, or interpreted and developed from your own research and which you write for yourself (not as an employee of a company which employed you to write a specific work) are your copyright, and remain in copyright for 70 years after your death. If you want to know more, go back to the exercise on the previous page. If you want to learn the intricacies, you will need the help of an intellectual property expert.

You wouldn't want someone stealing your work and selling or passing it off as their own. It is stealing. It is as much stealing as faking the recipe for a cola drink and selling it in bottles displaying the label of a famous brand. The consequences of that could probably bankrupt you and even send you to prison. Very few people really understand copyright, even those who are meant to be dealing with its issues and complexities on a day-to-day basis. With the advent of the internet, copyright protection is all but out of control. Photocopying, copying and downloading music, films and books is seen as cheeky or naughty – but it is actually piracy and theft.

Before you can legitimately reproduce any work that is still in copyright (written, photographic, electronic or otherwise) permission will need to be obtained in writing from the copyright holder. If the author or creator agrees to grant permission they will almost always expect to be paid and to get a name-check in your book. Before agreeing to write any commissioned, illustrated non-fiction work, check your contractual obligations with your publisher to find out whose responsibility it is to obtain and pay for permissions. It is vital that enough time is allowed prior to your book going into production for permissions to be sought and granted. Tracing the actual copyright holder of a work can be difficult and very time-consuming. However, if you do not have permission to use another's work, an expensive legal action could follow publication.

There are various ways to trace copyright holders, and sometimes persistence will be required. Sometimes you may even have to give up, and use something that is in the public domain (because all the copyright restrictions have expired e.g. the works of Charles

Dickens or The Brothers Grimm), or find an alternative that is more easily traceable or more affordable. Some copyright holders are fiercely protective of their work, and will not allow anyone to copy or use their material unless they can see a very valid reason for it.

To make your permission tracing easier there are organizations such as WATCH (Writers and their Copyright Holders) which is an independently funded expanding research project based at Reading University Library.

An email application via a permissions page on a website or a letter of enquiry (and as a courtesy, a self-addressed envelope) to the copyright holder should include the information about what exactly you wish to reproduce, whether it's text or images. You should also include details of your proposed work, its format and publication details (if you already have them). Copyright holders may reply with a form for you to complete, ask you to apply via a website, or request very detailed information before considering – let alone granting your request.

Sometimes, despite all your best efforts, it will prove impossible to track down the copyright holder. If this is the case, you will need to retain a file of all your efforts to trace the copyright holder(s) before your publisher might include a disclaimer in your book such as:

> *Every effort has been made to trace the owners of the copyright to XXXX. It has been impossible to trace the owner and the author and publisher would be glad to hear from them.*

Insight

Remember – copyright law, particularly in regard to photographs and artworks, is a complex area. Seek advice from your publisher if you are in any doubt, or from a media copyright expert.

Checklist

Before you enter the world of non-fiction, ask yourself the following questions:

▶ *How good are my research skills?*
▶ *How methodical am I?*
▶ *How tenacious am I?*
▶ *How accurate am I?*
▶ *Can I make seemingly dull facts fun or interesting?*

Non-fiction authors who are primarily researchers by profession or by nature can be given a theme or topic and will be able to produce an authoritative book on a subject in which they previously had little interest or knowledge.

Exercise 30

Make a list of non-fiction subjects in which you have a particular interest.

Do you have any qualifications or experience relevant to the subject that will impress a publisher?

On how many of these subjects would you be willing to do a lot more research? Your project is going to fail if it turns out you have missed out an entire branch of alternative wisdom.

If you have knowledge of a particular subject, how up to date is that knowledge? In the field of computers, for instance, cutting-edge knowledge from a year ago may be redundant by now. You will also need to know what technology is under development if your work is to be as current as possible by the time it reaches the bookshops.

Difficulties

We asked a number of trade and educational non-fiction publishers to answer the question, 'What percentage of your list is author inspired or editorially/in-house inspired?' Their replies are worth noting.

Most of the list is planned here and then developed with chosen authors! Publication of unsolicited material is rare. Once authors are contracted to a project, much of the inspiration comes from them.

Over 80 per cent of our list is in-house inspired.

In-house 80 per cent.

Up to 90–95 per cent of our non-fiction list is conceived in-house.

Less than five per cent is author inspired. Our staff editors – or freelance packaging companies – come up with most of our titles.

Almost 100 per cent in-house.

Our next question was 'How do you find authors or contributors?' Almost every reply was similar and along these lines:

Agents.

Directories, academic bodies, agents, colleagues.

Word-of-mouth and personal contacts; institutions such as universities, colleges, museums, agents, occasionally unsolicited applications.

From previous projects, by putting requests to agents, and from rejected proposals that showed ability but were rejected on the grounds of unsuitability.

The marketplace

As you can see, the non-fiction market is even more difficult to break into than the fiction market. If you're going to crack it, you'll need skill, practice, perseverance and a certain amount of talent.

We next asked the same publishers if they had any words of wisdom for new authors. Every single one said the same thing: research the market and study your selected publisher's list before starting work on a proposal. The following replies sum up the situation and offer a little more hope:

> *Do not be put off by rejection. Ninety per cent of the proposals that show some flair and ability are rejected because they are unsuitable for our list and not because they are simply awful! Study the market and think about what you are proposing. If you can show that you have thought through your ideas and investigated the market you may well be approached for some other project in the future.*

> *While many of our authors come from the usual sources we also take on many authors/contributors who have written quite modest pieces/parts of books/edited etc. – and are ready to develop on from there, based on past records!*

If you are an acknowledged expert in a particular field, publishers may approach you to write something or to endorse the work of others. If you already have had articles published in magazines and newspapers, this will certainly help open doors. Newspapers, magazines and specialist subject websites are good areas to consider. Periodicals are always on the lookout for new material; like television, they are great devourers of work and there's an enormous range of specialist magazines constantly needing their pages filled with new articles.

Even if these are articles aimed at the adult reader, publishers will be impressed that you've already been in print. Maybe the article could be expanded to become a children's book. This is not so unlikely as it may sound. As an expert ornithologist, you may be able to write a children's guide to birds by rethinking and reworking a published adult article.

The in-house method of creating books means that commissioning editors are always looking for authors. If you have presented a professional proposal to a suitable publisher, the editor will have your name on file. There are many reasons why your work may have been rejected, including the possibility that the publisher had already commissioned a similar project at the time yours arrived.

Presentation

Because of the nature of non-fiction works, it's not a good idea for a writer to try to present a publisher with an unsolicited piece of work in 'finished' form. The best way to go about this is to show the publisher an outline of your proposal, including topics to be covered, a sample chapter and perhaps a rough chapter or page-layout guide, along with a polite introductory letter. (See Chapter 9 for details of submitting work.) We asked our non-fiction publishers whether they preferred to see proposals or completed scripts, and what they appreciated in a covering letter. The replies were yet again similar and the following are typical:

I prefer proposals and sample text – that way I have an influence over the finished ms [manuscript]. Complete scripts are usually too wide of the mark – they usually aren't tailored to the company's needs or the needs of the marketplace. Scripts should be accurately typed and come with a CV and covering letter which gives me something about background and personality. An unmemorable letter gets forgotten!

Proposals which include full contents outline and some sample text. Always helpful if author indicates what he/she considers the appropriate age-level, readership, sector of the market, rough extent and treatment of illustrations to be. And supplies a brief biography.

Proposal – stating clearly and concisely the aim, market and main strengths of the book. A sample chapter', to show style and approach, is useful. Personal details and relative experience is useful. Covering letter – concise, with main points only.

The wide range of non-fiction

The markets for non-fiction break down in a similar way to those for fiction: trade non-fiction books are mainly sold through the usual bookstore, book club or school book fair outlets direct to children, parents or whomever. Non-trade non-fiction (think books which would be used as study guides or school textbooks) is aimed at schools, libraries, and other educational institutions.

The trade non-fiction market covers everything that isn't fiction. This is broader in range than you might imagine: it includes puzzle books, joke books, books on how to create your own theatre, books on how to become a racing driver, and books on how to make a working origami submarine, kite-making, knot-tying, juggling, bike maintenance, how to look after a cat and a gerbil, how to extract your gerbil from your cat's mouth, first aid for cat-scratches, living with a neurotic gerbil and a homicidal feline.

While the age-groupings are similar to those for the fiction market, non-fiction books may have a much broader age-range appeal. For example, a book on fly-fishing may well be bought by a seven-year-old and a 13-year-old, as long as it is written so that it appeals to and can be understood by children of either age. Non-fiction books primarily aimed at children will also be bought by adults who may be looking for a simple or basic, and perhaps more explanatory visual guide to a subject.

Books like these have to appeal instantly to a fast-food generation, and this includes dishing out the information in easily digestible chunks as well as making it attractive to the eye. Modern non-fiction books will be scattered with cartoons, jokes, information boxes, bullet points, interesting design layouts and so on. Anything, in fact, to catch the eye and interest.

Many non-fiction books are presented nowadays as being fun first and knowledge second. If a book can convey useful information without the child even knowing there is a learning process in action, so much the better. Such books can deal with topics as different as sport, art, the lives of famous people, 'true' ghost stories, 'real-life' mysteries, interesting historical events, and so on, with so light a touch that even the most willful underachiever can be hooked and reeled in.

For the older ages, say, eight and above, there's also a wide variety of more text-based books with little or no illustration, covering social issues from coping with grief to growing through puberty. A whole lot of serious issues can be approached this way, including peer pressure, problems encountered by stepchildren, how to survive divorce or how best to approach the job market. These books often include 'true-life' stories picked up by research with children who have encountered these things first-hand. (Research for a book like this would, of course, include many interviews with or responses from children.)

Other non-fiction is largely illustration-led. A bath-time book on pond creatures may have a picture of a fish with the single word, 'fish', underneath. A 'things to find in your local park' book could have a picture of a wriggly worm accompanied by the word 'worm', and similar pages for spiders, centipedes, beetles, etc.

Cookery books for children are another part of this illustrated genre. The book may explain the ingredients, recipe and cooking methods with simple text accompanied by large, colour photographs showing each stage of the process.

You could even write an illustrated book on how to make your own illustrated book.

As with illustrated fiction books, these illustrated non-fiction works are very costly to produce and a lot of the comments included in Chapter 6 are pertinent here. Publishers will be very selective about what they produce because of the cost of commissioning artwork, photographs, picture research and designers. Trade publishers in particular will be on the lookout for something with an international appeal, something that will suit as many different countries and cultures as possible, so think international sales potential and try not to be too parochial when you present your proposal.

This is not to say that a publisher would automatically dismiss a book exploring the flora and fauna of a particular country or region, or a book that explores that country or region's traditions or politics. Books like that have a place in the non-fiction market – they may just be a little harder to sell in large quantities. On the other hand, a well-produced book on the Antarctic or the Sahara Desert is likely to find a worldwide audience and sell in good numbers.

Payment

Many non-fiction authors are offered a flat fee or a one-off payment for their text work. This is because their input is seen as just one element in a complex production process. They are not generally viewed as the 'author' of the work but as a single contributor.

Advances and royalties are less likely to come from non-fiction publishers than they would be in the fiction world because of the extra preparation and production costs involved – which is something else to bear in mind before you head off for a six-month research trek across Siberia.

Educational publishers

Specialist educational publishers produce books mainly for the school and library markets, so they will be looking for projects that are linked to education. If you're interested in this field, you'll need to know what children are studying and at what age, so that books can be pitched appropriately. For instance, if children study ancient China only between the ages of seven and eight in your country at the moment, there's no point in preparing an educationally based proposal on this subject for 13-year-olds. No one will want it.

Books produced by educational publishers range from history to art, from science to social issues, from mathematics to special needs, from drama to literature, and all points in between. They will include books providing interesting information: technical know-how from photography to mechanics to quantum physics.

These books can include companion websites, photocopiable teaching aids, beginner readers, dictionaries, study books, encyclopaedias and DVD and computer disks.

Non-fiction multimedia ranges from learning a foreign language to 'how-to-draw' packages, from encyclopaedias to interactive games, and so on.

Essentially, you need to take a long look at your skills and carefully consider how best to use them. Those of you with teaching experience will find that this scores highly with a commissioning editor, assuming your projected book falls within the parameters of your expertise.

How to annoy publishers, part two

We asked the non-fiction publishers what their pet hates were. These included:

> *Ill-considered proposals, people who 'cold-call' wanting to discuss their project at length over the phone.*

> *Writing in a high-level, technical way when not appropriate. Writing too many words, even after an editorial briefing!*

Unreliability. Lack of clarity. We also never bring together authors who don't know each other and automatically expect them to work well together. So, if the author of a submission can work well with a co-author, suggest it.

Authors who draw their own pictures, or naively think they have to do all the artwork and take all the photos themselves.

And if you're still at all unclear what we're saying, check out these comments from publishers we contacted:

I will give a lot more attention to letters from people who have bothered to find out what we publish. I get irritated by people who haven't done the slightest bit of research before they write. Unrealistic proposals are a complete waste of time.

I received a two-line letter from someone who was proposing to write a history of Britain. The two lines contained four spelling mistakes (including the writer's address). The accompanying proposal comprised a box (in which I was supposed to imagine a picture of George III) and four bullet points of four or five words each about George IV. There was no CV, and no other clue to the author's identity. Nothing. Would I give any time to someone who treated such a huge project so feebly? Of course not!

Schedules are often very rigid in children's non-fiction, with very heavy initial investment costs. When an author doesn't deliver the goods, it causes a lot of problems. For this reason, most editors will tend to use authors they know and trust rather than try out new names who might not deliver what's wanted on time. What this means is that unsolicited material gets a lot less attention than it does in other areas of publishing. It doesn't take much for a proposal to end up in the trash. If you want to crack this market, you will need to present your work professionally having researched your selected publisher's style, and be persistent. One day, your idea might land on the commissioning editor's desk on the day they are looking for inspiration.

Co-writers

You may be asked to co-author a work of non-fiction with one or more other authors. But when it comes to dividing up the writing duties and the subsequent money, authors can fall out with each other permanently unless boundaries and percentages are agreed in advance. Your editor may be able to mediate. The same applies if you are asked to 'ghost write' a work – perhaps for a blind author who cannot key in text, or for a famous person who created a storyline idea but who cannot actually write children's books (in which case, their name is really being used on the cover as a selling feature).

10 THINGS TO REMEMBER

1 Non-fiction is based on facts and calls for research at a very rigorous level.

2 Research using different sources is vital when embarking on a non-fiction project.

3 Always make sure your research sources are accurate.

4 Consider whether your subject would work well with a 'faction' treatment.

5 Try to find an original angle or an unusual theme or topic.

6 Make your work popular and interesting.

7 When approaching a publisher set your thoughts out professionally.

8 Find out who is publishing the kind of book you are proposing, and make sure you approach the right publisher.

9 Learn what publishers expect from a proposal and present your idea appropriately.

10 There is a wide range of non-fiction being published – even if your first idea is rejected, if it has been well thought out and presented you may well be approached again.

9

....

Presentation and submission

In this chapter you will learn:
- *the importance of presentation*
- *guidelines to help you with your approach to publishers and agents.*

The sales pitch

You want to be published. That's why you're reading this book. To a certain extent, getting published will include selling *yourself* – your book has come out of your head, it's part of you. How do you get a publisher interested? There are ways to sell yourself to a publisher, and there are ways of digging a big hole for yourself and jumping in.

Check this out, for instance, from a cheesed-off publisher:

> <u>*Don't*</u> *talk about projects at social occasions; ask for a name and address/card.*

> <u>*Don't*</u> *then ring up the office – write.*

> *A DIALOGUE*

> *The scene: A supermarket checkout. Eddie, a man with many years' experience in children's publishing is waiting*

*in line to pay for his week's shopping. A would-be author
named Hope happens to have found out what he does for a
living, and sees the chance to advance her cause.*

*Scene opens. Hope shoves her way through the line of
shoppers.*

*Hope: Hello, there. My name is Hope. This is your lucky
day – I've written a brilliant book that will make us all rich.*

Eddie: Ye-es ... uh, is it a book for children?

*Hope: Well, it's got a message for everyone, really. Everyone
from eight to 80. Ninety, even!*

Eddie: I take it it's fiction. How long is the story?

*Hope: It's sort of fiction, and non-fiction, really. The story
revolves around my lovely old dog Bozo who sadly died a
couple of months ago. We've had him stuffed and mounted
in the hall if you'd like to come around and see him some
time. Anyway the really brilliant thing is that I've come
up with this stunningly original concept where Bozo
can speak!*

*Fantastic, huh? And he can fly and do just about everything.
In Chapter 6 he single-pawedly solves all the ecological
problems of the entire planet and discovers how to make
sure everyone loves everyone else. In the nicest way, of
course. No smut, you know. And then he flies off into outer
space in search of the almigh ...*

*Eddie: I see. Sounds interesting. How long would you
say the script was?*

*Hope: Uh, I don't know. I haven't actually finished typing
it out yet or anything. But my writing is really easy to read.
I mean, take no notice of my friends – they say I write like*

*a dyslexic spider in boxing gloves. It's just not true. My
next-door neighbour is a doctor, and she says she can read
nearly every word. And she thinks it's brilliant. Anyway, the
book is about 234 pages long so far and still going strong.
Would you like to read some of it? As it's the weekend,
I don't suppose you'll have much on, so I could get the first
12 notebooks over to you later this afternoon, if you like.
No problem.*

(Sound of Eddie slumping to the floor.)

*Hope: Oh dear, he seems to have fainted. It must be the
excitement! Help! Call an ambulance, somebody!*

This scene could also take place in line for the drinks at a party, in
a crowded lift or in the office of an editor who forgets to put his
voicemail answering machine on, and unsuspectingly picks up the
ringing telephone.

*I went to a convention at a big hotel in America, with well
over 500 budding authors. I got in a packed lift at the 35th
floor. As the doors closed on me, I realized I had already
put on my badge saying that I was the commissioning editor
for the biggest publisher there. I still have nightmares
about that.*

*I went to the funeral of an author who had also become
a long-time friend. Afterwards, as I said my goodbyes
to the family, I was accosted by a bookseller, and a
would-be author and harangued for my advice on various
publishing things when all I wanted to do was escape for
a snivel.*

It need not be an editor on the receiving end, either. It could
be anyone whom Hope happens to know is involved in some
way in children's books. A lot of 'wannabe' writers make contact
with their favourite authors and ask them to read something
they've written. In ten years' time you could be that author.

A LETTER

We put the following letter together to give you some idea of the kind of stuff agents and editors regularly receive through the mail. The most important thing to understand about this is that no one is kidding around here. This kind of thing is real.

Dear Sir or Madam

I have looked at all the meterial avaliable for chidlren and a lot of i'ts at the best unsuitable and at wort itter grabage, I no i can do much better ans so i wrote a series of books about a little school bu called Mister Toot-Sweet dn all the fantastical going on he comes acorss in his erevyday journies. I have reed it to my next door neigfhbour who is a supermarket manger and nobodies' fool, and he says its a sur-fire woinner and I going to get Mister_Toot sweat trademarked and the quartersize salt-dough model I have made also patented,

I also see Mister Toot-Sweet as a cartoon which Dizney could animate and also it has a million marketting and merchandising pissibilities!!!

This idea miust be treated in the strictest confidense and i await your reply by return of post otherwise i shall take it to someone else and then you'll be sorry..

Your sincerey
Jack Ass.

Neither Hope nor Jack are going to find themselves in print, unless they pay for it themselves, or unless they learn how to approach publishers in a professional way.

In a competitive market like children's publishing, you have to work on your presentation. You can't wrap a bad idea up in pretty paper and get it through the net – but you can make a good idea better if you take the right approach.

Let's go back and take a look at exactly what those two would-be authors did wrong.

HOPE: THE CRASH AND BURN APPROACH

Timing
Everyone knows the story of the professional comedian buttonholed by someone at a party and asked to tell a joke. 'What do you do for a living?' asks the comedian. 'I'm a plumber,' comes the reply. 'Okay, then,' says the comedian. 'Let's see you fix a ball-cock.'

Hope has done something similar by approaching Eddie about her writing ambitions out of working hours. You should only ever make contact about work with professional people at their place of work, and in an appropriate way. Of course it's all right in a social situation to discuss shared interests, and maybe mention your ambitions. The person you are chatting with may offer you their card, and really mean for you to get in touch. But if they look like they are desperately trying to get away, don't hang onto their arm and bore them about the book you haven't yet written. When off duty, people who work in the book, film and media world most likely want to stay off duty.

What's wrong with Hope's 'book'?
The age-range for a start. Not many books are read by people of *all* ages. As you know, children's books are fitted into specific age-range categories. The fact that Hope imagines that her book will be read universally shows that she doesn't understand the market.

She hasn't even finished her book, let alone typed it up. In fact, she has no clear idea of how long her book is or how long it will end up being.

She also makes another big mistake. What if she really does have a good idea, a totally brilliant idea – something that doesn't involve a talking dead dog flying around and saving the universe. The very last thing she should be doing is shouting about it in public before her idea is in a finished and presentable form.

There are several reasons for keeping a good idea to yourself. Ideas spoken aloud have the strange tendency to resurface elsewhere – written by someone else. They aren't stolen on purpose, but an idea that you put in someone's head, might pop out months later in slightly different clothes, and that person may not even realize they're pulling the rug out from under you when they write their own story based on this idea. There's a familiar phenomenon in the publishing world whereby several stories or proposals on virtually the same subject, by authors who have never met, will land on an editor's desk in the same week.

If you have a good idea, just jot it down, keep it private, and only discuss it with people you trust. Hope wouldn't like it if her neighbour the doctor had a book published called *Bozo the Superdog*, but she might not be able to do anything about it. (We'll cover safeguarding your work later.)

JACK ASS: THE IDIOT'S GUIDE TO LETTER-WRITING

Addressee
Jack hasn't even found out the name of the person he should be sending his letter to, or the contact line which might be described on a website. In fact, for all Jack knows, he could have made contact with a publisher who deals solely with Russian-to-English translations of build-it-yourself outdoor activity equipment manuals.

Spelling and typing
Jack can't spell. Not all writers can spell, but there are dictionaries, spell-checkers on computers and even little electronic gizmos to help you out, not to mention literate friends or colleagues. Jack can't type either. Everyone allows the odd 'typo' (typing or typographical error) to slip through, but there's no excuse for anyone to send a letter that looks like someone has spilt a can of

alphabet spaghetti onto a sheet of paper and then sealed it in an envelope.

Anyone receiving this letter will instantly realize several things about Jack. He hasn't re-read his letter, and he hasn't bothered to spell-check or sort out the worst grammatical errors. He has a really bad attitude. He's far too aggressive and he needs to get over himself before anyone is going to take him seriously.

As we said, no matter how great your book is, hooking a publisher depends on getting the sales pitch right. Be professional about this.

The market
Jack says he's had a good look at the market he's writing for. Do you think he has? Anyone who thinks everything currently available for children is 'garbage' has a pretty skewed point-of-view. Even if you do think your new book is better than anything you've seen, you don't want to be saying so – because the editor on the receiving end of your letter is someone who was involved in publishing the 'garbage' you're dismissing.

Jack also needs to know that the opinions of family, friends and neighbours aren't always of great value. The supermarket manager might be right about Mister Toot-Sweet – but he's just as likely to be wrong. The fact is that unless your friends, neighbours and family are involved in children's publishing, nothing they say is likely to carry much weight. Be honest with yourself – your family members and friends are not usually going to tell you your own work is garbage – they wouldn't want to hurt your feelings. (We did say 'usually'. You might have a cousin who hates you and is prepared to give it to you straight, but their response will still not be objective – and objective with the relevant experience is what you're looking for.) Normally, you'll get enthusiastic or polite responses from the people around you, most of whom will be eager to tell you what they think you want to hear.

Plenty of submission letters include the comment '… I've shown it to all my friends, read it to my children, and they think it's great.' Well they would, wouldn't they?

My publisher boss once said that he would love to get a non-fiction proposal from someone that started 'I've shown it to all my friends and they all think it's a load of rubbish, but I still think it's a good idea.' At least then you'd feel you were getting something original, something the author really believed in.

Expectations

Maybe Jack's idea would make an amazing action movie; and possibly children throughout the world will think the coolest thing to own is a Mister Toot-Sweet pencil case. But merchandising comes later – much later, if at all – and the first thing Hope and Jack need to do is begin by selling their books. Even experienced and widely published writers will be told to get a grip on their horses if they approach editors with multiple spin-off concepts.

Know the publishing style and philosophy of a house before you submit your work; you can get a sense of this by requesting a publisher's catalogues and by reading the books they publish. If your work doesn't suit a particular publishing house, don't submit it; find a publisher that's compatible with your style. Be selective and target your submissions carefully.

Research publishers' lists through bookshops, libraries, catalogues, to discover if the project is likely to be suitable for them before sending it off. Also research the competition and consider how your project would/could stand up to it. With non-fiction, try to understand the difference between an educational list and a non-fiction trade list.

I hate unsolicited email submissions addressed to info@ which begin 'Hi' and go on to suggest that if I want to read some of their work, I'm to check out their website. You just know every publisher and agent in town, if not the world has received the same round robin untargeted, lazy email, and it's the fastest way to get me to hit the delete key.

The finished product

Before we get to your covering letter, let's look at an example of how to lay out the first page of your book.

SHADOWBACK

Chapter One: The Voice From Nowhere

'Are you all right?'

Dominic Carroll almost jumped clear of his chair as that faint,

hissing voice broke the silence. A girl's voice. A projected,

urgent whisper, like someone trying secretly to get his attention

without being overheard by anyone else.

Except that Dominic was alone in the room. There wasn't

anyone else.

(Contd)

He listened intently for a few seconds, turning his head this way and that: trying to home in on the source of the uncanny voice.

Maybe it had been someone passing by out in the street. Maybe it had been a voice on the television down in the living room. Maybe he was just hearing things.

He shook his head and went back to his impossible maths homework. The strain of an hour with numbers that simply <u>would not</u> add up or divide or multiply the way they should was enough to make anyone start hearing things. It was as if those numbers had taken on a mischievous life of their own.

He grabbed a pencil and wrote: 10 + 10 = 92.4.

He gazed down at the paper. Ninety-two point four?

He tried again. But this time, although he thought 10, his pencil wrote 66.

He threw the pencil down with a snort of annoyance.

He decided to give up on his homework. Maybe all those disobedient numbers were beginning to damage his brain? Whatever was going on, he needed a rest from maths: that much was certain.

He slipped off his chair and sprawled out on his bed, staring up at the sinister trapdoor in his ceiling. Dominic's room was small, its walls pushed inwards under the roof. There was only a narrow stretch of flat ceiling, and it was dominated by that trapdoor. He had never felt <u>entirely</u> at ease with it. He knew that it led only to the dark and dusty roof-space, but he couldn't help the fact that his imagination believed otherwise. His dreams were often darkened by images of the trapdoor opening silently in the deeps of the night, and of the crouched hulks of the things that would come slithering down to get him.

Your typescript (which is still often called a 'manuscript' in the publishing world) must be presented professionally. You can vary this layout a little, but the above sample page shows you the basic idea.

WHITE PAPER

There may be occasions where you are invited to submit
your work via email. You may have written a personal and
targeted email, or you live overseas and your recipient can't
wait for the post. But this is going to be a rare event, and with
email overload for most children's publishing people the old-
fashioned approach is more likely to be considered and receive
a response. So despite everything we've said about the rise of
computers, your manuscript should first of all be submitted to
a publisher as a hard copy on good-quality white A4 paper.
Thin paper, which is easily torn or damaged, will start to look
scruffy after one or two read-throughs. But avoid expensive,
heavyweight paper: it costs a fortune to send through the mail
and will be wasted if the manuscript needs to be rewritten –
which it probably will. Standard photocopying paper does the
job perfectly well.

BLACK PRINT

Your manuscript must be printed in black ink. This photocopies
better than any other colour, as well as generally being easier
on the eye. Choose a typeface of a size and style which is clear
and easy to read, such as Times New Roman, Garamond, Arial
or similar; 12pt is the best size to use. If you are working on
a computer, be sure not to use draft printouts for your final
presentation copy. Check that your printer is working properly
and that every line of every page is clean and legible.

LAYOUT

The layout of a page is all-important and pretty much standard
throughout the publishing world. Use double-spacing: this means
you must leave a full line gap between every line of print. Also be
sure to leave wide margins on either side of the text and at the top
and the bottom of the page.

Wide margins and double-spacing are there to allow an editor to make notes as they read, and a copy-editor enough room to make notes and alterations and to write down instructions to the typesetter/printer, which usually will be done in red or sometimes blue ink, which will stand out from the black type. Should you get to the editorial stage of being published your manuscript will almost always end up as a computer file – and changes may will be done on screen. The reason you should use this format at this point is to show you know the rules. And even on a computer screen, a double-spaced page is easier to read and alter than close-set print.

Also note that italics are not used in the example above; the words to be set in italics are underlined – the editors know what this means. Unless it is relevant to the text it might also be better to avoid bold print or different typefaces in the text of the manuscript – the general rule is to keep any kind of fancy formatting to a minimum. That said, the computer-age means you could probably get away with *some* use of bold type and italics, and you may want to distinguish a relevant text message or an email from the main prose, but keep in mind that your primary aim is to make the manuscript as unfussy and easy to read as possible.

The copy-editor, by the way, is the person who makes all the finer alterations and corrections in the code understood by typesetters. We have included overleaf a page of our second draft script, from the first edition for this chapter, which was patiently edited by a long-suffering freelance editor, Iain Brown.

The front and title page of your manuscript should include the title of the work and your name or the pseudonym under which you would like the work to be published. It should also include your address, telephone/fax numbers, and email address.

If an agent represents you, their name and address should be included at the bottom of the title page instead of yours. It's also a good idea to show the word-count of your script, although most editors will be able to guess it from the number of pages. (Again – you're doing this to show you know the rules.)

In general, the text should have a straight margin on the left (ranged left this is called). It should not be "justified". A "justified" script is one where there is/are straight ~~line~~ down both the left-hand/sides of the script, as in a book. ~~An unjustified script looks~~ much ~~like a more widely-spaced business letter.~~ If you are working on computer, do not "justify" your script as this may cause ~~spacing~~ confusion for the typesetters/~~later on~~.

You should leave one blank space after ~~the full~~ stop, ~~of~~ ~~one sentence and the beginning of the next.~~ Don't use "bold" print for emphasis or italics, but simply underline words you wish stressed/~~or put them into~~ ~~CAPITALS/~~

You may have been taught to /indent/ new paragraphs and dialogue ((i.e.), leave five letter spaces before starting a fresh paragraph or piece of dialogue.) This is no longer strictly necessary as a copy-editor will alter the layout to suit their requirements / Publishers prefer a one-line gap between paragraphs.
Likewise,
~~However,~~ each new piece of dialogue in a conversation should be given a fresh line. It looks better (on the page) and makes it easier to follow the conversation than would be the case if ~~it~~ was all strung together in a single paragraph. dialogue

Every new chapter should be started on a fresh page.
[LESLEY: CRIKEY! REALLY? YOU NEVER TOLD ME THAT.] This
Delete!

Never date the manuscript, either at the beginning or on every page. You might have to send it to several publishers before someone likes the look of it. This process can take weeks or months, and a printed date will only go to show commissioning editors further down the line that they were not your first choice. Not a great idea.

As your manuscript goes through this process of passing from editor to editor, whether inside a publishing house, or because it is returned unread and in good condition to begin with, it will start to show its age and lose its appeal. Now you can see why good quality paper helps – you may be able to send out a script more than once.

TEXT FOR TYPESCRIPTS AND DISKS

Once your work has found a home you can check your contract or ask your editor for details of how they would like the final draft of your script delivered – do they want several hard copies, as an email attachment, or on disk? Many publishers have briefs and guidelines on how to submit final work. In general, the text should have a straight margin on the left (this is called 'ranged left'). It should not be 'justified'. A 'justified' script is one where there are straight edges down both the left-hand and right-hand sides of the script, as in a book. If you are working on computer, do not 'justify' your script as this may cause confusion for the designer or the typesetters.

You should leave one blank character space after a full stop or any punctuation mark. Follow the guidelines and remember not to use bold print, italics or fancy type fonts unless you have already been told this is okay. Simply underline words you want stressed. You may have been taught to indent new paragraphs and dialogue (that is, leave five character spaces before starting a fresh paragraph or piece of dialogue). You don't necessarily need to do this – the copy-editor will alter the layout to suit their requirements. Publishers prefer a one-line gap between paragraphs. Each new piece of dialogue in a conversation should be given a fresh line. It distinguishes it from the prose on the page and makes the conversation easier to follow.

Every new chapter should be started on a fresh page. This fresh page should include the chapter number and its title (if it has one).

Your computer will have a header and footer facility. It is a good idea to use it, to save loose pages getting entirely lost: all you need to do is include your name and the book title.

PAGE NUMBERING

> **Insight**
>
> You have got to number your pages. Don't do it chapter by chapter. The first page of your manuscript has to be '1', and the numbers should then follow consecutively through to the last page.

The best place for these numbers is in the centre of the bottom of the page, or alternatively in the top right hand corner. This is easy with a computer, but it will only do it if you click 'insert' and then 'page numbers'. Don't assume your work will be automatically numbered. This could lead to unnecessary work if you print out your book before you realize there are no numbers. If this happens, write them in neatly by hand. Under no circumstances send an un-numbered manuscript to a publisher.

There's been more than one occasion where a script without page numbers has fallen off my desk and I've had to put it back together. There's also been more than one occasion where the fact that chunks of chapters were in the wrong order (while they've puzzled me after a while) have made no real difference to the story. Which then highlighted the fact that the storyline wasn't making any sense in the first place!

We mentioned asking a literate friend to transcribe your work for those of you who can't type, for whatever reason, or paying for a professional freelance typing service. There are also literary consultants and constructive editorial criticism services available if you would like and can afford a professional opinion of your work before you send it to a publisher. You might find it useful to have an outsider's viewpoint to edit, tidy up and make constructive or even detailed editorial suggestions on your work – especially if you've been submitting your work and receiving negative feedback, or none at all, and are beginning to wonder if a professional and objective editorial eye might pinpoint where you could be going wrong. These services as well as those of typists, can be found through various author associations, magazines, and websites, but compare prices and use a recommended service if possible. Be wary and be wise – paying for some help if you are really stuck could result in your completing a marketable piece of work. Look for endorsements by well known professionals, or ask around at your local writer's group. Beware the literary criticism service disguised as a vanity publisher or unscrupulous money-making scheme. You do not need to sign up to a proofreading course, or any other kind of expensive service if you've followed the basic advice in this book.

FICTION SYNOPSES

Once you've had contact from an interested editor, you'll probably be asked to send in a detailed synopsis of your work, along with the first three chapters, especially if it is a work of 8,000 words or more. You're going to think your book needs and deserves to be read from start to finish, but commissioning editors don't have time to read every unsolicited submission all the way through. They will want to know the general storyline and they'll want to see a sample of your writing. These two things will help them decide if they want to see more. If the editor likes what they see, you'll be asked to send the full manuscript. The synopsis shouldn't be shorter than half a page, and it could run to a few pages in a complex novel – but don't get carried away: the job of the synopsis is to present the story clearly and briefly – too much detail at this stage might mean your basic plot gets lost in unnecessary background info.

Non-fiction products

The title page for a non-fiction manuscript should be the same as for fiction, but you should also give an idea of the type of material contained in the manuscript. Explain what it is that you want to do, and who is your target audience. For example:

Edible Bookmarks for Beginners (working title), a proposal aimed at the 5–7 year age-group on how to make, bake and create bookmarks which can be eaten.

It's up to you how you lay out the title page, but the best way is to use a slightly larger typeface than the rest of the book, so it stands out, and centre it on the page.

WHAT TO INCLUDE

A contents page will give a quick impression of your book. Include chapter headings with perhaps a sentence or two about the material contained in each chapter. Remember that it isn't a good idea to submit completed material. It may turn out to be the same as another recently published work, or possibly your ideas may suit a publisher while your style does not. A synopsis will give you the opportunity to present your ideas and allow a prospective publisher to guide you in the actual writing of the book so that it fits in with the house style. This could save you having to write the book twice.

Exercise 31

Write an introduction and summary of your proposed work.

It should not be more than one page long.

It must be informative and interesting – what can you add to catch a prospective publisher's eye?

Imagine this is just one of 20 proposals to hit the publisher's desk that morning. Why should they follow your idea up in preference to the others?

Your proposal or synopsis outline could also include a section on any marketing ideas you may have for selling your book. Potential sales areas for *Edible Bookmarks for Beginners* would include the usual trade and non-trade markets, but might also appeal to supermarkets, with a promotional link to a particular product or range of products, or to schools or groups who run healthy eating classes. The more innovative, but realistic and practical ideas you can come up with, the more your publisher will know that you have done your homework, and the more they may be convinced that your project is worth publishing. (We'll tell you more about marketing and promotion in Chapter 12.) You'll also need to include a sample chapter, or some example page layouts of your proposed work.

ILLUSTRATIONS

If your book needs photographs or illustrations, then send photocopies or scanned images, preferably on A4 paper, to give the script a well-packaged look. Colour copies or printouts can be produced easily and cheaply these days. Remember to get permission to use photographs and art and to send in copies of the permission documentation along with your submission. Only send your images on disk or as an email attachment if your editor has asked you to do so.

If you have a very specific idea for the layout of your work (if it is to be highly illustrated, for example), then send in a design plan to the publisher. This can be done by using some A3 paper (420 mm × 297 mm, the size of two A4 sheets placed side by side), folding it in two and then showing the proposed design for a typical spread. In this case, text could be typed or neatly handwritten with copies or hand-drawn illustration layout suggestions ('roughs'). It doesn't matter if you're not an artist, or you're not planning to illustrate the book yourself, simple drawings should be enough to show what you mean.

Never submit unsolicited original illustrations or artwork, or your only copies of photographs. At the very least, they may well be out of your hands for several months; at worst, they could get lost in transit. Even if they arrive safely at their destination, your illustrations could still get battered, knocked about and trodden on, and have coffee spilled on them, or simply disappear forever between publisher's offices. Colour photocopying or the purchase of a computer scanner may seem expensive, but in this case, the financial outlay will at least ensure that your original work survives intact and in perfect condition.

Editors prefer not to have the responsibility of being given original artwork – at least, not until the book has been commissioned, in which case they will often ask you to bring the work or artwork/ photographic portfolio to them in person.

AUTHOR/ILLUSTRATORS OF ALL WORK

If you are an author/illustrator familiar with the technicalities of producing an illustrated children's book (as explained in Chapter 6), then you can go about presenting your work in one of several ways. If you have completed the artwork, then you could submit colour photocopies or scans, numbered to correspond to the script. If you don't own or have access to a scanner, and colour photocopying the entire book is too expensive, a better option may be to submit one or two colour copies of the illustrations you think will best represent the book as a whole, and then copy the rest in black-and-white. (Publishers' abbreviation for black and white is 'B/W' or 'B&W', by the way.)

You may want to present a 'dummy' book, by which we mean a mock-up of your book showing the page layouts, style, size and even examples of any paper engineering if the book is intended to include cut-outs or additions. A dummy book like this can range from a stapled-together booklet in pencil, to an A4 page of simple sketches or a 'zig-zag', which is a length of paper folded concertina-like. We won't go into any more detail here, because if you don't know what we mean, you probably shouldn't be submitting your own artwork.

Presenting your work

You have a completed manuscript in front of you and you've been asked to send it in. What do you do next?

Insight

Here's what you don't do: hole-punch it, ring-bind it, staple it chapter by chapter, paperclip parts of it together or do anything else to it at all. The same rule applies to your synopsis and initial three chapters, as mentioned above. Your manuscript must be left *loose-leaf*, no matter how uneasy that makes you feel.

Your work is almost guaranteed to pass through several pairs of hands. Punched holes can easily tear; the paper will show creases, curls and scuffs from being folded over staples; and any kind of binding will make the script look 'used' – which is something you definitely want to avoid. Editors may well 'speed-read' your manuscript to get a general feel for your work – and paper clips and staples slow this process down and will be irritating. You don't want to irritate your editor.

Simply put the manuscript or the synopsis and opening chapters in page order, give it a quick shuffle and thump to make it look neat and tidy, and slip a couple of elastic bands around it. Two elastic bands side to side and two top to bottom should do the trick and will ensure that the pages stay together in transit. Place your work in a simple cardboard folder that will fit into, usually, an A4 padded envelope. (Illustrations can be sent in an A3 size package, but be very wary of sending a publisher anything too large: huge packages that won't fit on a desk might be put somewhere out of the way and then forgotten.) For additional security you could add card sleeves to either end of your work before putting it in the folder.

On the outside of the folder, write your name or pseudonym, your address, the title of the work and, this time, the date of submission.

Why date it now when we told you not to before? Simple. A date on a folder will remind an editor that it's about time they read the book. And if the work is returned, all you need to do is put it in a new folder with a new date. And don't forget a stamped addressed envelope if you want your material returned.

THE TITLE

It's not vital for your work to have a definite title at this point: it could have a 'working title', which is a word or phrase by which you can identify it – *The Earwig that Flew to the Moon*, for instance. In this case, write on the folder: 'THE EARWIG THAT FLEW TO THE MOON (working title for 32 pp children's story) by L. E. Fant.' In the case of non-fiction: 'PIRACY FOR BEGINNERS – proposal idea for 7–11-year-olds, by R. Jimlad.'

Before you settle on a final title, be sure to check that it is original. There's no copyright in titles (trademarking of original typography or titles is an exception), but it would be silly to select a famous published title or one very similar to something already in print. *The Earwig, The Witch and the Wardrobe* will not get very far. Neither will *Lord of the Earwigs*, *Earwiggy Sickert*, *His Dark Earwigs* or *Earwig Quest*. On the other hand, there's no point agonizing over a title at this stage, especially as publishers may have their own ideas as to what your work should be called.

COVERING LETTERS

Your proposal is prepared, packaged and ready to go in the post to your chosen publisher.

You may have found your publisher's address from an annual writer's reference book or website. This is as good a place to start as any, but the speed with which things change in the world of publishing could mean that a commissioning editor name-checked in the book may be gone by the time you want to write to them.

The safest thing, if you have any doubt about your information, is to telephone the publisher and ask the receptionist the name of the senior commissioning editor. Be certain to ask for the name of the editor in the particular field in which you are interested. Large publishing houses are split into several departments so make certain you have been given the name of the right person. 'Could you give me the name of the editor in charge of children's non-fiction, please?' will do the trick. If, for some reason, the receptionist is unable to help you, they may put you through to someone in the appropriate department.

Do not use this as an opportunity to buttonhole an editor: it won't go down well. Briefly, politely and professionally ask for the name you need, and check the spelling and title (Mr, Mrs or Ms) if you are at all unsure.

Of course, if someone asks you why you are enquiring, then by all means give a very brief outline, but don't treat this as a pre-interview. Remember Hope.

Insight
The submission letter is possibly the most important item in your package. It can instantly intrigue or antagonize the reader. It must be well written; it must be professional.

All the publishers we contacted with our questionnaire, both fiction and non-fiction and from all over the world, said precisely the same: that they want to receive typescripts and proposals in hard copy, in the manner we have described, and never just as a computer disk or an email attachment. They all said they didn't want telephone calls describing your work at length. They all said that they didn't want to receive original or amateur artwork. They all agreed on what they do and don't like to see in a submission letter. The following two responses are typical:

> *Badly written letters, or proposals containing poor spelling and punctuation get rejected. If a writer is*

incapable of checking an introductory letter then there's precious little chance that he/she is going to take care over a manuscript.

[Non-fiction publisher]

Covering letters should be kept as brief and to the point as possible. It's easier to say what I do not appreciate in them:

a) I do not want the author's life history.

b) I do not want to know that several kids next door/their son's class at school or whoever think this is the best book ever written.

c) I certainly do not want emotional blackmail. It makes me uncomfortable and annoyed if I get letters telling me that the author has recently been made redundant/has multiple sclerosis/suffers from depression. I've had all these more than once.

[Fiction publisher]

I like to see a correctly addressed, typed and decently laid out letter in the first instance, with a little bit about the writer, and a reasonable overview of the proposal – which could be told in a paragraph or so. A synopsis and first chapter will probably be enough for me to assess whether I can find the idea a home in the long run, but often I can make an educated guess on that first letter.

[UK agent]

Type or print your letter on good-quality white paper, preferably A4, and with a legible, standard typeface (avoid handwritten letters). The letter must include (at the top) your name, address, telephone and/or fax number, email address and the date.

Start your letter by giving a very brief explanation of the material you are submitting, include its title (in capitals or italics so that it stands out) and a very small amount of relevant information about yourself. Include any previous successes you have had in getting into print, and any press or marketing angles you may have come up with. In the case of a non-fiction work, give appropriate background information about yourself so the reader can understand why you've written the book. Keep your letter to one page if you can (if it is more than one, paperclip it together), and if you are also submitting work, attach the letter to your folder with another elastic band.

Exercise 32

Compose an introductory letter to a prospective publisher.

Choose a publishing house you have researched and know would be interested in the kind of thing you are proposing, include the full address, plus the department you want, plus the name of an actual commissioning editor.

This letter should differ from the previous introductory exercise, in that it needs to be briefer and to cover less detail. It should be no more than a single clearly laid-out page long.

Include the following:

▶ *Who are you?*
▶ *Why have you chosen this particular publisher?*
▶ *Who is the book/project aimed at?*
▶ *What is it about?*
▶ *What is special about it?*

Show the letter to a friend who does not know anything about the book or project you are trying to promote, and see if they can grasp the basics of what you are proposing.

CONFIDENTIALITY

You can reasonably assume that the publisher you write to will treat your submitted work with complete confidentiality. But if you feel that your project is especially innovative, then it might be wise to reinforce this element: 'This typescript is submitted to you in confidence' will do, but only use it in very special circumstances.

On the other hand, if you truly believe that you have created the next world bestselling idea, then find a media copyright expert and ask them to draw up a letter of confidentiality, or a Confidentiality Agreement. This will cost you of course; but the letter of confidentiality will be sent to, and signed by the prospective editor before you deliver any material. These letters are more commonly submitted in connection with material that could be deemed libellous or controversial, something we don't normally expect to see in connection with children's books.

RETURN POSTAGE

You must include enough stamps to cover the return postage of your package if the publisher rejects it, and you want it back. Mention in your letter that return postage has been included and then tuck the stamps securely under the paperclip. Better still, include a stamped, self-addressed label or envelope. Get yourself an up-to-date copy of postal rates and an accurate set of scales so that you can weigh your package at home and put the appropriate number of stamps inside. If you have to go to the post office to find out what the postage will be, leave the package open and take some sticky tape with you so you can insert the stamps and seal the package there rather than having to haul it all the way back home again.

You could also include a stamped, self-addressed acknowledgement card, which on one side has the name of the publisher and a line saying 'We acknowledge safe receipt of *A Bucket of Sludge* by Pete Bog, dated ...' Some publishers don't automatically send out these cards, and you're going to want to know that your package has arrived safely.

KEEP A COPY

Never, ever, under any circumstances send off your one and only original copy of a manuscript. Publishers cannot be held responsible for the disappearance of your work, and although the postal service you use may be held liable for things that go astray in their hands (if proven), no compensation is going to make up for the absolute loss of many months' hard work. If you're working with a computer, you should make a second 'hard' copy and also save your work to a labelled disk or memory stick to save you from the results of a serious hard-drive collapse, and then you should keep that disc or stick in a safe place.

Be cautious about carrying your memory stick around with you. A librarian friend of ours has a big box in the computer section of the library where he works – and every day up to six lost or forgotten sticks are added to the pile already in there. In many offices nowadays where it's important to keep information secure, employees are either not allowed to use memory sticks at all, or are not allowed to take them out of the office. If you do need to take a memory stick out of your house, be very careful with it and try to come up with some fail-safe method to ensure you can't forget or lose it. As good an idea as any is to hook it onto a long chain or strap that is either kept permanently around your neck or is linked to your belt or key-ring all the time you're out. Another option for keeping your work safe if you're using a computer, is to attach it as an email to someone you totally trust and have them squirrel it away on their computer. That way, if your house is burned down or whatever, your work will survive. But make really sure you can trust this person with your greatest secrets. You don't want your 'best pal' getting rich on your ideas.

There's no need for you to go to the additional expense of insuring or registering your package. If you have addressed it clearly, put sufficient stamps on it, given a clear return address on the back of the parcel and sealed the package securely, then you should have no worries. Don't hand-deliver either, not unless you're passing by anyway. You probably won't be able to put it directly into your editor's hands, and it may become detached from the normal internal mail system. Leave the parcel with the receptionist, ask for a receipt and leave. *Never* cold-call a publisher expecting to be welcomed in for a cup of coffee and a chat.

TWO WEEKS LATER

If at the end of two weeks you haven't heard from the publisher, it's okay to write a short, polite follow-up letter to check your package has arrived safely. Try not to phone or email, however anxious you may be at this stage. Your editor may have been away from their desk on holiday, at a sales conference or attending a book fair and has returned to a huge pile of work demanding attention, and an even bigger pile of unsolicited manuscripts. You don't want to come across like you're nagging them, or suggesting they should drop everything else to read your stuff.

SIX WEEKS LATER

Assuming your initial follow-up letter proved that your manuscript had arrived, you should then wait a further six weeks before your next follow-up letter. In this case, there's no point in telephoning. Write another polite enquiry about your manuscript. A brief letter sent after an appropriate gap may jog a busy editor's memory. But remember to leave at least six weeks between letters. An editor who feels pressured into making a decision will usually decide to reject.

> *People who pester do not endear themselves to me. So please don't send me a manuscript and then phone up two days later to see what I think and try to discuss it with me. I will get around to looking at it, but my first responsibility is always to the books we are actually publishing and the authors already on the list.*
>
> [UK publisher]

I do not appreciate people phoning and demanding to see me that day because they happen to be nearby, with the idea that they can sit there while I assess their work. A good submission may be considered and discussed by several people and that takes precious time. The author took time to produce it, so they don't really want a ten-minute pressurized consideration, do they?

[UK agent]

Remember this: if you demand an immediate reaction from an editor, that reaction will very likely be 'No.' Editors are always under pressure. If someone keeps sending them nagging letters asking about their manuscript, what's the quickest way of bringing this to a stop? Send the manuscript back. And what if your editor liked your book, but they weren't entirely sure and they wanted to think about it for a while, or get some other opinions? Your complaining letters could put a stop to that by putting the editor under more pressure.

It may be that your project really does require that you meet the editor face to face to explain some computer innovation or distinctive new DVD animation showreel or laptop computer display. In this case, send as much information as you can and ask for an appointment to meet with the editor if your initial approach interests them. Make sure that you give the editor some idea in advance of what you want to discuss. It is a waste of everyone's time for you to arrive at an appointment only to find within the first few seconds that your idea does not fit in with that particular publisher's requirements or list. Don't expect a decision on the spot. Even if the editor is enthusiastic about your project, any purchasing decision will have to be made by a whole team of different people.

TIMING OF SUBMISSIONS

The last thing on your mind is going to be an appropriate time of year for submitting your work. All the same, it's as well to know that there are definite 'black holes' in the year. Editors are always busy, but some times are busier than others. For instance, the weeks surrounding major national or international book fairs are especially fraught. The main ones are the Bologna Children's Book Fair, the Frankfurt Book Fair and the London Book Fair; and in the USA, the BookExpo.

The summer is also a peak sales conference and holiday period that will take editors away from their desks. Some European publishers and agencies actually close for two or three weeks completely. If you submit material in March/April or September/October, give it a little longer before you start to worry.

There's no perfect time to submit your manuscript; the best approach is to fill in the waiting time by getting to work on your next project. January: send off project number one. February: start on project number two. March: send off project two. April: start on project number three. May: get a publisher's response for project number one. It shouldn't take that long for your first project to get a response, but you can see what we're getting at: don't just sit around – keep working.

MAKE A SUBMISSION INDEX

To help keep track of things, you could make an index using a card, book or computer filing system.

If you use a card index, it could look like this:

The Zany Zoo (96 pp) 2010

Submitted to:

<u>*Zaney Books*</u>*. Contact: Eddie Torr. Sent: 14 January 2010. Acknowledged 23 January 2010. Reminder letter: 1 March 2010. Material returned: 1 April 2010. Editor commented: 'It's too zany for us.'*

<u>*Animal Crackers Publishing*</u>*. Contact: C Lion. Sent: 2 April 2010. Mat. retd. 11 April 2010 with comment: 'We've decided to publish only picture books.'*

File your submission details any way you find useful, in alphabetical or month order or whatever, just so you can keep track of what's where and when a reminder letter could be sent. Note the dates in a works diary on your computer, and set pop-up reminders to let you know when to make follow-up enquiries. Your submission file should also include any information that might be useful. For example, you now know that Animal Crackers Publishing is only looking for picture books. Maybe you could write one for them?

If your contact, Eddie Torr moves to another publisher before you've sold *The Zany Zoo*, it will also remind you that he has seen it before. He might want to see it again if he is now commissioning books about zoos, but if *The Zany Zoo* has been doing the rounds for a year without being sold, he might wonder why no one else has bought it. In which case, send him something else.

MULTIPLE SUBMISSIONS?

Impatient? Want to cut corners? Want to cover all the bases? Here's our handy three-stage method of how not to do it:

Stage one: Hand write an all-purpose letter headed 'Dear Publisher'.

Stage two: Copy this letter and send or email it off to a whole bunch of publishers at the same time, along with a few pages of your typescript or a link to a website. Accidentally cc all the addresses in the world of publishing on your email so that the each recipient knows they have not been carefully selected.

Stage three: Enroll in an origami course so you have something constructive to do with all the rejection letters that you'll get back, or twiddle your thumbs while listening to the silence of an empty email inbox.

Our point being that there's no way of cutting corners in publishing. Publishers like to feel special; they get all huffy and irked if they think you've sent your manuscript or project off to anyone else at the same time. They like to feel chosen. Never send a photocopied submission letter. Print or type a fresh one out for each publisher, no matter how time-consuming this may seem.

If you really can't bear to wait, or if one publisher seems to be taking an unreasonable length of time considering your work, then send your work to no more than three publishers in total. If you feel the need to do this, then make a careful note of who has what, and when they got it, in your index system. If you're not careful, you could end up in a terrible and potentially embarrassing and damaging muddle.

COPYRIGHTING YOUR WORK

There's obviously no way of copyrighting ideas or concepts (meaning an idea thought or spoken about) but as soon as you commit your idea to paper it's automatically a tangible thing which is now your own copyright. If you really feel the need additionally to protect the copyright in your work, then by far the simplest way is to post it to yourself. Seal your project in an envelope and take it off to the post office. Ask the staff to date stamp it across the sealed flap, and ask for a certificate of posting.

When you receive the package through the mail, don't open it. Store it away safely somewhere unopened. If you are feeling especially nervous, you could even store it with your bank or with your solicitor, although you will most likely have to pay for this additional security. If you think you have a potentially multimillion-dollar idea, and are concerned that it could be stolen, the additional expense may seem worth it. Should it then ever become necessary to prove that you were the first person to write down this idea, then the unopened and date-stamped envelope should provide sufficient proof when opened, for instance, in court.

Things to remember

Before you finally submit your finished work, check out the following.

KEEPING IDEAS SAFE

Don't go around explaining all your best ideas to people. Get them down on paper first, and then keep them to yourself. Any other medium (a computer disk, for example) is easily alterable, or could become corrupted or wiped, and is nothing like as safe as a sheet of paper in a secure place.

PLAGIARISM

Stealing other people's copyrighted ideas is called plagiarism. It means you've copied or used another person's work without permission. If you want to quote other people, or copy their artistic style, always seek permission first. Otherwise someone, somewhere, someday may knock on your door with a legal action.

Copyright is an involved and specialist branch of law, and becoming more so all the time. There are books available on the subject and experts in the field. If in doubt, *always* seek advice from an 'intellectual property' lawyer or copyright consultant.

LIBEL, DOUBTFUL TASTE AND OTHER THINGS

Libel is another subject that we don't have the space to cover at any length here. Children's books have been withdrawn from public bookshelves because of libel action. The neighbour you hate and who you included as a nasty character in your children's novel may well recognize himself or herself. They may also have little difficulty proving it to a court. Your characters and situations might well come from real life, but use your common sense and imagination to mix them up into unrecognizable and untraceable people and events.

You can also create expensive trouble for yourself, in terms of reputation as well as money, if you pretend to be someone or something you are not. Never claim to be a university professor in an attempt to impress a publisher. Don't pretend to be a child prodigy if you're a grandparent.

Your publisher will most likely edit out any unsuitable language, situations or views you may hold which could upset others. These days, book contracts contain extensive libel and other warranty clauses. Check your facts if you're going to be contentious, and be moderate and sensible in other areas, for example, cooking recipes and scientific experiments must include clear safety instructions and guidelines. You don't want an angry mob and a gang of reporters on your tail because a child has been hurt by doing something you suggested in your 'How to learn chemistry at home' book. You don't want a child to be hurt *at all*.

TRADEMARKS

If you come up with a great character or concept (or even in this case a title or name) which you want to protect more firmly than can be done by copyright, then you may wish to consider having it trademarked. There are specialist trademark agents who will do this for you, at a price, or you can do it yourself – in much the way that it is theoretically possible for you to negotiate your own house sale or purchase, if you have the time, diligence and patience. The best place to start your research into this subject may be the government trademark website on the internet, or you could try a reference library or an up-to-date writers' reference book.

Agents

You might think employing an agent as a go-between for you and a potential publisher is a waste of time. If you know the publishing business inside out, you might be right. But if you're just starting out, an agent might be just what you need.

In the publishing world there are literary or authors' agents, illustrators' agents, theatrical agents, merchandising agents and so on. These are specialists who know every detail of the field in which they work.

Of course, they don't work for free. On average, an authors' agent will take between ten and 25 per cent of basic commission as well as asking you to sign a contract making them your sole representative. An illustrators' agent may take 25 to 50 per cent, and a merchandising agent from 40 to 60 per cent.

'No way!', you may think, but bear in mind that 80 per cent of something is a lot more than 100 per cent of nothing. And that may be the choice you are faced with, as many publishers these days don't even look at unsolicited work unless it has come to them via an agent. There's a practical reason for this: publishers don't have the time or the staff to go through heaps of unsolicited material. At least when they agree to look at a manuscript or project recommended to them by an agent, they know that someone in the business has already seen it and thinks it's worth publishing. An agent will have a reputation to protect, so they're not going to send half-baked ideas to a publisher – and the commissioning editors know this.

The problem is that it's not much easier to be picked up by an agent than it is to get published. But there is a difference. If an agent thinks you have potential, they may well be prepared to spend time helping you to improve your chances of publication. The big publishing houses hardly ever do that. If an agent agrees to try to take on a piece of work by you, then they must think they can sell it.

You'll be able to find the names of agents on the internet or in a writer's reference book, or the Authors' Agents Association, or by meeting them at book talks, book societies or conferences. Another way could be to write a brief, polite letter to a publisher who handles the kind of work you're producing, and ask them if they could recommend any agents to you. (If you do try this route, remember to supply a stamped, self-addressed reply envelope.)

You should submit your work to an agent in exactly the same way as you would to a publisher, but first of all ensure that the chosen agent accepts unsolicited manuscripts. Many agents these days have a full client list and are unable to expand that list.

If an agent does show interest in your work, do ask for a copy of their commission schedule. This will outline their commission percentages and detail any extra charges, say, for emergency delivery or copying. Commission will be deducted only from work they act for and sell on your behalf. These details will usually be contained in an Agency Agreement.

An agent who likes your work will want to arrange a meeting with you, if it's at all possible. (Not so much if you're in Hong Kong and they're in Chicago.) This might be the first time you meet a professional face to face, so it should be an interesting and useful experience for you.

Remember, this may turn out to be a career-long relationship. Agents tend to stay in one place, unlike most publishing editors. Your agent may well end up as a friend, confidant, editor, accountant and security blanket as your career progresses.

If you sign up with an agent, you can expect editorial advice, representation, legal and contractual negotiations, invoicing and chasing of monies and royalties, mediation, as well as information on work required by publishers which may be suitable for your talents. They will also work to make sure you get at least the market rate for your work.

An agent will also be able to go over the contract and check that everything is okay. Things can go wrong, and you're not likely to notice if an error or glitch has crept into the fine print of your contract. An agent should spot that kind of thing at once.

So: do you need an agent? Here's a checklist to help you decide.

▶ *Are you clued up on the ever-changing world of publishing and contractual law?*
▶ *Do you know what to do if you're having problems with a publisher?*
▶ *Are you an expert accountant?*
▶ *Do you understand how the royalty system works?*
▶ *If the answer to any of those questions is no, then maybe you need an agent.*

10 THINGS TO REMEMBER

1 *Make your proposal/presentation look professional – number each page of your script or proposal.*

2 *Have the right materials for your package – good-quality white A4 paper, black ink etc.*

3 *Make your submission letter of introduction polite and brief. Double check for spelling errors and omissions. Enclose a stamped addressed envelope if you want your work returned.*

4 *Include a stamped addressed acknowledgement card. Your recipient may have the resources to send this, but they may not.*

5 *Find out the name of the relevant commissioning editor to whom you should send your proposal from website or directory details.*

6 *Don't forget to include your name and address. Add your name as a header or footer to each page of work in case the package comes apart.*

7 *Decide when and how to date your work.*

8 *When the envelope has gone off, keep working on new projects while you're waiting.*

9 *Create an index record system so you know who has what, and when they got it, but don't chase for news to early, or too often. Busy people could suspect you could be a hassle and just return your material unread.*

10 *Think about whether you might need an agent. Approach them in the same way that you would a publisher.*

10

Dealing with rejection

In this chapter you will learn:
- *how to cope when a publisher rejects your work*
- *the importance of addressing constructive criticism to improve your writing skills.*

> *I had a meeting with a commissioning editor of a large and well-known publishing house to discuss my first book. I was told that they were interested in it but that they thought it needed a different title and a lot of rewriting. I agreed to make all the required changes – but a few weeks later, when I resubmitted the manuscript I found that the editor who had liked the book no longer worked there and no one else was interested in it. The book was rejected. It took approaches to a further six publishers before it found a home! You just have to accept that these things will happen.*

The closer you get to the possibility of publication, the harder it may seem to jump those final hurdles, and the more annoying, stressful and depressing it will be if you are ultimately a victim of circumstances and get rejected ... yet again. There are plenty of things that could go wrong between an editor showing interest in your book, and your book appearing on bookshop shelves.

An economic situation might force your publisher into rethinking their output – and you, the new kid on the block, might be the first to be cut from the list. A new editor might take over from the one you've been working with (the major publishing houses can feel a little like the editors are playing an endless game of musical chairs), and the new editor might insist on changes you're either not able to make or not willing to make, or your work is just not their cup of tea. The publishing house might get taken over by a larger corporation with resulting staff and lists being cut. The plot of your book may be negatively impacted by a real or tragic event in the outside world – and the timing of your publication is delayed or even cancelled as it might be seen as insensitive. For example, your book might be about a pop group or famous celebrity, and something happens to them, either tragic or that makes them inappropriate as role models to young people. Events like these are way beyond your control, and any one of them could stampede your book into the ground. But let's go back a step or two. Let's imagine an editor has shown initial interest in your book, and asked you to send it in. A few tantalizing, crazy-making weeks go by, filled with hope and expectation and possibly a lot of praying to whichever deity you trust in. Then one day, you get a parcel. Your book has been rejected.

One thing you can be sure of – the rejection letter will usually be very polite. In the world of publishing, everything is done with a smile. The cut-throat nature of the business is hidden behind a thick veneer of courteous and respectful behaviour and of glib and gushing compliments – and it can be tricky sometimes to get behind the facade and work out exactly what is going on.

In order to get some idea of why your work has been rejected, you really need some basic understanding of the way that the world of publishing actually functions. To get some insight into this, here's a reminder to make sure you've taken a look at books like *Inside Book Publishing* (4th edition) by Giles Clark and Angus Phillips. They will give you a broad understanding of who does what, when, where and why in publishing, as well as offering an extended bibliography and a lot of useful addresses and links.

So, how come you've been rejected?

The commissioning editor of the publisher you made contact with liked the idea enough to want to read it. Then you got it back. Unwanted. Let's find out what went wrong and why.

The first thing you need to understand is that your book was probably handed over to a junior editor for a first report. Your manuscript might even have been read by an intern or someone on unpaid work experience, or a freelance reader or someone brought in especially to help with a large backlog of work, or even the receptionist who happens to have a spare five minutes.

Face it, your unsolicited manuscript is not going to be on the top of the editor's priority heap. It may be read 'in-house' (that is, by someone on the publisher's pay roll), or it may be sent out to an outside 'reader' or possibly two, if you are lucky. This reader will be someone whose opinion is trusted by publishers and who will be given a set fee for their report on your manuscript. They may be a teacher with known experience on the subject you've written about, or a freelance editor or some other well-read person whose views have some weight with the publisher. The idea is that this reader will give as objective an opinion of your work as is possible.

If your manuscript is given to an outside reader, then you have to bear in mind that it might have been mailed to them, read by them, reported on by them, and sent back to the publisher again. That's a few weeks gone. And if the reader's report is undecided, the book may be sent out again. Six weeks can easily slide past while all this is going on.

Maybe the commissioning editor who asked to look at your book totally adores it – but you're not home yet. That editor has to present your book to the kind of committee we mentioned in Chapter 1 – and they are going to be on it like hungry sharks. They'll want to know whether your books can be fitted into their marketing strategies, whether it 'rides the Zeitgeist' (publisher's speak for 'jumping on the bandwagon'), whether it can be produced reasonably cheaply, and whether it will make big bucks quickly.

These acquisition meetings probably only happen every couple of weeks, often only once a month. You're not going to hear back from your editor until after that meeting has taken place. Your script could be out of your sight for quite some time, but this is not a reason to worry. In fact, if your manuscript comes back to you very quickly, attached to what looks like a standard, impersonal letter, then the chances are that one of the following has happened: your manuscript has not been looked at; your manuscript has only been glanced at; you have chosen the wrong publisher; your material is way off-target; or the editor hated it and is simply being polite.

Such a letter will read:

> *Thank you for the submission of your script, but I am afraid it is not suitable for our list.*

Or:

> *I enjoyed reading your submission and found it rather sweet, however the storyline is not strong enough for our requirements.*

If you submitted a non-fiction work about capital punishment down the centuries, then the use of the word 'sweet' would suggest that the person responding has not actually read your work. And 'strong' is a frequently used word that means whatever the publisher wants it to mean, usually not a lot.

Other 'standard' rejection letters include the wording:

> *We are not looking for unsolicited scripts at the moment.*

Or:

> *We are not publishing new authors in the current economic climate.*

Your first reaction to this might be: 'The fools! I'm going to give them a piece of my mind! They need to understand the terrible mistake they've made by rejecting me!'

Seriously, folks: don't bother. If they're not interested, then they're not interested. An angry letter demanding an explanation won't make any difference, and might make it unlikely for you to get their attention for some other piece of work further down the line. Move on! Remember that publishers and agents receive hundreds of unsolicited submissions every week. Some with good snappy introductory letters, synopses and samples of the work with stamped address reply envelopes which have followed the company's submission guidelines, plus a majority which are way off mark. If the company is overworked because it's a busy time of year, then you may just get a standard rejection response.

On the other hand, a *long* rejection letter, coupled with a lengthy gap between submission and response, means the publisher liked your work. No, really – this is going to sound weird at first, but think about it. If the publisher only writes a couple of lines, it's because they don't think they have anything helpful to say. If you get two pages of criticism, apparently tearing your work to shreds, that means the editor was so impressed that they not only spent time going through your manuscript in detail, but also thought it worth while giving you the benefit of their experience and opinion.

For an author this can be a difficult thing to handle, but the more your work is criticized the better it is for you in the long run. One well-known children's author told us the following:

> *I once wrote a TV sitcom and sent it to the BBC. It came back accompanied by the following 'though there's the occasional good line, your dialogue, if literate, is too literary, and often in the form of a paperback novel. Situation comedy means what it says: comedy arising from and furthered by a strong situation. Here we have only endless conversation, mostly with the same subjects under discussion, resulting in some heavy-handed plotting of a feather-weight storyline.'*

The author responded positively, as you should in the same circumstances. He says:

Useful advice? Definitely! I'd been told I could write good lines; that I had the style of a novelist (albeit minor); and that I was literate. My writing ambition switched overnight. There were still plenty of failures to come – but it was a turning-point for me.

Readers' reports

Your rejection letter will probably be signed by the commissioning editor, but that doesn't mean he or she actually read your book. They are just as likely to be quoting from a reader's report. In fact, if your work is non-fiction, it is more than likely that your work will have been read by a third party with some expertise in the field. If the report is constructive, the editor may send you a copy. This can be very helpful; just remember that it wasn't intended for you to read, so don't take any criticism too harshly.

If the book is fiction, the reader's report will include a brief summary of the plot. Then it will cover strengths and weaknesses, comment on particular points the author needs to look at again, and then end with a brief verdict. This could be the suggestion that the book has potential, but needs some major rewriting, or that it's such a mess that it's beyond all hope. On the other hand, the report might tell the editor that this book is exactly what they've been looking for.

If the rejection letter mentions that the editor liked your work and that they would like to see other work by you, then you can feel you've scored a hit. This is a huge step forward for you. It means that although this particular book wasn't right for them, they were impressed enough by your writing skill or concept to want to see more.

This publisher is worth following up.

If you receive a helpful and reasonably lengthy rejection letter, some of which you may genuinely not understand, or if you believe the editor has completely missed the point, then a brief, professional letter or email to that editor is okay. You may be lucky and get through on the phone – but don't hassle by leaving more than one voicemail message. Write instead. Don't be surprised if you find that the editor hasn't actually read your script and that their rejection was based on someone else's recommendation. Be friendly when you approach them. Explain the problem or the misunderstanding. Editors have been known to ask an author to resubmit their material.

On the other hand, if your rejection letter is brief and definitely dismissive, you might want to take that editor off your mailing list. Try a different editor in the same publishing house, if possible. Or try a different publisher.

Exercise 33

Write a 'reader's report' of a book you have recently read.

Here are the main elements you should include:

▶ **Author:** *One author? Two? An author and illustrator?*
▶ **Word Count:** *You know how to work this out now.*
▶ **Genre:** *Horror? Teen Romance? Sci-Fi? etc...*
▶ **Target audience:** *What age-group or type of reader do you think the book is aimed at?*
▶ **Synopsis:** *One reasonably short paragraph.*
▶ **Style and storyline:** *A more detailed synopsis with positive and negative critical comments, plus any typos or other obvious problems.*
▶ **Libel or doubtful taste:** *The libel should have been taken out already, but there may be elements in the book that you think are in doubtful taste – sex or violence or bad language etc. – comment on them.*

(Contd)

- ▶ **Remarks:** *This is the place to give general comments such as 'This book is* Twilight *meets* Prince Caspian*' etc.*
- ▶ **Verdict:** *Did you enjoy reading it? Do you think it is a bestseller?*

This exercise will give you a valuable insight into how books are read and reviewed by professionals.

The returned manuscript

If your manuscript is sent back, check it carefully before you mail it to anyone else. Make sure that it's all still there. Check that the pages are in the right order and the right way around. Make sure no one has left wine or coffee stains on it, or let their pet dog or cat leave footprints on it. It's also not unknown for editors to scribble uncomplimentary comments on the actual script (very rude and unprofessional, but it does happen), or accidentally leave a page of damning comments in the text. The last thing you need is for the next publisher to see that it has been read and rejected before.

If you do find scribbles or accidentally enclosed notes, steel yourself for what is said. Rejected authors who read the publisher's notes are not going to find anything pleasant or comforting. Try not to take it too much to heart. One agent we know scribbled a note to her editor, following the cold-calling of an overenthusiastic, scary and eccentric author. She realized that the work he had presented her with was not good. She wrote a note intended for her editor: 'This stuff's rubbish, the guy's bonkers, send it back at once to me with a nice thanks-but-no-thanks note.' A temporary member of staff returned the note, too, and the author was quickly back in touch – not in a good way. Temporary members of staff who don't know the publishing system can be responsible for some classic mistakes, including returning only half of your material. Double-check your returned package.

Some would-be writers think it's smart to check on whether their manuscript has really been read properly. They'll put a thread between the pages, or place one page in upside down or back to front. The problem with these sneaky tactics is that editors have seen it all before. They're just as likely to replace the thread and leave the pages upside down.

You need to understand that an editor won't need to read all of your manuscript to know whether it appeals to them. They'll have figured that out in a few pages. You might think this is unreasonable – that your book needs to be read as a whole. But remember what we told you in Chapter 5: grab your audience on page one. It's no good telling an editor the book doesn't really get going until chapter three. Your book needs to come out of the blocks like a sprinter. Most experienced editors or agents will know whether the whole script is worth reading by the time they've read the submission or covering letter and the first chapter or two.

Say your book has made its way successfully through the reader's report stage and has been presented to a committee at an 'acquisition meeting'. Time drags by for you. Say the committee votes in favour of your work. But maybe someone on the committee wants to go away and look at your work in more detail before making a decision. They may say they'll report back at the next meeting – and so another month slips away.

Even if your book is given the green light, more time will pass while your editor goes away to do some 'costings'. They'll need to decide how much they can afford out of their annual budget for the initial printing, artwork, design and editing. They'll need to decide what grade paper to use and whether to print in hardback first, a trade paperback, or a mass market paperback publication with all the expense of a large print-run. They'll need to decide whether it needs illustrations and who should be commissioned to do them and how much they will cost. They'll need to take a look at their long-term publishing plans and find a suitable publishing date, usually in the following year – maybe even the year after.

And then your work could be rejected for no other reason than the publisher has been caught up in a global recession, as happened in 2008.

Even if you get a letter or email telling you that the acquisition team love your work, you could still be kept hanging about for weeks while all this goes on. Your formal acceptance letter could take weeks and weeks to arrive.

This is where we stop. This chapter isn't about what happens when your manuscript/project is accepted. This chapter is about coping with rejections, so let's carry on coping. The authors we consulted said the following:

> *Don't take any notice of anyone. Just write.*

> *A degree does not mean one is automatically a writer. I had to do my apprenticeship, just like anyone else. It took me seven years to produce a saleable book.*

> *<u>Don't give up</u> if you have any signs of real encouragement from publishers. But if every returned manuscript is accompanied by a rejection slip, or a bland and vague letter, take a long hard look at your submissions.*

> *Keep at it! Writing is a craft as well as an art and needs to be practised assiduously if you want to get published.*

> *Write, write, and rewrite, however long it takes. Keep working at it until you make it.*

> *Nothing is ever wasted, because it helps build writing technique.*

Responding to positive criticism

Insight

If you've sent your book or project to three publishers and have got back three brief and impersonal rejection letters, it might be time for a rethink. Perhaps you're doing something wrong? Maybe it's time to try something new or different.

If you still have faith in your work, you could keep going for another couple of tries. If those come back you are either very unlucky, and the office junior is just sending all scripts back or, maybe you need to re-think your submission – approach it from a different angle, or aim it at a different age-range. Is it time to get more professional advice before submitting it again?

But what if you've had three longer rejection letters from publishers? What if it's clear from these letters that your work has been read and considered carefully before being sent back? And what if the letters are all saying similar things? Now's the time to take the criticisms on board. These criticisms should be seen as constructive.

You want to be published. That's the whole point of reading this book. Well, then you have to pay attention to professional opinions – whether you agree with them or not. Editors can get it wrong, but on the whole they do have a pretty clear idea of what's going on in the market and whether your work is going to sell.

Tastes and fashions change. You may have written a book that would have sold ten years ago, but no matter how brilliantly it's written, nothing that seems dated or old-fashioned will be published. A book written a year ago may no longer be fashionable, or topical. All the authors we spoke to said, 'Study the market.' All the authors said, 'Keep at it, keep on writing.' All the authors said, 'Revise and rewrite until you succeed.'

Let's say three publishers have seen your work and have rejected it for more or less the same reasons. There's no point in you sending the book out again and again without making any changes. All you'll do is spoil the market for your work. Three publishers have seen it and rejected it. You need to take a hard look at your work, and revise it before you send it off to anyone else.

Unless one of the rejecting publishers has actually asked you to revise and resubmit, there's no point in sending them a rewritten version. Send it to someone new and see what they say.

It's almost like being on a treasure hunt. The prize is publication, and all along the route you pick up clues that help you move on to the next stage. One publisher may tell you your work is far too long. You shorten it. The next publisher may tell you the language is too complicated for the target age group. You make it more straightforward. The third publisher may point out unnecessary characters and confusions in the plot line. You deal with them. See what's going on? By taking on board these constructive criticisms, you are honing your work for the market.

Insight
If you have patience, natural talent and the ability to learn from criticism, then you're well on the way to getting your name in print.

In the past, an editor might spot your potential and take time out to nurture it. Not so much these days. Time and money considerations have cut the time an editor has to work with new writers. Some publishers, media and film/TV companies are so busy that they no longer accept unsolicited material unless it has been submitted by an agent who they know will already believe it to be marketable – because successfully selling work is their business. Commissioning editors nowadays need material of a high enough quality that they could almost send it straight to the printer without even having to touch it. We did say *almost* – in much the same way that anteaters eat ants, so editors edit – they really can't help themselves. A full-time writer we spoke to said that editors were like the road crew for a rock band – they don't have the talent to make a living writing, but they want to be near the action, so they become editors. We're not saying this is true, but it's an interesting point of view from someone inside the business. Once senior commissioning editor of a large publishing house commented that no writer had ever produced a sentence that she couldn't improve. Another was of the opinion that every book needed editing; he also added that some publishers over-edit, some under-edit, but that he gets it just right. Speak to any editor, and they'll tell you exactly the same thing.

If you can't make head nor tail of the criticisms of your rejected work, then maybe this is the time to present it to one of the criticism services we mentioned earlier. Or if you're in a writers' group, maybe you should take it along for them to take a look at (if you aren't in a writers' group or class, this may be the time to join up).

Just remember that the nearer you get to possible publication, the more the criticism will be stepped up as editors start fine-tuning and adjusting your work for the marketplace.

This may be the time to approach an agent. If you have several near-miss rejection letters from different publishers, these may help to gain an agent's attention, bearing in mind that an agent will usually be better able to give you long-term advice and encouragement than a publisher. Send these letters off with your manuscript: agents understand how hard it is for a new author to get started and can read between the lines of an editor's rejection letter. They are familiar with the good old catch-22 situation: 'Come back when you've made a name for yourself and we'll publish your stuff.'

One author we know had a middle fiction humorous novel submitted to a publisher via an agent. The story revolves around a girl who wants to be a secretary when she leaves school, marry a hunky super-hero and live happily ever after. Her mum, who is a boot-wearing, green, feminist labourer, has other ideas, and her home-maker step-dad is no help at all. The first publisher who saw the script rejected it along with a disgusted two-page letter to the agent. Missing the point much? They thought it was a serious book. The second publisher telephoned to say that he thought he ought to buy the story but he hadn't been given the chance to read it yet. His staff had hijacked the script and all he could hear was shrieks of laughter.

Even among professionals, it all comes down to different strokes for different folks. One editor could hate your work, another might love it to bits. So, let's take a look next at what happens when you find an editor who loves you to bits.

10 THINGS TO REMEMBER

1 *If your work is returned, take a cold hard look at why that might be? Was it the wrong recipient, the wrong style or 'just not strong enough'?*

2 *More than one person makes buying decisions at acquisition meetings. Your work will need to please the majority. Is there anything you could do more of to achieve this?*

3 *Read between the lines of rejection letters. Is it a standard letter or card because the publisher does not have the time to deal with unsolicited work, or has it been read? Take serious note of any editorial or reader's comments.*

4 *Be patient, and be proactive. The more good pieces of work you have on submission the increased chance of someone spotting it. Luck can play a big hand.*

5 *If you get a Reader's Report, realize that an experienced reader has probably taken time and consideration to report. Value their words.*

6 *Most criticism should be useful to you in some way. Use it constructively.*

7 *Know when it's time to move on and let go of an idea. Responses to your work are subjective, but if a whole heap of rejections come back it may be simply because your work is not publishable at this time. Shelve the idea and save for another day. Nothing is ever wasted.*

8 *Check your returned manuscript. Are there any hidden notes? Can it be re-sent out, or do you need to produce a sparkling new package?*

9 *Don't be afraid to revise and rework your material.*

10 *If you believe you've done the best you can and the work is the best it can be, research your target market and resubmit.*

11

Acceptance

In this chapter you will learn:
- *how to react to an offer from a publisher*
- *about the complexities of contracts, royalties and rights*
- *about the publishing process*
- *about forming a relationship with an editor.*

You've written something which you believe to be marketable, you've targeted the right publisher, you've submitted a professionally presented proposal – as per the submission requirements for that company or as we've suggested. An editor or employee has spotted the merits of your work and asked to read the whole thing. They've had their reports and discussed the book with colleagues. They've suggested a few revisions and you've reworked all those revisions and more, and delivered the book back to their satisfaction. They then may have asked to meet you – to see if you and they could work well together. Or, they have wanted to know what else you have been writing, what your goals are, and what it is about you and your ideas which could be marketed in such a way that your work is going to have a chance of selling in viable quantities, and then...

The Scene. A room in a house. Anywhere. Anytime.

FX: Phone rings.

Hope picks up.

HOPE: Hello?

EDDIE: Hello, there. Could I speak to Hope, please?

HOPE: Speaking.

EDDIE: Hi! It's Eddie Torr, here. I have some wonderful news for you! I took your book to our acquisitions meeting this morning, and I'm thrilled to be able to tell you that everyone totally loved your work and we really want to publish it!

FX: Thud of Hope hitting the floor unconscious.

It's going to happen something like that: a phone call out of the blue to tell you that all your hopes, desires and dreams have finally come true. Maybe you're not the collapsing unconscious type, maybe you'd prefer to run around the room, screaming. Or there's the running down the street screaming option. A big favourite with new authors is calling your friends and family and screaming down the phone at them. Or you could opt for just standing there, clutching the phone and screaming at Eddie.

Whatever works for you.

> *I entered a competition with the opportunity of getting published by a real publisher. The organizer rang. I thought: Here it comes, thanks but no thanks – if I'd won, they'd write. Then she said 'We'll be writing to you, but I thought I'd give myself the pleasure...' I've no idea what she said after that. I didn't come down to earth for weeks, I was walking around 6 inches off the floor and singing 'I've won the competition, I've won the competition.' The kids moaned, 'Mum, stop that. We know!'*

Insight

Keep your feet on the ground. This phone call is not a signed contract. It's an *offer*. Many things could still go wrong, and

(Contd)

sometimes they do. There's a big gap between Eddie calling you up and a parcel of printed and bound books arriving at your door.

There's a true story of an author being promised he could expect a six-figure sum as an advance for his first book, and on that basis he sold his house and put in a bid for a bigger one. Some agonizing months later, his book was rejected, and no one else wanted to buy it.

Next you need confirmation of this offer. Tell Eddie you're looking forward to his offer *in writing*. This is really important. What if Eddie goes sick? What if he gets chewed up and spat out in a company 'downsize'? What if he gets hit by a truck? Who else knows about the offer – how can you prove it ever happened?

The letter should look something like this:

Dear Hope

THE EGG-WHISK'S REVENGE

Subject to contract

I am delighted to be able to make you an offer for the above title which we propose publishing in our My First Book series in the spring of 20XX. We all think this is a wonderfully imaginative and well-crafted story.

I can offer an advance of ££$$ payable as to half on signature of the contract and half on first publication against royalties of X per cent of the published price on paperback copies sold in the home market, and X per cent on copies sold for export. We require World Volume rights.

I do hope this offer is acceptable and look forward to hearing from you. I will then arrange to have the contract drawn up as soon as possible.

With best wishes,

Eddie Torr

Senior Commissioning Editor

There are things in the letter you probably won't understand. That's not important right now. What is important is that this letter will most likely lead directly to your book getting published.

Money, money, money

What exactly is an 'advance'? Let's say your publisher offers you an advance of £1,000. The actual offer may say something like: 'an advance of £1,000 set against a royalty of ten per cent of the published price of the hardback edition for home sales.' (Home sales means sales in the domestic market – the country usually where you and your publisher are based; export sales means sales of the book in the home language but in other countries, and foreign sales means sales of the book which has been translated into other languages.)

This £1,000 is the amount of money you'll be paid in advance of any actual sales of copies of the book. You'll be asked to sign a contract. We'll come to that in a while. The advance may come to you as, say, £500 when both you and the publisher have signed the contract, and a further £500 on publication of the book. This money is paid in acknowledgement of the work you've already done in producing the book. So long as you fulfil your part in the deal as set out in the contract, this money is yours to keep.

PUBLISHED PRICE AND ROYALTIES

The published price referred to in the offer is the recommended retail price. Say your book sells for £10 in the home market (the country where you live or where the book is first published).

For every copy of your book sold at £10, you will be entitled to a 'royalty' of ten per cent, in this case, £1. However, the £1,000 advance you receive is an advance 'set against a royalty of ten per cent.' That means you will not see any more money until enough £1s have accumulated to cover the £1,000 advance. Which therefore means, in this case, that 1,000 copies of your book have to be sold before you will see any royalty money. Your actual contract will be a whole lot more complicated than that.

Okay, you've had the publisher's offer and you've read the rest of this chapter so you know what glitches to look out for. Happy? Fine. Now you need to reply to your editor, also in writing and on paper. You should accept the offer and say something along these lines:

Dear Eddie,

Re: THE EGG-WHISK'S REVENGE

Thank you for your letter dated XXXX regarding your offer to publish the above title in your My First Book series. I am pleased to accept the offer as outlined, subject to contract.

I look forward to receiving and considering the contract in due course, and to working with you.

With all good wishes,

Hope

Insight

Obviously every book and every offer letter will be different, and you're reply will need to be changed to fit the circumstances, but the basic wording you need to include is 'I accept the offer as outlined' and 'subject to contract'. This will give you an opportunity to examine the contract and perhaps negotiate some changes before you commit yourself.

The same thing applies at this stage if you are being offered a 'flat-fee' payment (a flat fee is a single payment without royalties). In this case, the offer letter from the publisher might look like this:

> *We would be delighted to include your text piece on THE HISTORY OF EGG-WHISKS in our Encyclopaedia of Kitchen Utensils.*
>
> *We will pay a flat fee of £$£ for your 800-word contribution upon delivery and acceptance of the text, for exclusive rights in all languages, all forms, editions, versions and adaptations throughout the world, and an acknowledgement will be given to you in the front of the book. We aim to publish in October 20XX, and will give to you one copy of the title upon publication.*
>
> *Please sign the attached copy of this letter where indicated as acceptance of our terms.*

In this case, the payment for your contribution is all the money you will receive. Because the publisher wants exclusive rights throughout the world, they can sell as many copies as they like, in whatever form, and you can't sell that piece of text anywhere else. Make sure you understand all the detail, the meaning, and the consequences of this letter. If you are happy with this, sign and date the copy of the letter and return it to the publisher.

'We all love it!'

What if Eddie tells you that although everyone is very enthusiastic about your book, they'd like you to make some specific changes before they're prepared to make you an offer?

This kind of approach might go something like this:

> *We all really loved your story about the little girl who didn't get the egg-whisk for Christmas, but we all thought it*

would work a whole lot better if she DID get the egg-whisk, and that it was a birthday present rather than a Christmas present. And does the main character have to be a little girl? We all felt that a little gerbil would work much better. What do you think?

You might think, 'No way!' You're perfectly entitled to respond that way, especially if you think your story is about to be changed beyond recognition.

But it's unlikely that the suggestions will be as radical as that. It's more likely, for instance, that if you've set your story around a Christmas party, the editor might suggest you make it a birthday party instead. Why? Because it's not easy to sell a book about a Christmas party in midsummer – but you can sell a book about a birthday party all year round. It may be the story would sell successfully to some overseas countries – but they don't celebrate Christmas as a big holiday festival. You need to ask yourself if the story still works despite the changes, or if it all falls apart. If the former, why not go with it? If the latter you can still call it quits at this stage and walk away.

But think long and hard before you turn your back on the offer. You may still have your Christmas party book – but who's going to benefit from it? Not the children who might have enjoyed your book if it had been published. Be tough, be realistic. You want to be published: bending a little at this stage will help you in the long run.

Perhaps you can negotiate the changes with your editor? If a snowy landscape is really vital for the story to work, then maybe the birthday party can take place in midwinter? Then the editor doesn't have to worry about the company trying to market a Christmas book in summer, and you get the weather you wanted. Listen to the reasoning, and if you can't see the point, make your case to the editor. Be assertive – you are the author and creator – but don't be aggressive. If it comes to a face-off, the editor always has the power to pull the plug – they believe they know what will sell and what won't. You want to have your books sold and you don't want to get a reputation for being difficult.

Revising your work

Let's say you've agreed to take your manuscript away and do some revising. The editor will probably send you a letter or an email telling you what they'd like you to do. If your book is on a computer file by this stage, they'll add their comments and suggestions in among the script – usually in blue or red type as tracked changes – and they may even put lines through sections that they think should be taken out. If it's on paper, they may attach Post-it® notes to relevant pages or even make pencilled suggestions in the margins along with a very detailed letter. Make sure you understand exactly what they want you to do before you start. If some of the comments seem a little vague or confusing, give the editor a call, or send an email asking for more explanation.

Before you start revising, make sure you keep your original version intact, either as a clean paper copy or as an unedited and unrevised file. If you're working on a computer, which you probably will be by now, just copy the file, rename one 'EGG WHISK Original' and the other 'EGG WHISK Working Copy'. Chances are by now you have three different EGG WHISK files – the original, the one with editorial notes, and the working copy. Leave the first two intact – work only with the third one – that way you always know what the book looked like before the changes, and you'll also have a clear idea of exactly what the editors asked for, because as you go through revising, you'll obviously be taking out the editorial comments as you go along.

Insight

It's useful to keep an untouched original, because editors will often make what they consider to be 'minor' changes without

(Contd)

even telling you, and you need to be able to go back to the original book if you spot phrases or sentences that you know you didn't write.

One writer we spoke to told us that extra lines were added to a scene in his first book because the copy editor thought it improved the look of the page concerned. It's also possible that words and sentences and entire paragraphs can vanish – especially when the editor is working on a computer file. A slip of the fingers, and quite big chunks of prose can be deleted in an instant. An original copy, backed up on a memory stick or CD will prevent mistakes like this from becoming disasters.

REWRITE AND RESUBMIT

Rewriting and resubmitting your work may not be the end of the road. Your editor might like what you've done so far, but he might also think you need to take another swing at it. You might well get another batch of editorial comments to work on. If this happens, try to look at it in a positive way. The editor has a specific market in his mind – he just wants to make sure the book works as well as possible. Nit-picking to you is polishing to him. Open yourself a new working file ('EGG WHISK Working Copy 2') and see if you can give him what he wants. It's part of your writing learning curve, and you can still negotiate if this second batch of changes doesn't work for you.

DEVELOPMENT MONEY

If at this stage your editor is still asking for major changes (and assuming you've agreed to do them), it wouldn't be unreasonable of you to ask for some 'development' money. This is a payment that you get to keep if the publisher finally decides the book just isn't working. If the publisher does finally accept your work after two or three rounds of rewrites, then that money will be usually be deducted (or offset) from the advance or flat-fee offer they then make.

There's no guarantee that your editor will agree to pay development money to an author (though it is much more likely for an illustrator who is trying to give an editor the style they seek), but if you're going to put in a lot of work, plus have your hopes raised, and possibly still face the ultimate rejection of your work, then you're entitled to try for some sort of compensation. It will also show you just how committed the publisheris to you.

Once everything is in writing and the editor is happy with your revised book, you'll get a 'contract'. If you're working through an agent, they'll be able to sort out all the fine print and do all the negotiations on your behalf, but it is still useful for you to understand a little of what goes on behind the scenes.

Contract time

When you are sent the formal offer letter, the editor will also arrange for a contract to be sent to you. Depending on the publisher, the contract may be negotiated and drawn up by the editor, a contracts department or a freelance contracts consultant. You could wait some time before receiving the legal documentation. Progress could also be delayed by the type of contract the publisher uses. It could be a simple, single-page document or a standard 20-pager (often referred to as a 'boiler plate' contract). Or it could be an incredibly complicated, closely typed, 40-page chunk of paper, in which your book is called a 'media-neutral format product'. Unless you're up on legal terminology, you're probably not going to understand all of it.

NEVER SIGN ANYTHING YOU DON'T UNDERSTAND

....
Insight
If you don't understand legal jargon then we suggest you seek advice before accepting an offer, or signing a contract or contractual letter.
....

The benefit of having an agent (or a media contract advisor) at this point is that part of the agent's job is to understand the small print and make sure you're getting the best and fairest possible deal.

There are books available on contracts and copyright, and information in writers' reference books and on the internet, but unless you're sure you can take this kind of information on board quickly, and keep up to date on legal changes as and when they happen, then you must seek the advice of published authors, authors' societies, writers' advice centres or groups. Your best bet is to find yourself a book publishing and media contracts and copyright expert. Paying for expert advice at this stage can save you money in the long term. Don't be tempted to cut corners by consulting your family solicitor. Unless they're experts in the specifics of publishing contracts and intellectual property law, they probably won't be able to unravel the jargon and terminology any better than you can. Plus, how would they know what a fair offer was, anyway?

Insight

It's not easy for an inexperienced person to negotiate points in their first contract. You may even be so excited by the prospect of getting into print that you'll sign anything. Take a breath. Step back and think about your long-term writing future.

There is very likely going to be a clause in your contract allowing the publisher 'first refusal' of your next work. ('First refusal' means they must be allowed to see your next work and consider whether to publish it before anyone else can see it.) What if you decide you never want to work with them again, but you've tied yourself to them for your next work? They could hang onto this work for months or make a really lame offer. What can you do about that? What if your next piece of work isn't suitable for this publisher? What if another publisher contacts you with a better deal? You need to think about these things before you sign that contract.

I was offered a deal for a series of books, but the contract stipulated that I had to give the publisher 'first refusal' of my next work – and also stipulated that I could not present further work to the publisher for two and a half years! My agent renegotiated this for me, cutting the time down to six months.

Your offer from the publisher could be a flat-fee payment to use your short story exclusively in an anthology for a specified period of time. The offer may be non-exclusive, which means you can sell the story again, say, to a magazine, even while it is still available in the anthology. The offer could be for an advance giving the publisher the right to sell your book in one language throughout the world, or it may be for all languages and all media throughout the world, beyond the world, and forever. (We're not kidding with this 'beyond the world' stuff. Some publishers do now ask for rights throughout the cosmos. Think about it – we may not be that far from a manned moonbase. Who has the rights to books sold on the moon, or audio book downloads transmitted from antennae on Mars?)

Back on earth, you may or may not be entitled to a share of additional sales made from translation of your work into another language, audio versions, television, films, merchandise and so on. Even if you do get a share, the percentage may not be as generous as it should be. If you don't know what counts as a fair and reasonable offer or contract, if you don't understand what every clause actually means, then you can't make a good judgement. Your publisher wants to make money, as much as possible, and you don't want to give away your entitlement to the money that might be earned if the book became the next media phenomenon.

We asked some contracts and copyright experts (including publishers, consultants and society advisers) for their comments:

The trouble with most authors is that they don't ask any questions about contracts. The usual remark is along the lines of, 'It looked so official I assumed it must be okay.' Alternatively, they consult their own solicitor who has never seen an author contract before and who asks a mass of niggling little questions. Some authors then try to change the basic terms of a contract once it arrives: 'Yes, I know I agreed to a seven per cent royalty but I've heard that ten per cent is more normal.' Please point out that such things should be agreed before contract stage.

No one ever asks me anything, except what 'special editions' means.

Children's authors often ask me why their royalties tend to be lower than those for other trade books. They also get confused over collaboration with illustrators, and the implications of electronic rights.

A contract is a legally binding document. Even if a publisher says, 'This is our standard contract' or the contract is (or appears to be) printed, contracts are negotiable. If in any doubt, consult a specialist. That almost certainly does not include your local solicitor.

Most authors will confess to never actually reading their contracts properly, if at all, when pressed!

We also asked these same experts if they could give us a few instances of unusual experiences with contracts. Check these out:

The blind author whose contract expected him to read and correct proofs.

The Australian author who was expected to return corrected proofs to the UK publisher within seven days of their dispatch to the author.

The commissioned illustrator whose contract obliged her to deliver her material two weeks prior to the date of the contract (thus putting her in breach as soon as she signed it).

The agent whose contract provided for the advance to be on account of 'the aforementioned royalties' but the royalty clause came after the advance clause (the page was reprinted before the contract went off!).

The publisher's contract commissioning an author to write a work which contained a clause stating that the contract was null and void if the author had not delivered the typescript prior to signing.

Spend! Spend! Spend!

You might well be yelling: 'Show me the money!' by this stage. Hey, we've come this far together – let's keep our cool and we'll all get there safe and sound. Think back to when your editor first sent you the offer. You completely understood and agreed to the terms in the contract; you've signed and returned the contract, you've received a copy back, countersigned by the publisher for you to keep safely. You may be required to supply an invoice along with your contract if you are being paid a flat fee. Your invoice should contain similar information to the following:

INVOICE no. 111

Date:

To: Eddie Torr   From: (your name and address)
Senior Commissioning Editor
(address)

Payment due on delivery and
acceptance of short story
entitled WHAT IS IT WITH ALL THESE EARWIGS? By

B. Tell   £1,000

Total: £1,000

PAYMENT ON RECEIPT OF INVOICE

If you're a UK resident registered for value added tax, or need to include any other information, then add it to the bottom of the invoice.

It could take six weeks for the publisher's accounts department to send you the cheque for the money due on signature of the contract. (Or, increasingly, UK publishers make payments by BACS – direct bank-to-bank transfers.) Several different people in a publishing house may have to authorize a payment before it can be made. If you're working with an agent, then add a week or two on to this time, as your cheque will be sent to the agent first in order that they can check the details, ensure the payment clears, note their records system, and subtract their commission before you get the balance.

It could take several months between the contract arriving, being signed and the money due on signature of the contract turning up. Don't panic that the deal has fallen through, as in some circumstances, where major revisions are needed or there are lengthy contract negotiations, this could take months. Meantime, the title has been changed, the book jacket redesigned, and the proposed publication date delayed. You're unlikely to have to wait that long, but it's as well to remember that writing is not a great way to get rich quick – and for any five names of wealthy writers you can come up with, we could name five thousand whose income from writing is less than the minimum wage.

Things don't speed up much once you've earned your advance payment. Publishers tend to make up their accounts every six months. Some even do it annually, particularly publishers of foreign editions. This means that the £1 coming to you for a book bought by a child in a store in January, may not actually get to you until, say, October of the same year, if the accounts are made up half-yearly, or, possibly, March of the *following* year for an annual accounts system. This really is an over-simplification but it gives you an idea.

ROYALTY STATEMENTS

Royalty statements are documents that show how your book is selling, and also show any other sales agreement payments the publisher has made. They will show a date from which the accounts are being calculated, but you may not actually receive the statement for up to four months *after* this date. This statement will include things like home sales and export sales, sales at a greater discount (to book clubs, perhaps), any other income from rights sales made by the publisher (for example, large-print rights or translation rights), monies that have been held back as a reserve in case books are returned unsold from a bookseller, and possibly any deductions for copies you may have ordered at a discount for your own use. If you don't have an agent to check these statements for you, then you'll have to do some careful checking yourself or find a friendly bookkeeper who may be able to help you ensure everything is in order. As well as your writing file, you will now need a paperwork file for correspondence, contracts and royalty statements. File it under the title of the published work.

These statements of accounts are usually accurate, but mistakes can creep in. If you have any doubts, your contract should entitle you, or someone on your behalf, to examine the publisher's books. If you have any other worries, including payment delays, an author's society may be able to advise you how next to proceed.

Rights

There are a variety of other ways in which you and the publisher can earn money from your book, and these include the selling of 'rights'. Here are some examples of potential rights sales areas:

- ▶ *hardback, trade paperback, mass-market paperback editions*
- ▶ *anthology rights*
- ▶ *first serial rights (for newspapers or magazines)*

- ▶ *translation rights*
- ▶ *large print (books for those with impaired vision)*
- ▶ *audio (single-voice readings, or dramatized readings)*
- ▶ *radio, television, film, video and so on for dramatization*
- ▶ *animation*
- ▶ *merchandising (everything from greetings cards to curtains)*
- ▶ *electronic (computer games, online downloads, e-book and so on).*

If you don't have an agent to sell these rights for you, or if you don't know how you would go about selling them for yourself, then the best people to try to sell them are your publishers. If you have any helpful suggestions or contacts, the rights sales people would be glad to hear of them.

Surviving the edit

You'll be working closely with an editor. This may not be the person you've been corresponding with so far (probably the senior commissioning editor). Once your work has been accepted for publication, you may find yourself working with an editor holding a less senior position.

This editor, who will now be your front-line contact with the publisher, will probably check your revisions and be the person you exchange emails with and speak to on the phone. (Chances are the Senior Commissioning Editor is off signing someone else up by now.) This new editor may also be looking for an artist if your book is being illustrated.

ILLUSTRATIONS

If your work is going to be very highly illustrated, you're going to have to share your royalties with the artist, usually on a 50/50 basis, depending upon the nature of the work, and sometimes on how well known the artist is. By the way, if you're sharing royalties, the chances are that your contract is going to look even more complicated.

Some publishers will ask for your approval of a chosen illustrator, while others will assume they know best. The level of your veto should be outlined in the contract – if you have any veto at all.

Your editor may invite your comments on the work of several artists while a final decision is being made. You and the editor will be able to discuss which artist seems most suitable, but when it comes to the bottom line, unless you have an absolute contractual veto (not much chance of that), the editor will have the final say.

Once an illustrator has been chosen, the first things you are likely to see are 'roughs' – sketches of the events in the book that are going to be illustrated.

BOOK JACKETS

You'll usually be asked to approve cover artwork and design. This is an area where the publisher will believe they know best and, with their experience and the input from their sales teams, and bulk book buyers, they probably do. Your job will be to double-check that all the details of the artwork, design, cover 'blurb' and any biographical details are correct. The 'blurb' is the text usually found on the back of a book jacket, which may describe the book, and include some enticing sales points. You might also want to check at this point whether your name is being spelt correctly on the cover – and we're not joking about that, either.

PROOFS

You may not see anything again until the 'proofs' turn up. Proofs are, or are like, photocopies of how the book will look with the final layout and all the illustrations in place. If you spot that your heroine has been drawn as a gerbil, now's the time to mention it.

The proofs will come with an accompanying letter asking for your comments and giving you a specific period of time to respond. It's important that you get your comments in before this deadline; silence from you might be interpreted as approval, and the print-run could start without your input. Your editor will explain how to correct these proofs, especially when it comes to typos and similar 'copy-edit' problems.

By proof stage, the production costs are starting to rise, and your contract will probably explain how many changes you're allowed to make. This is usually about 12½ per cent, due to the time and cost involved in such changes (unless you are prepared to foot the bill yourself). This is to stop you going into a panic and wanting to totally rewrite the book at the last moment.

EDITED SCRIPTS

You may receive a copy of your manuscript edited by a copy editor and marked up for the designer or typesetter. The chances are that this is going to look like something out of your worst nightmare. Don't panic. Most of the mess covering your script is probably only instructions to the designer or typesetter about removing typing errors and unwanted indentations.

Some of the scribbles may be grammatical corrections or minor improvements in the flow of the text. If some of the editorial changes go beyond simply tidying the text or making copy-editing alterations, you may want to talk to your editor about them. If your book comes back via email, there may be hidden changes, so read it very, very carefully – and cross-reference it with your original if you spot anything strange. This is why we told you to keep your original file.

> *Being micro-edited by editers just out of uneversty who can't spel, and wouldn't kno a cool piece of prose if it bit them on the backside. I won't names names. Well, I will if you buy me a drink.*

Before you go ballistic over what they're doing to your book, take a deep breath, go for a walk or better still, leave the script overnight before you respond. Yell at your partner or a friend or the cat to get it out of your system. Then write to your editor or call or email them in a calm and polite fashion to see if some compromise can be reached. Your editor's changes might have driven you crazy – but your negative response to their suggestions might do the same right back at them. This is when things can start to get tricky. Put your position, let the editor put their position – see if a compromise can be found so that everyone goes home happy.

On the other hand, your editor might have noticed something in your book that is guaranteed to offend your potential readership. For instance, you may have characters doing a Tarot Cards reading – in the UK, this might not be a problem, but American publishers probably wouldn't let it through. Take your editor's advice and ditch it – keeping something like that in could seriously damage your sales, especially if the people being offended are the major book chains etc. If it's practical, your editor may invite you to the occasional meeting at their office, or even lunch, if you're lucky. It's worth your travel costs for the free lunch – because in a face-to-face meeting, you might be able to pitch some new ideas to your editor and gauge their response. You could come out of this kind of meeting with a better relationship and a pretty good idea of what to work on next.

I was writing a teen romance for the American market. I was told hand-holding was fine, but kissing was a tricky area, because kissing could lead to more physical intimacy and cause problems. I negotiated this and in the end I got away with a few chaste kisses. It's worth giving the editors a nudge over things like this.

I wrote a scene where the father of the main character was having a quiet glass of whiskey while watching TV in the evening at home. I was asked to change the whiskey to coffee

*because the American market frowned on any depictions of
people using 'hard liquor' in books for young people.*

Writers are a strange bunch. They often work away in solitude for
night after night and month after month, with only their pen or
computer as a companion. So when their book is finished and they
hand it over to someone else – all kinds of neuroses and traumas
can pop up. You need to get a grip before you decide to pester
your editor with daily progress phone calls or emails. This kind of
thing has exactly the opposite effect to the one you want. It will
slow things down if your editor has to talk you down off the ledge
all the time. Try to be a bit Zen about this – the journey is as
important as the arrival.

If you have a genuine problem or query and your editor seems to
spend their entire life in meetings, then write, fax or email if you
really do need a response. Calm down. Be patient. Yours is not the
only book on your editor's desk.

Troubleshooting

If something has gone wrong and you feel confident enough to
speak to the person involved, then go for it. If the problem is
particularly difficult or if you can't reach a compromise in person
or over the phone, then write to or fax or email the publisher,
making your concerns very clear. You'd probably be wise to put
this on paper – emails can get deleted or lost, and a hard copy is
going to make sure that attention is being paid.

Exercise 34

Imagine that the editor has suggested that your main
character should be changed from a boy to a girl
(or some other major change that would drive you crazy).

Write a letter, letting the editor know that you're not happy with this, and why.

Try to imagine yourself in the shoes of this editor, and receiving your letter.

Have you been diplomatic and friendly? Would you be offended by this letter?

When you have finished the letter, show it to a friend and ask how they would react if it was addressed to them.

If the reaction to this letter doesn't satisfy you, then write to the managing director and send a copy of your letter to the person you have the problem with.

Be firm in your letter, but also try to be as fair and as objective as possible. Make sure your point relates directly to your book, and hasn't been blown up by a clash of personalities or from some simple misunderstanding. If even this doesn't work, then you do have other options.

You could approach an authors' or illustrators' society, an advice centre, a media contracts expert, an agent or even a solicitor with the relevant experience in the publishing world. This advice could end up costing you money, so be sure the point you are arguing is worth it.

Just remember that publishers are heavily invested in keeping their authors happy. After all, they're spending a lot of money on that first book of yours, and if you and your publisher get on well, this could just be the first of a whole series of bestselling books.

10 THINGS TO REMEMBER

1 *Confirm your acceptance of the publisher's offer in writing.*

2 *Make sure you understand all the 'small print'.*

3 *Your first payment may be in the form of an 'advance', with further payments as royalty.*

4 *You may be offered a flat fee for your book, or part of it.*

5 *The publisher's offer may be subject to editorial changes.*

6 *When revising to editorial suggestions, respond positively and negotiate sensitively.*

7 *Read your contract carefully and never sign anything you don't understand.*

8 *Familiarize yourself with the publishing process and how long each stage could take.*

9 *Keep a copy of your original book on file to refer to if necessary during the copy-edit – you may want to check you are happy with the changes that have been made.*

10 *If you have a problem, consider the most appropriate way of dealing with it. Be firm, but try to be as fair and as objective as possible.*

12

....

Publication day – and afterwards

In this chapter you will learn:
- *what happens when your first book is published*
- *about publicity and promotion*
- *how to deal with tax demands*
- *about self-publishing.*

You've climbed Mount Everest, you've walked on the moon, you've won an Olympic Gold medal and your first book has a scheduled publication date. What do you do now?

It's a bit early to consider tax exile. You might want to think about setting up a website or joining an online forum or social networking site to promote yourself and the book. You should also be working on your next project. The first thing your publisher is going to ask is: 'What are you working on next?' You need to have an answer. You're a writer – you *should* have an answer. In fact, by the time your first book hits the stores, you should have your next book up and running.

If you want to have a career as a writer (even if only part-time), you need to jump three hurdles.

1 *Getting a publisher to read your first work.*
2 *Getting a publisher to publish your first work.*
3 *Getting a second (and third and fourth and ...) piece of work published.*

You've already jumped two of the hurdles. We don't want to rain on your parade, but word has it that the *third* hurdle is the real killer. Some authors throw so much energy and soul into their first book that they have nothing left in the tank for book two. You can understand how this happens. Your first book may have taken ten years to write – night after night in the cupboard under the stairs, or on a laptop at the launderette or in lunch breaks at work. You've thought about it and worked at it and changed it and tinkered with it forever. It includes all you best ideas and thoughts, because you couldn't bear to leave anything out.

And now there's a commissioning editor sitting across a desk from you saying, 'What's next?'

The publishers are not going to wait years for your next project – they want it right now so they can get working on it for publication 12 months on from your first book. Then they'll want your third book. And so it goes. Your young reader loves your first book, and they want to read your next and become a dedicated fan. Your sales people want to keep the promotional interest going about you.

You freak out and write something as fast as you can, and the editor says that it's not as good as the first book and of course it isn't. That took you two years – this one has been churned out in three months. The book is rejected. You have the weird feeling of being right back where you started.

Welcome to the world of the published writer.

Publication

Let's look at the day-to-day practicalities for a moment. You've seen and corrected the proofs. You've been given a publication date. The title of your book will probably have appeared, along with a picture of the cover, in your publisher's sales catalogue some six months in advance of this date. The date will have been chosen by your publisher to make sure it stands the best chance of gaining attention and selling well: for instance, a wintry tale might come out in October to attract Christmas sales. It's also traditional to publish in spring and summer (to attract summer holiday sales – sometimes called 'beach reading') and to put books out on the middle Thursday of the month. Your book may be published to coincide with an event or anniversary related to your work.

UNEDITED BOUND COPIES

A couple of months or so before publication, you may receive a bound 'unedited' copy of your book, often with a white cover. These copies are normally sent out for review purposes and to let booksellers know what's coming. Of course, it isn't actually 'unedited' – but it will perhaps contain typos and glitches and odd mistakes that will be cleared up for the real print-run. There's probably no real point in you going through this edition with a fine tooth comb – minor mistakes will be spotted by copy editors and put right. But if at this stage you notice some major problem, let your editor know about it as quickly as you can. We're not talking about plot-holes or problems like that – it's too late for those to be put right unless the book goes to a second edition. We mean technical errors – like where a paragraph has been left out, your name has been forgotten – or where chapters have been paged up in the wrong order.

ADVANCE COPIES

A finished copy of your book will usually be sent to you about six weeks in advance of the actual publication date. This is called an advance copy.

Check it thoroughly, but keep calm if you find that things are not absolutely perfect. You may find some minor errors: misspellings in the blurb, or your biography may even be missing. These things may seem like major nightmares to you, but a publisher isn't going to recall all the books and start again to correct that sort of mistake or omission – it would be too expensive. Minor problems like that will only be put right if there's a second print-run – and that isn't going to happen unless the first print-run sells out.

On the other hand, if you spot that the book jacket has been attached upside down, that pages of the text are missing or out of order, or your name has been misspelt, then these books will definitely need to be reprinted. Call the publisher immediately in case no one else has noticed.

Problems like that don't happen very often, but it's possible that the author will be the first one to spot what went wrong.

One agent said this:

> *I have seen book jackets upside down, names spelt correctly on the front cover, and incorrectly on the spine. But I once got a call from an author to say, 'Thank you for my advance copy, but the last page containing the climax of my story is missing!' Three thousand copies were promptly reprinted, at the printer's expense.*

Most recently a co-author's name was left out. You can imagine the hurt that caused, and the embarrassment to the publisher.

FREE COPIES

Your contract will explain how many free copies of your book you will be sent. You're going to feel the urge to hand them around to friends and family – and possibly to work colleagues who have been sniggering about you spending your lunch breaks in a corner, crouched over your laptop for the past 18 months.

Insight
Make sure you keep one copy for yourself of every edition. In 20 years' time you might have trouble tracking down a first edition of your first book to show your grandchildren, let alone various versions.

As well as these freebies, you'll be able to buy pretty much as many copies as you want at a discount price. But you're not supposed to sell these. If you need copies for a school talk and book signing visit or whatever, a local bookseller will provide them, or the publisher will be happy to supply you or the school with them for sale or return.

LEAD TITLES

In the publishing world, a 'lead title' is one that's going to be promoted in preference to everything else. You're not likely to be the one getting this level of attention. We know of one new author whose first 32-page picture book was published at the same time as a biography of a major celebrity. The celebrity biography hogged the media limelight for days – the new author couldn't figure out why news-hounds weren't camped out on his lawn day after day. Do not expect a champagne launch party and TV promotion.

> *I was invited as a surprise guest on a TV programme where children had been asked to review books. I was hiding behind panelling awaiting my cue while one girl finished her favourable review of my book. The presenter asked 'Would you like to meet the person who wrote the book?' 'Not particularly', she replied as the panelling sprang open and I stepped out before millions of viewers.*

You need to get things into perspective. To you, the publication of your first book may be the climax of a lifetime of ambition, but to the publisher it's just another book on their list, another chocolate Santa on the conveyor belt, another piece of the corporate jigsaw. To the wholesale buyers, it's one more title amongst the tens of thousands published in a year.

SALES AND PUBLICITY

By publication day, you should have been sent a publicity questionnaire. If you are with a large publisher, you may already have spoken to someone in the publicity department to discuss ways in which your book can be promoted.

When costs are being cut, the publicity departments are often the first to suffer. This is particularly noticeable in the publicity departments that deal with children's books, and some publishers will employ freelance publicists for special titles or a new series of titles.

Your publisher's sales team will have attended sales conferences and book fairs and will have been pre-selling titles (including yours) to bookstores, wholesalers, library buyers and so on. They will have been adding advance information to online bookstore listings and giving out advance information sheets, sometimes nine months before publication day. Hundreds or even thousands of copies may be pre-sold or subscribed (known as 'subbed') prior to the big day. These copies are not definite 'sales' though until someone actually buys them.

RETURNS

Retailers sometimes return unsold copies of books to the publisher. These will show up as negative amounts on your royalty statement. Publishers hold back a percentage of royalty money to cover this possibility. It's called a 'reserve against returns'. You'll find the exact details of how this works in your contract.

REVIEWS

Your publisher will send copies of your book to appropriate reviewers. If you're really lucky, you might get a glowing review in a magazine or a newspaper, or on the website of an online bookseller or reviewer. If this review is read by booksellers, teachers, librarians and children, it could make a big difference to your sales.

Try not to be too disheartened by a bad review. Although this will be demoralizing, remember that it's only one person's opinion, and in these days of the ever-expanding internet, we're well past the times when a single reviewer can bring a book down with a bad write-up.

You also need to remember that you can't please everyone; the fact that your book has been published, means that plenty of people have faith in it. The internet can work for you and against you in this. Check out the amateur reviews on sites such as www.amazon.co.uk – some reviewers will give a book a five-star rave-review, while others will give it one star and totally trash it. Even with huge bestsellers like *Harry Potter* or *His Dark Materials* or *Twilight*, someone is going to hate it – and they're going to say so online.

Most publishers have access to a 'cuttings' service, usually provided by a firm specializing in going through newspapers and magazines for reviews, comments or whatever. Everything they find is copied and sent to the publisher, who will forward copies to you. They may range from coverage in a local paper to mentions in national newspapers and magazines. Prepare yourself. You'll be sent the reviews whether they're good or bad.

Insight

Keep a publicity file. Good reviews and publicity might be useful later; perhaps when you contact a different publisher a few years down the line.

There isn't much space or effort made in newspapers and magazines for reviews of children's books, so don't be surprised if you don't get reviewed at all. This isn't the end of the world. Children's books, particularly the 12+ titles, have become bestsellers through word of mouth, and if children latch onto a particular book, it can quickly become a vital fashion accessory. Children also like to collect: so, if they like one title in a series, they are quite likely to buy and read the whole lot.

You may wonder why your publisher doesn't seem to be putting much effort into letting people know your book is out there. No billboards on buses. No full-page magazine advertisements. No TV spots. This is because your publisher is going to concentrate most of their publicity budget on books that they already expect to become bestsellers. It's frustrating to be on the wrong end of this policy, but you have to understand that this is the way the business works. Who knows, you might be the next big thing – in which case you'll be the one benefiting from all the publicity. If that's the case, steel yourself for a roller-coaster ride of magazine interviews, TV appearances and nationwide book-signing tours.

PRIZES AND AWARDS

Children's books attract plenty of prizes and awards every year. Your publisher will know all about these, and will know when to make submissions. You could ask your editor where they're sending copies of your books for reviewing purposes and whether there are any suitable prizes for it. Be prepared to discover that your book has not been entered because the publisher can only enter a limited number of titles – and it's just not your turn this year. Depending on timing, these prizes could be awarded in the year, or even two years, after the publication of your book. In any event the press attention and publicity surrounding the presentation of an award is guaranteed to increase sales.

Self-publicity and promotion

You may have already considered sales opportunities for your book and outlined a few when you first delivered your proposal. As publication day draws nearer, give this some more thought. Does your book have some topical angle that could attract publicity? Is there a 'hook' to hang some PR on? (PR = public relations: another way of saying publicity). Is there something in or from your life that will make the publication of your book of particular interest to the media? Does your book connect with some anniversary, event or topical issue; most books, whether fiction or non-fiction, have something about them that can be used. Alternatively something might happen by coincidence in the news that you can link your book to for some useful publicity.

Postcards with a picture of the jacket of your book on the front and a few details on the back are a really good way of spreading the word about your book around the country, as is a two-line blurb about your book and your website details if you have them as a 'signature' on all your emails.

Speak to your publisher's publicity department and see what ideas they can suggest. If you find that your publisher does not have the time or the budget for you as a first-time author, then have a go yourself. Local newspapers are often eager to write about a local celebrity – 'Local Hope Whisks Up Book Success!' – and publish a photograph of you signing books at a local library or book shop. Local radio stations may also be interested, particularly if there's an extra newsworthy angle. If your publicist is unwilling or unable to produce a press release or information sheet on your book, then think about writing or designing one yourself. First double-check that your publisher is happy for you to reproduce their book jacket in print or on the web (you don't want to breach the designer or illustrator's copyright), make photocopies and give it to any group you belong to, and email it to friends. Make it fun, make it appealing, but remember how uncontrollable the internet can be and try make sure you are targeting the right audience. It's worth setting up a search engine 'alert' with your name and book title, and searching at least once a week too to see where these details are appearing.

I occasionally Google my name, but with some trepidation. On the plus side, I may find my book reviewed by some fans on the other side of the world, or some press I didn't know about. On the down side, there might be some really bitchy comments between fellow writers on some group chat site, or my audio book illegally available for free download on a site which also advertises pornography.

A word of caution here: if you do join a writers' online chat group, be wary of writing something critical or libellous about anyone or anything. If you wouldn't say it to that person's face, or if it's untrue, don't write about it on the net. Once out there, you can't take it back, and it may haunt or damage you for years to come at the very least.

It's really scary the amount of information available about you on the web, from your date of birth from a friend's face page to the letter you wrote to the council meeting complaining about the dustbins. Then there's the embarrassing photo someone took at the local fete while you were frowning, and the quote taken out of context from a speech at a conference. You need a thick skin these days if you want to put yourself in the public eye – and even if you don't, it's almost impossible to protect your privacy these days.

Does any organization you belong to review members' books or publish articles about members' activities. Is your non-fiction book on earwigs relevant to national or local wildlife trusts?

Exercise 35

Imagine you've researched and written a story centred around the ghosts of a legendary Robin Hood-style highwayman and his young stable lad, who reputedly haunt your local highways and byways, riding their spectral horse and pony through the bars of your local pub, and who have allegedly manifested themselves to children on school visits to a nearby stately home. Do a little research and make some notes of potential publicity interest this story could attract.

Always think big, and don't forget the small and the silly ideas. Is there a local event or an annual celebration of this highwayman? Is there a TV or local news programme that might do a feature on the legend alongside interviewing you and those who claim to have seen the ghosts? Does the stately home have a bookshop?

Might the local pub have a freebie postcard rack for your promotional postcards? Would your local history group welcome a talk from you and a book signing session? How many websites (think laterally, and think diverse – local history, pony club, national heritage houses, myths and legends?) might welcome some comments from you or add reviews of your book?

Visit your local bookstore or make an appointment to meet with the person who runs the children's department. Tell them you'd be willing to visit the store and sign books for customers. If it's a story or poetry book, you could also read from it. Plenty of independent booksellers would be glad of the local press publicity from an event like that. You may have to make personal arrangements if you want a photograph taken, and in some cases, you may even be asked to do the write-up (the article) yourself for the local newspaper if there's no reporter on hand.

Signings like that don't have to be limited to bookshops, either. You could get yourself some publicity by signing copies of your book at a school fair, writers' conferences, a garden centre, supermarket or boat/ferry trip; anywhere, in fact, where books are being sold.

Signing sessions can be hit-and-miss affairs, and no one really knows why. You could sell out all the copies of your book in half an hour, or find that a huge local media blitz only results in half a dozen sales in an entire day. Still, what have you got to lose? It all means more sales, more publicity and eventually, more money.

Your library may also be interested in a visit from a local author if you are prepared to read your storybook to a group of children at a storytelling session. Contact the children's librarian for your area.

These days many authors have their own websites – so you might like to consider setting up your own site, where you can give information about yourself, update fans on your writing activities and maybe even have a questions-and-answers page. Unless you have the necessary know-how, you will probably have either to get a knowledgeable friend to set the website up for you, or pay a professional to do it – but you may find the long-term benefits are worth the expense.

And while we're talking about the internet again, go onto one of the online bookstores and write your own review of your book, or contact one of the growing number of 'amateur' reviewers to be found online. Once you plug yourself into this world, you'll be surprised at the feedback. You may be asked to do online interviews, podcasts, and question-and-answer sessions. You might even find that your book has been video-reviewed – that is, talked about in an online video. If you have your own website, you could blog regularly to keep fans interested in what you're doing. They even like to know what you have for breakfast and where you go on your holidays and what kind of pets you have. If you're writing a series with the same characters, you could blog something along the lines of: 'Jennie is having trouble choosing between hunky Ben and brainy Bart – who do you think she should end up with?' This will certainly get a response from your fans.

> *I suggested on my website that fans might like to come up with actors to play the characters in my books, were they ever to be made into a movie. Little did I know the effect that would have! Fans were posting suggestions for weeks afterwards! It certainly proved to be a great way of getting people to make return visits to my site. No movie, so far, though!*

And the beauty of internet publicity is that it can all be done from home, which may be a big plus if you're worried about losing writing time racing around the country. Social networking sites are another way of reaching people, whether you chatter or share pictures or link into network groups. Is there a mad craze going on at the moment for virals, or lying down in silly places and having your photo taken, or taking photos of stuff piled on top of your cat and adding them to a website, or whatever? Think outside the book box and the traditional ways of book promotion – and add a photo of your cat laying down in a washing basket reading your book!

VISITING SCHOOLS

You might find that local schools are interested in inviting you to visit them to talk to students, to read to them or to work with them, say, on a book project or as part of a book sale/fair or event. While some schools can't afford to pay you for these visits, others can obtain funding, and you can find out what to charge for time and travel costs by contacting any one of the authors' societies. This fee could also include expenses and you may find that some schools are able to pay you quite well for a day or two's work. Once you are published, you can add your name to various listings and directories as an author who is willing to do school or group visits. As we write this, there are some noises being made about visiting authors needing clearances to work alongside children, in the same way as is required for those who work with children. Do not be alarmed therefore if you are asked for references – especially if you are not yet a well known writer. For some established authors, the fees from school visits make up a useful percentage of their income.

Ask the headteacher if it's okay for you to sell signed copies of your book to the students. If so, then ask your editor or the publicity department to inform your local bookseller or if there is no bookseller available let you have copies of the book for sale or return, and provide some promotional material. Give everyone plenty of notice if you're going to do this, and make sure the students have been asked to bring some money along so they can buy your books.

If you've arranged this visit yourself and it's a non-paying event, it may still be worth approaching your publisher to see if they are willing to pay some travelling expenses for you. They will probably prepare some promotional material, such as posters, postcards, badges, leaflets or bookmarks. Your publisher might have a press release that they can give you, or perhaps a mail-order leaflet. Let them know that you're available and eager to do publicity work. If you're really keen and able to self-promote your work, then further research into publicity and marketing will help you with ideas. There are some great books available. Help your publisher to help you.

Tax and accounts

Whatever your circumstances, whether you're a taxpayer or not, or wherever you live, the tax situation for authors can get complicated. Your local tax inspector or an accountant may be able to help. There are also media accountants who specialize in the taxation of authors. If you have any doubt about your position, get some expert advice.

We asked London Chartered Accountants H. W. Fisher & Company to provide the following guidance notes for UK-based authors. This is what they replied:

WHO IS AN AUTHOR?

For tax purposes, someone is a professional author if they are writing regularly with a view to making a profit. Their taxable income is the amount receivable, either directly or via an agent, less expenses wholly and exclusively incurred in exercising their profession. If expenses exceed income, the loss can generally either be carried forward and set against future writing income, or set against other income in the same or previous year. If a writer receives only occasional payments from books or stories, it may not be possible to argue successfully that these are profits from a profession. In this case, only expenses directly incurred are likely to be deductible.

ALLOWABLE EXPENSES

The following are expenses that can normally be claimed. Note that it is essential to keep detailed records, including receipts wherever possible.

- *agent's commission*
- *secretarial, proof-reading and research*
- *telephone, postage, stationery, printing*
- *periodicals and books*
- *research assistance and materials*
- *photographic expenses*

- software, CDs, internet charges
- travelling and accommodation
- car hire, car running expenses or mileage allowance
- publicity and advertising expenses
- illustrations
- subscriptions to societies
- rent, business rates, mortgage interest, council tax, lighting, heating, etc. in proportion to the number of rooms used exclusively for the profession – most authors do not claim exclusive use of rooms and restrict their claim to a portion of home expenses in order to avoid capital gains tax upon the sale of their home
- accountancy and legal costs (incurred in the course of the profession)
- TV and DVD/video rental, and relevant cinema and theatre admission
- capital allowances can be claimed for business furniture and equipment as follows: cars – 20 per cent in year of purchase, and 20 per cent of reducing balance each year; other business equipment – 100 per cent in first year up to a maximum of £50,000 and 20 per cent of reducing balance
- courses and conferences
- copies of own books for publicity.

SETTING UP IN BUSINESS

There are a number of important matters that new (and existing) businesses should be aware of. These include:

- registering to pay National Insurance or claim exemption or deferment
- registering for VAT including joining the Flat Rate Scheme and Cash Accounting – it is almost always beneficial to register for VAT; the compulsory registration income limit is £68,000 in any consecutive 12 months, including reimbursed expenses
- preparation of VAT returns
- preparation of tax returns
- preparation of accounts.

Delays with any of these matters attract penalties.

Increasingly, authors are coming to realize the tax and National Insurance advantages of trading as a limited company. However, incorporation is an important matter, and it is essential to take professional advice.

AVERAGING INCOME

Anyone who is new to the writing profession should take expert advice about the date to choose for their accounting year end. An author may average earnings over two consecutive tax years if the net profit in one year is 75 per cent or less than the other year. It is also possible to average income within the terms of a publisher's contract. Income is the amount earned in the year rather than the amount received.

UK AND OVERSEAS TAX

If an author is resident in the UK for tax purposes, all income from literary work, whether domestic or foreign, is subject to UK income tax. The UK has double taxation treaties with most countries. After completion of certain formalities, no tax is usually deducted by the overseas publisher or other payer, but is taxable in the UK in the ordinary way. Where tax is withheld abroad, this can usually be offset against UK tax.

GRANTS AND PRIZES

Certain Arts Council grants and literary bursaries are deemed to be taxable, but most prizes and awards are not.

What next?

You're a newly published author with a book in the stores. Your publisher probably isn't going to give you a contract for your next piece of work until they've seen the early sales figures for your first book. But as we said before, they're going to be asking you what you're working on. Check your contract to see if there's a clause allowing them first refusal of your next work 'of a similar nature'. The 'first refusal' clause may give a time-scale for presenting your next work, or a time-period by which you should expect a decision from the publisher. If the publisher rejects your next book, then you are free from the contractual obligations and can submit it to other publishers. Before you do that, you might want to think about why it was rejected.

Chances are you will already have been talking to your editor about your next book, and they might even have ideas for what you might write next. For instance, if your book is for the young adult market, they will be probably be expecting something that targets the same readership. They will be looking to 'brand' you – so that readers who liked your first book will buy your next one, knowing it will be in a similar genre, whether that genre is romance, fantasy, thriller, horror, comedy or whatever. But if you're desperate to follow up your teen romance with a storybook for children aged four to eight, your editor might not be interested, or if they really like it, they may even suggest it's published under a different name to avoid confusion with your readers. Remember, you worked very hard to get your first publisher and they too have invested time and money in you. They will be interested in building up a long-lasting profitable relationship with you. Think very carefully before you decide to make a break with them.

Depending upon the type of market you're writing for and the size of the publisher's list, your editor might be hoping for several new titles from you per year – assuming your material continues to suit them. On the other hand, you might be the sole author of a major series with a new title every month. In that case, you're going to be working flat out and to scary deadlines. Before agreeing to delivery dates in contracts, make sure you've given yourself enough time to do the work. Add time for holidays and unforeseen problems. You could have a computer crash that could cost you half a week. Give yourself plenty of time too, for working on editorial suggestions.

A 65,000 word book might take you half a year to write – but it might also take a whole month to revise once your editor has seen it. Keep this in mind when you sign contracts. Asking for plenty of time up-front is better than having to go back to your editor and beg for extensions. They will have programmed your book into a whole line up of other projects, and an extra month tacked onto the end of your first draft could cause all sorts of chaos for your publisher – especially if you don't tell them about it until the day before the due date.

If you're writing more books than your publisher can cope with, you might want to make some alternative arrangements. Could you branch out into fields that might interest different publishers? If you can broaden your scope by writing for different age groups or by writing on different subjects, then you'll increase your marketability. You could find yourself working for several publishers at the same time without competing with yourself, and without upsetting your first publisher. Remember what we said about those contracts – plot your working time out very carefully, especially when you're working for different publishers.

Self-publishing

You know in your heart that you've written a good and worthwhile book, but somehow no publisher you make contact with shares your vision. You are certain that there is a viable readership that would pay to enjoy your book, if only they had the opportunity. What do you do when all the obvious options have been closed off?

Should you self-publish? Be realistic and honest with yourself: is there really a market for your book? A non-fiction title which covers a neglected subject, or which has definite niche-market appeal, is more likely to be successful than a typical novel or collection of poetry. Why do you think your book or project has been rejected? Is it because publishers have said it's too technical, or too expensive for them to produce, or because they're not prepared to spend money on a new author in the present economic climate? Is it simply that they don't think it has mass appeal? In other words, is it a good book that lacks broad commercial appeal, or are you being told it's badly written or badly plotted? If the former, some kind of self-publishing could be worth considering. If the latter – perhaps you need to consider improving your writing skills, or totally re-thinking the book.

A self-published book we heard about, explaining the intricacies of croquet, sold out its initial print run and made a profit in no time – and of course the internet is a great way of letting the world know that your book is out there, especially if you can plug into an existing worldwide market. You want to write an instruction manual on croquet? Make contact with every croquet website on the internet and you could find yourself spending most of your spare time packaging and mailing books to every corner of the world where croquet is played. You may be obsessed with getting into print at any cost – you may have spent half your life desperately wanting to see your book between hard covers. This is good, up to a point. But the joy of finally getting into print might fade very quickly if all you end up with is a large bill and an attic full of unsold books.

Let's assume you decide to go for self-publishing. Fortunately, with the existence of desktop publishing facilities and highly competitive printing prices, it is far easier now to publish yourself and less expensive than you might imagine. But do you have the time to learn the business? And do you have the necessary capital to cover the initial production costs? Self-publishing may not cost the earth, but it is a time-consuming business, as you need to absorb everything from how to get an International Standard Book Number (ISBN; you will find one on the back of every book published since the 1970s), to supplying copies to national libraries for copyright registration, to finding a distributor for the finished product.

Given the time and money to set up the business, your next biggest headache will be figuring out how you are going to get your book

in front of your potential customers in sufficient quantities to cover
your costs and maybe even make a profit.

There are excellent guides available on how to go about publishing
your own work and, as with everything in this business, you'll want
to do some research before you make a final decision. You'll also
discover the existence of small publishers (known as 'small presses')
who may be able to help you publish and distribute your book if
you can 'sponsor' them (that is, help out with the costs). It's helpful
for publicity and distribution purposes if you can have your book
on a publisher's list, no matter how small that publisher might be.

PRINT ON DEMAND

Before you get too disheartened by the complexities of self-
publishing, ISBNs and weights of paper, take heart and read up
about the success story of *The Long Tail* by Chris Anderson.
There are now print-on-demand companies that can take your
work from a disk, design the typography and page layout, help
with jacket design, advertise and make your work widely available
electronically. In this way, your book will be printed literally
'on demand' – it doesn't exist as a printed and bound book until
it is ordered. The main sales area for this will be via the online
bookstores, to which most print-on-demand companies will
arrange listings and links. There are also growing numbers of
bookstores that have super-fast, high-tech machinery from which
you can select online listed titles which are printed while you wait.
It works this way: your potential reader finds your book on the
web and orders it. That order connects to the print-on-demand
publisher who then prints a copy and sends it to the customer.
Some print-on-demand publishers are only interested in dealing
with a number of titles, and work only with professionals within
the business rather than with individual authors. But there are
growing numbers of other companies with good reputations
providing the individual author with a good value service.

Before you're tempted to publish a teaser sample of your work on
your own or another website (or chapters or even whole books

online), ask yourself 'How am I going to make any money from this exercise, and is my work safe from theft and corruption?' These are important questions.

Before you self-publish or take the print-on-demand route ask yourself the following questions:

▶ *Why am I doing this?*
▶ *Is there a real market for my book?*
▶ *Is it the best it can be and have I really tried every recognized publisher, and would it now benefit from the hand of a professional (potentially expensive) editor?*
▶ *Have I the time and resources to understand the business?*
▶ *Can I afford the costs and the risk of making a loss?*
▶ *Will I be able to promote and sell the book to anyone other than my friends and family, who will expect free copies anyway?*

An agent told us this:

> *For autobiographies and family histories, for niche market books, for the frustrated, the impatient or even the vain, self-publishing and print-on-demand publishing can be very satisfying and sometimes successful. But I've seen awful jacket covers badly illustrated and designed by the author which would put most buyers off, dreadful typos and unedited, unreadable novels. These books did not get bought and published because they are simply not good enough to warrant a publisher's attention. I'd rather work with the raw script material and help an author turn their ugly duckling into a swan, than try to rescue a badly self-published book.*

VANITY PUBLISHING

Be careful about approaching a 'vanity' publisher. These people advertise regularly in magazines, newspapers and online, and they can look very convincing, but you need to understand a few things about them. For a start, these 'publishers' are sometimes nothing more than unscrupulous printers out to make a fat profit. They'll print as many copies of your book as you're prepared to pay for – and they don't much care about what's inside. They might tell you how much they like your book without even reading it. They might tell you that your book has a big market, when they have no idea what it is about. The enormous upfront fees for their work may not include 'extras' like editing, copy-editing, cover design, distribution etc. Unfair as it may seem, a book published in this way does nothing to impress a genuine publisher, and may have the opposite effect. If a 'vanity' publisher of this kind takes your eye, try this simple exercise before you go further. Search the internet – type the company name and type the word 'complaints'. Read and learn from what turns up on your screen. It may include posts from enthusiasts (be cynical about their origin) and from people who are less impressed. One you've read both sides of the debate, you can then decide what you want to do. Finally, bear in mind that at any given time, several vanity publishers will be under investigation for fraud.

You may also sometimes spot deals advertised in newspapers and magazines, etc., where you can get your book published for a fixed fee. But be wary of these offers – the quality of the finished product is often very poor, and once you have your books, you still need to come up with a method of getting them out to potential buyers/ readers.

The bottom line

Now you've almost finished this book, does the life of a published author still look good to you? Even after everything we've warned you about? Are you kidding? You still want to go ahead with it?

In that case, at least you're now armed with a lot more information than you were 12 chapters ago. The things we've written about here only scratch the surface of the business of writing for children and getting published. As we've repeated, go and check out articles and books that detail specific aspects of the business that you need to know more about. The more research you do, the better your chances of hitting the target.

Hopefully, we've given you a few pointers about how to go about collecting and organizing your ideas, producing a product that will attract a publisher and dealing with all the failures and successes that may come from your desire to see your name or your work in print. Over the years we have learned the hard way, and made all the classic mistakes. With the aid of this book, your learning process should be much faster than ours was.

In the end, it's all down to you. We can only provide the signposts: it's up to you to make the journey. And for that journey you're going to need persistence, determination, stamina, talent and a whole lot of luck. Just keep one thing in mind: for a writer, nothing beats holding your first published book in your hands.

Writing for a living can be a rollercoaster. Don't take the highs for granted, because you might be about to fall off a cliff. Don't despair when things go wrong – something might be just over the horizon. Enjoy your writing, and keep going.

Exercise 36

What are you waiting for? Publishers are crying out for new talent. Go get that book published. And when you're rich and famous and living in tax exile, remember we had faith in you all that time ago when everyone else thought you'd never make it.

ENDNOTE

It took dozens of letters, faxes and emails, hours of phone calls, months of time and research and several drafts and revisions of the script to complete this book and deliver it to our publisher, in between our normal day jobs, sleeping, eating, parenting and putting the cat out. We also used and abused friendships and family above and beyond the call of duty and are forever in their debt. One of the authors questioned added the following to the bottom of his returned questionnaire:

> *The question that really interests me is: how to write my own children's books – the satisfying and necessary ones – and to make contact with an audience? There are plenty of books and evening classes which only talk about market research and how-to-please-the-little-brats. (Don't write one of those, will you? I know you won't.)*

There's only one way to sign off

> *… and they all lived happily ever after*

says Allan.

> *I'm leaving my last word to someone else*

says Lesley.

> *It does no harm to repeat, as often as you can, 'Without me the literary industry would not exist: the publishers, the agents, the sub-agents, the accountants, the libel lawyers, the departments of literature, the professors, the theses, the books of criticism, the reviewers, the book pages – all this vast and proliferating edifice is because of this small, patronized, put-down and underpaid person.'*

Doris Lessing

10 THINGS TO REMEMBER

1 *Find out what actually happens on publication day.*

2 *If you spot errors in your published work, know when to be calm and when to hit the panic button.*

3 *Find out what is expected from you to promote your book and increase sales.*

4 *Be prepared to deal with good and bad reviews.*

5 *The internet will be an important tool for you – learn about its rampant uses and abuses.*

6 *Talk to your publisher about opportunities you may have to do your own publicity.*

7 *Make sure you understand your tax position as an author – and seek advice or professional help if necessary.*

8 *Start thinking about your next step if you haven't already – your publisher will want to know your plans.*

9 *If you are considering self-publishing or vanity publishing, research your options carefully.*

10 *Go and do it!*

Taking it further

Listings for UK-based authors

BOOKS

Books in Print 2008–2009 (published annually) New Providence, NJ, USA: R. R. Bowker (8 vols).

Clark, Giles and Phillips, Angus (2008) *Inside Book Publishing* (4th edition), London: Routledge.

Crofts, Andrew (2007) *The Freelance Writer's Handbook* (3rd edition), London: Piatkus Books.

The Publishers Association, *Directory of Publishing* 2010 (35th edition, published annually), London: Continuum.

Richardson, Paul and Taylor, Graham (2008) *A Guide to the UK Publishing Industry*, The Publishers Association.

Ross, Tom and Ross, Marilyn (2010) *The Complete Guide to Self-Publishing* (5th edition), Writers' Digest Books (F&W Publications).

Shay, Helen (2009) *The Writer's Guide to Copyright*, Contract and Law (4th edition), How to Books Ltd.

Shepard, Aaron (2007) *Aiming at Amazon: The NEW Business of Self Publishing, or How to Publish Your Books with Print on Demand and Online Book Marketing on Amazon.com*, Shepard Publications.

Turner, Barry (ed.) *The Writer's Handbook 2010* (published annually), London: Macmillan.

Writers' & Artists' Yearbook 2010 (published annually), London: A & C Black.

PERIODICALS

The Author
(In-house membership magazine of the Society of Authors, see below.)
www.societyofauthors.org/the-author

Books for Keeps (BfK)
1 Effingham Road, Lee, London SE12 8NZ
www.booksforkeeps.co.uk

The Bookseller
Fifth floor, Endeavour House, 189 Shaftesbury Avenue, London WC2H 8TJ
www.theBookseller.com

Carousel
The Saturn Centre, 54–76 Bissel Street, Birmingham B5 7HX
www.carouselguide.co.uk

Directory of Writers' Circles, Courses and Workshops 2010
www.writers-circles.com

Publishers Weekly
360 Park Avenue South, New York, NY 10010, USA
www.publishersweekly.com

Times Educational Supplement
26 Red Lion Square, London, WC1R 4HQ
www.tes.co.uk

CONTACTS AND SOCIETIES

Arvon Foundation
Free Word, 60 Farringdon Road, London EC1R 3GA
www.arvonfoundation.org

Association of Illustrators (AOI)
2nd floor, Back Building, 150 Curtain Road, London EC2A 3AR
www.theaoi.com

Author's Licensing and Collection Society
The Writers' House, Haydon Street, London, EC3N 1DB
www.alcs.co.uk

Booktrust
45 East Hill, London SW18 2QZ
www.booktrust.org.uk

Children's Book Circle
www.childrensbookcircle.org.uk

Contracts for Publishing Limited
1 Jeffery Close, Staplehurst, TN12 0TH
www.contractsforpublishing.co.uk

Federation of Children's Book Groups
2 Bridge Wood View, Horsforth, Leeds, West Yorkshire LS18 5PE
www.fcbg.org.uk

H. W. Fisher & Company, London Chartered Accountants
who prepared the tax and accounts summary in Chapter 12.
Barry Kernon: bkernon@hwfisher.co.uk
www.hwfisher.co.uk

**International Board on Books for Young People [IBBY]
(British Section)**
PO Box 20875, London SE22 9WQ
www.ibby.org.uk/

Public Lending Right
Richard House, Sorbonne Close, Stockton-on-Tees,
Teeside TS17 6DA
www.plr.uk.com

The Publishing Training Centre
Book House, 45 East Hill, Wandsworth, London SW18 2QZ
www.train4publishing.co.uk

Society of Authors
84 Drayton Gardens, London SW10 9SB
www.societyofauthors.org

Society of Young Publishers
c/o The Bookseller, Fifth floor, Endeavour House, 189 Shaftesbury
Avenue, London WC2H 8TJ
www.thesyp.org.uk

The Writers' Advice Centre for Children's Books
16 Smiths Yard, London SW18 4HR
www.writersadvice.co.uk

Writers' Guild of Great Britain
40 Rosebery Avenue, London, EC1R 4RX
www.writersguild.org.uk

Index

Image credits

Front cover: © Nikreates/Alamy